Janet Balaskas *was born and educated in Johannesburg, South Africa and emigrated to England in 1968. She is well known internationally for her pioneering work as a lecturer, author, childbirth educator and activist. In the late 1970s she introduced a new approach to prenatal preparation with Yoga and the concept of 'Active Birth' which focuses on women's self empowerment in pregnancy, and freedom and autonomy in birthing. Her work has influenced change in maternity practices in many countries and helped to further understanding of physiological childbirth.*

Janet Balaskas coined the phrase 'Active Birth' and founded the Active Birth Movement in the late 1970s. She is the principal of the Active Birth Foundation for Professional Training and the director of the Active Birth Centre in London. This is a resource centre for pregnant women, specializing in Active Birth, Yoga for Pregnancy and Water Birth. The Active Birth Centre website, www.activebirthcentre.com, provides e-mail information and coaching contacts or associates worldwide. Janet is the mother of four children, one stepdaughter and has two grandsons. She lives in North London.

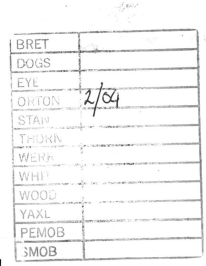

Preparing for Birth with Yoga

Janet Balaskas

Thorsons
An Imprint of HarperCollins*Publishers*
77–85 Fulham Palace Road
London W6 8JB

The website address is: www.thorsonselement.com

and *Thorsons* are trademarks of
HarperCollins*Publishers* Ltd

First published in 1994 by Element Books Ltd
This edition 2003

1 3 5 7 9 10 8 6 4 2

Photographs by Anthea Sieveking
Line drawings by Michael Cole
Medical drawings by Michael Courtney

A catalogue record of this book is
available from the British Library

ISBN 0 00 716676 1

Printed and bound in Great Britain by
Butler & Tanner Ltd, Frome and London

CONTENTS

FOREWORD

By Sandra Sabatini

When a pregnant woman joins one of my yoga classes, I always look forward to her first lesson. I know with certainty that after the first few words she will step right into the true essence of yoga. She will immediately realize how natural it is to feel the contact with the ground through her feet, and the subsequent impulse to grow and spread in her own space. She is already in a wholly creative state. She is constantly listening to what is happening inside her. She is glowing with an inner smile which pervades her whole being, from the centre to the surface. She needs yoga only to maintain this 'light from within'.

Yoga gives the pregnant mother the capacity to adjust to inner and outer changes with extraordinary flexibility. The constant presence of the breath as a means of connecting her to gravity discharges tension and tiredness into the earth, whilst her body maintains a state of cleanliness and lightness. The daily practice of simple, effortless yoga positions leads her into childbirth with a clear mind, interested, even curious about the coming event. As the birth gets closer, her whole being opens up and the five senses are stimulated to perceive new dimensions: time and space dilate. Giving birth becomes a unique opportunity to get in touch with her inner power as a woman. Once she has experienced it, she will always remember its intensity and, like an everlasting spring, she will draw from it for the rest of her life.

Thanks to the work of Janet Balaskas over the years, this immense natural gift need no longer be taken away from us. In writing this book, she shares her profound perception of the ways in which we can benefit from the cosmic forces that surround us. These influences are not confined to yoga positions. They are transplanted into our daily life and become our way of being.

Janet not only pours all her personal experience into these pages as someone who practises yoga, but also passes on the scientific knowledge needed by those who may assist in a birth. It is only when you are helped by someone totally aware of the beauty of the whole process of childbirth that you can abandon your last vestiges of resistance and step consciously into motherhood.

With these few lines I would like to express my gratitude as a woman to Janet Balaskas, and her colleagues Lolly Stirk, Yvonne Moore, and other Active Birth teachers for their work in showing pregnant women a better approach to childbirth.

Sandra Sabatini
FLORENCE
1993

FOREWORD

By Yehudi Gordon MD FRCOG FCOG SA

I am very pleased to write a foreword for this book. Janet Balaskas and I share a lineage. We have both been taught by Mina Semyon, Mary Stewart, Sandra Sabatini and Vanda Scaravelli: we have practised together, and we have shared our discoveries and our experiences with parents during pregnancy, birth and infancy.

Yoga is wonderful. The style taught in this book is inspiring and magical and focuses our awareness on the universal pull of gravity. Once in gravity we are taken, step by step, breath by breath, through the discovery of our feet, heels, spine, and finally our head. The exploration is an adventure which is safe because we acknowledge the anchor of gravity to the earth and this allows our bodies to fly. This yoga is not about how far we can stretch, it is about discovering gravity and feeling the infinite ocean from which 'the wave' of the breath originates and returns.

Practising yoga is accompanied by many benefits. It awakens our spine, releases the tension in our joints, ligaments and muscles and releases our energy and vitality. As our body relaxes actively we discover the space within. It is always safe because every posture is carried out on the wave of the breath.

The discovery of the ocean and the waves with the breath arising and returning is a priceless gift. It allows us to find our self whatever circumstances our lives are in. The breath is present whether we are calm and relaxed, during a stormy labour when the ocean waves are high, in the middle of the night when our baby is crying, and during lovemaking. The wave of the breath is always there, it is always accessible provided we are attentive to its presence. It calms, centres and energizes us. The practice of yoga is one way to discover the wave, and once discovered it empowers us throughout our lives.

This is a practical and inspiring book. The excitement, joy, richness and benefit of yoga is in doing. This book acts as a guide along the path.

Yehudi Gordon
LONDON
1993

KALI GIVING BIRTH TO THE UNIVERSE
This wooden carving of the Goddess Kali
comes from a prayer cart in a temple in
India. She tells us that the birth giving
regenerative power of women is sacred.
Her body symbolizes the feminine source
of all life and renewal. She is a symbol of
the active autonomous
birth giver – standing in the squatting
position to give birth in full possession
of her own strength and power.

ACKNOWLEDGEMENTS

It is a great privilege to receive the wisdom of a living tradition through the generosity and enthusiasm of a personal teacher. I would like to thank my teachers John Stirk, Sandra Sabatini, Mina Semyon and Dominique Moorsom for their inspiration. I am honoured to pass on what I can, for the benefit of the reader, of their innovative ideas, poetic metaphors, attention to detail and care of the practitioner.

Thanks also to all my colleagues, in particular Alice Charlwood, Lynn Murphy and Natascha Laing for the exchange we share in our practice of teaching yoga for pregnancy.

I greatly appreciate the contribution of the graceful women who provided the photographs and illustrations in this book: Marigold Gordon Gray, Mooli Ten-Tusscher, Jocelyn James, Erika Klemperer, Linda Coggin, Jennifer Stariski, Shelley Latham, Jill Fricker, Kate Mulchansinge and Judy Lawson. Anthea Sieveking has done full justice to their power and beauty with her photographs. I am also especially grateful to Anthea for her loyalty, friendship, and enthusiasm for this book over the years.

Thanks to my family, for providing the support at home which made it possible for me to write this book.

Thank you to Nikki and Sienna Oakley for the beautiful cover photographs and to John Oakley for his spiritual guidance and encouragement. For their help while I was writing this book I would like to thank Judy Hargreaves and Julia Naish.

Finally I am deeply grateful to the late Vanda Scaravelli who is the pioneer and originator of this approach to yoga, which provides the fertile ground for all of our practice and teaching.

PREFACE

Pregnancy is the beginning of a major life change. You are becoming a mother. Like someone who is on a journey, each day takes you into new territory and brings you closer to the birth of your baby. Whether this is your first or a subsequent baby, a single or multiple pregnancy, there is now a whole new and deeper dimension to your life. You are bringing a child into your family and into the world. What a joyful task and what a great responsibility!

Almost as soon as pregnancy begins, your body calls your attention inwards. Now your priority is not only to care for yourself, but also to nourish and protect this little person who is sharing your body. Everything you do, think, feel, dream or eat is shared with your baby. Being conscious of this doesn't mean that you need to be super-vigilant or overly worried. Babies are meant to share their mother's world and life is never perfect, much as we would like it to be. It does mean that you have a wonderful opportunity to pay special attention to how you are living and to do your very best to look after yourself and your baby. You have the months of pregnancy ahead to prepare yourself for birth and motherhood.

I would like to offer you in this book the gift of yoga. Over more than twenty years of working with pregnant women, I have learned how deeply yoga can transform the quality of a pregnancy. This is not ordinary yoga, but yoga that is especially kind and gentle to the body and is ideally suited to pregnancy. It is also very effective preparation for labour and birth. By practising for a short time every day, you will be choosing a powerful way to help yourself to integrate the changes you are going through and to develop confidence, trust and a positive attitude to the challenges that lie ahead. This is the way to maximize your health, to heal yourself and clear the way for a new chapter in your life.

In an ideal world, preparation for birth would begin before conception. All of us carry fears, patterns from the past and unconscious barriers that may limit our potential. Sometimes we doubt whether we will be able to surrender to the natural opening of the body for birth, the nurturing of breastfeeding, the holding and giving of motherhood. In pregnancy a natural clearing happens in preparation for this. Our emotions and feelings well up and pour out of us, our fears and worries emerge and demand our attention. Yoga gives you the time, focus and space to surrender to this spontaneous emotional clearing, this natural preparation for what lies ahead. At the same time it is a marvellous way to release physical tension in your muscles and joints, to prevent or ease any discomfort from the extra weight you are carrying and to get your body ready for birth.

How does it work? Well, firstly yoga draws you deeply inside yourself. In addition to being physically beneficial it is also meditative and prayerful. The word 'yoga' means 'union' of body, mind and spirit. It connects you with the elemental forces of nature and at the same time, with your own internal resources. In our patriarchal culture, the power of the feminine has been suppressed and denied for centuries. This is especially evident in childbirth, which, for the most part, became a medical event managed by professionals and doctors. Women have forgotten, lost confidence in their innate ability to give birth. But now this is changing – more women are discovering their potential to give birth normally and naturally, actively or in water. Midwives, doulas, birth educators and pregnancy yoga teachers are there to encourage and guide them.

Yoga takes you directly to the elemental sources of life and connects you with the feminine power and wisdom that has helped millions of women before you. It invites you to approach the experience positively, from a position of autonomy and strength, to grow more confident in your ability to give birth normally. It also helps you to keep an open mind, to be without expectation and to use your intelligence and intuition to know when, if and how you might need help. Whatever the circumstances of your birth, yoga can help to calm, relax and empower you.

Pregnant women who have never done yoga before often ask me if this is a good time to start. My answer is that this is a wonderful time to begin to learn yoga. Your body is especially intelligent and responsive in pregnancy. Once you are familiar with the positions and can relax into them, I invite you to pay attention to the rhythm of your breathing. This leads you to discover the connection between your body and the earth. You will begin to feel calmer and more grounded. You will learn how to release tension and make more space in your body and your life. You will feel lighter and more energetic. You will soon realize that the breath and the earth are like best friends, just waiting for you to become quiet and still enough to receive the abundant nourishment that is there for you and your baby.

In India there is a name for this energy – it's called *prana* or 'life force'. As a pregnant woman you are part of the natural impetus that generates new life – that makes spring follow winter, seeds begin to sprout, flowers bloom and fruits ripen. Yoga will help you to sense that connection, to feel one with it, to receive it and to trust the flow of *prana* or energy that is bringing your baby to birth through your body. This will prepare you for the intensity of labour when you will need to surrender and open to the powerful waves that open your womb and then release your baby.

One of the greatest benefits of yoga is that you will find peace and stillness inside yourself. This allows you to get much more deeply in touch with how you feel and what you want. It also enables you to pay attention to your thoughts and to develop the skill of creating positive rather than negative thoughts. The mind has incredible power to affect the body. Negative thinking can all too easily become a self-fulfilling prophecy. The positive affirmation of being that yoga brings is empowering and validating. You are about to learn a lot about yourself: your courage, endurance and energy. You are stronger, more resilient and more capable than you may realize.

Then there is your baby to consider. Like a little Buddha inside you, your baby is a sentient being who already feels, senses, hears, tastes and – in a kind of deep cellular way – even remembers. I often think that perhaps babies in the womb are more sensitive, more highly conscious, and more intelligent than we are. My yoga room, where unborn babies have come with their mothers for many years, has the most incredible atmosphere. People often comment that it's as if there is a divine or enlightened presence around.

Think for a moment about the timeless, almost 'cosmic' world your baby experiences inside the womb. The stillness within that you can find during deep yoga practice helps you to get onto the same wavelength as your baby – to tune in to him or her in a natural way. The silent space, the possibility that yoga creates, means that you can actually listen, respond and inwardly communicate with your baby. You are going through the journey of birth and life together. For your baby birth is going to be a huge experience. Leaving the shelter of the womb, being squeezed through the birth canal and then propelled into the world is the first and greatest change in life. This deepening of your inner connection with your baby before birth will help you to lead the way.

I discovered this connection in a special way myself when I was just a few weeks pregnant with Iasonas, my third baby. It was only 18 months after the birth of my second child and initially I was thrown into a state of emotional turmoil and ambivalence about having two children so close together. Then, in the quiet moments I spent during my yoga practice, I sensed that inside my body there was a wonderful person who was going to enhance my life beyond measure. Very soon the shock of being pregnant again was replaced by a warm certainty that the child I had inside me was a wonderful gift and it was completely appropriate for him to be there at that time. I discovered that I could 'talk' to him while he was in my womb and I could hear his 'answers'. By the time he was four weeks old *in utero* I had apologized to him for my initial ambivalence, and we have never looked back since. Ias, as we call him, was born easily at home and weighed in at 10.5 lbs.

Number four, my son Theo, surprised me by arriving ten years later when I was 42 and thought my childbearing career was over. I did consider for a few weeks the screening procedures recommended for women my age and had tentatively booked an appointment for an amniocentesis. The day before the test I had a startling experience at the end of my yoga practice. I distinctly heard Theo 'telling me' that he was not only fine but also was a magnificent specimen and I did not need the test. So I cancelled the appointment and sure enough he turned out to be a robust and healthy 11 lb baby.

This was a very personal experience. In some cases going through with the test may be the best thing to do. The essential point is that when faced with a choice, a dilemma, it's really helpful to be able to become quiet with the help of yoga and thus find the guidance within to make the right decisions for yourself and your baby. Theo was born at home beside the fire, after a short intense labour that was eased by the use of a water birth pool in my bedroom. Despite his size, the second stage was over in seven contractions. I did not tear and was ecstatic for several days after the birth. Without yoga I do not believe I could have achieved this outcome.

Discovering yoga while you are pregnant is just the beginning. For the rest of your life you have a marvellous health-giving anti-dote to the stresses and strains of living. You can continue after the birth and also play with your baby using natural yoga movements to gently enhance his or her development.

I started to practise yoga just before my second pregnancy 25 years ago and still do. I have become looser, lighter, more flexible, happier and more youthful as a result. Since then I have had the privilege to introduce many pregnant women to this path and to witness the profound and positive effect it has on them.

It's my great pleasure to pass this on to you and your baby. My wish is for you to receive the gift of yoga through this book and to be empowered by it. This will enable you to respond with your whole being to your baby and to the transformation you are experiencing as you evolve and are being reborn yourself as a mother.

Janet Balaskas
LONDON
June 2003

INTRODUCTION

Before you embark on practising yoga during your pregnancy, you will want to know a little more about its history and the benefits it can introduce into your life. You will also need to know what sort of yoga I am recommending and why I believe it is so suitable for the childbearing year.

It is generally thought that yoga originated in prehistoric India. Evidence of ancient seals decorated with carved figures seated in the lotus position were found in the Indus valley, in what is now Pakistan, and are thought to date back to between the fifth and second centuries before the birth of Christ.

The earliest written reference to yoga comes from the Sanskrit hymns of the Aryan people, known as The Vedas (3000BC–1200BC). The Upanishads are later Vedic hymns dating from 1200BC to 600BC, in which yogic teaching was passed on from teacher to pupil. This tradition of passing on the wisdom of yoga philosophy and practice from guru to disciple has ancient roots and has spread to many parts of the world, adapting along the way to the cultural needs of the time and place. It is still very much alive today and is flourishing in the West as well as in India.

At the end of the Vedic period, The Bhagavadgita was written in about 600BC. This is an epic poem which describes the philosophy of yoga in the form of a dialogue between the god Krishna and the warrior prince Arjuna. Around the time that The Bhagavadgita was written, the Buddha (born in 568BC) lived and taught and many of the great religions of the world were flowering. Buddhist teaching absorbed the yogic practices and carried them throughout most of Asia, leading to the evolution of Tantra.

One of the most famous yoga texts is the classic Patanjali's Yoga Sutras. Written between 200BC and 200AD, these are short passages or aphorisms composed so that they could be easily memorized. They contain the essence of a well-established practice discipline of yoga postures, breathing, meditation and spiritual guidance for everyday life, as well as the attainment of self-realization and enlightenment.

In the Middle Ages, later texts such as the Hatha Yoga Pradipika were written which expand further on the purification of body and mind with physical exercises, breathing and meditation. When India was invaded and colonized, these texts were translated and this led to the great interest in Eastern religion and philosophy and in yoga which is thriving in the West today.

Western women's interest in yoga in this century is, as far as recorded history tells us, unprecedented. Most of the documents I have referred to tell us of a mainly male tradition of yoga practice. However, it is possible that yoga goes back much further in history than anyone has so far realized and is as old as civilization itself. There are indications that it may even have its roots in our own culture and may have been invented and practised by women long before the evidence confirms its existence on the Indian subcontinent.

It is possible that yoga goes back much further in history than anyone has so far realized and is as old as civilization itself.

The revolutionary work of the archaeologist Marija Gimbutas has more recently revealed the existence of ancient 'matristic' (female centred) civilizations all over old Europe (see *Gods and Goddesses of Old Europe* and *The Language of the Goddess* by Marija Gimbutas). She provides evidence in the form of thousands of clay figurines of the goddesses and other related artefacts, dating from the Paleolithic (as much as 30,000 years ago) and Neolithic (7000–9000 years ago) periods, which she discovered in different parts of Eastern and Western Europe from the Ukraine to the Mediterranean. Interestingly, some of the figurines of these matriarchal goddesses are clearly seated in yogic meditation postures which suggests that the roots of meditational yoga practice in women's circles might go back thousands of years and are to be found in our own prehistoric culture.

While it is not possible to tell whether these goddesses were pregnant or not, it is possible that we are not the first women to think of

This early pregnant goddess from Neolithic Crete (6000-5500 BC) is seated in the lotus position. The crown on her head is a symbol of her wisdom and wealth. She represents the goddess as the source of all life, who takes her energy (through meditative and 'yogic' practices) from the springs and wells, from the sun, moon and moist earth.

practising yoga in pregnancy. Perhaps in those ancient times, women knew how to connect with the invigorating energies of nature by means of some basic 'earth centred' meditation. Thus they maintained a ritual practice which empowered them to respect and nourish both body and soul, in harmony with the rhythms of nature and the creative powers of the feminine.

Historical accounts of these ancient matriarchal civilizations tell us that they were 'gylanic', which means that both sexes were regarded as equal. The feminine, or the 'Great Mother', was worshipped and honoured as central to life. Women were deeply respected as birthgivers and nurturers. In matriarchal cultures all over the world, the body of a woman is often depicted as a sacred vessel or container holding the mysteries which create and sustain new life. Her fertility both symbolizes and reflects the regenerating power of living nature itself, not only human, but all life on earth and within the whole cosmos.

These ancient civilizations were also renowned for their high standard of art and lifestyle and for their political stability, living for thousands of years in peace and harmony with the laws of nature.

We are now approaching an era when the need to awaken and transform our consciousness is being felt all over the world. At no time has a re-emergence of the feminine been so urgently needed in order to create balance, harmony and peace on earth, in accord with the creative energies of nature.

Marija Gimbutas, in the Introduction to *The Language of the Goddess*, says:

> *The Goddess-centred religion existed for a very long time, much longer than the Indo-European and the Christian (which represents a relatively short period of human history), leaving an indelible imprint on the Western psyche. This is in stark contrast to the 5000 years which followed, in which patriarchal values of conflicting warlike tribal and national interests have dominated social life, wreaking havoc and ruin on our planet.*

> *We are now approaching an era when the need to awaken and transform our consciousness is being felt all over the world. At no time has a re-emergence of the feminine been so urgently needed in order to create balance, harmony and peace on earth, in accord with the creative energies of nature. We are still living under the sway of that aggressive male invasion and only beginning to discover our long alienation from our authentic European heritage – gylanic (both sexes equal), non-violent, earth-centred culture.*

YOGA in the WEST

As we have seen, yoga has evolved over the centuries mainly in India, a culture in which matriarchal religious values remained intact longer than in most parts of Europe. While there is some evidence of yogic practices among women, particularly in tantric art, it is generally presented as practised in India by male yogis. Yoga in its modern form was introduced and popularized in the West during the twentieth century, mainly by male teachers from India who have kept the tradition alive through recent centuries.

There are many different kinds and traditions of yoga, but it is largely hatha yoga which has become popular in the West. The main focus of hatha yoga is to develop the potential of the body and to bring it into balance in preparation for meditation. The means to this end are through practising breathing (pranayama) and postures known as asanas.

The approach to yoga which you will learn from this book has been inspired by the teaching of Vanda Scaravelli and her pupils. Vanda, now in her eighties, lives near Florence in Italy. Her book *Awakening the Spine – A New Way of Yoga* was published in October 1992. Vanda Scaravelli was taught yoga originally by B.K.S. Iyengar, the world famous Indian yoga teacher who visited the West and introduced and popularized hatha yoga. Vanda then originated her own style of hatha yoga which, as yet, has no formal name but might, I think, be called 'Gravitational Yoga' because of the emphasis it places on understanding the way that gravity affects us at all times and particularly when we practise the yoga postures.

I have had the good fortune to study yoga both in London with Mina Semyon and Mary Stewart and recently in Italy with Sandra Sabatini (see Acknowledgements). Their teaching is the source and inspiration of my work in teaching yoga to pregnant women.

The NEW WAY of YOGA

The new way of yoga is based on the understanding of the way that the spine in a human body naturally extends in two directions. The lower, heavier part, from the waist down, is drawn towards the earth by gravity. The upper, lighter, more delicate part from the waist up lengthens towards the sky.

When you practise the yoga positions, your awareness will be drawn to this by focusing on your breathing. First you will learn to feel the pull of the earth, of gravity in your body. Then, as the lower part falls into harmony with this 'attraction' to the earth, you will begin to feel the energy which arises from the ground and brings balance, lightness and vitality to your whole body.

Most people, without fully realizing it, feel 'top heavy' before they begin to practise this kind of yoga. A lifetime of tension in the upper body, neck and shoulders gives a feeling of being very tight and constricted on top while the lower body may feel stiff and ungrounded.

All too often, we live in our heads and only partially occupy our bodies. Sometimes the upper body feels so heavy that it is an exhausting task simply to keep upright. Over time chronic mechanical imbalances develop in the body as muscles stiffen and joints become less mobile.

The new way of yoga brings the body back into balance so that the weight of the lower, heavier structures slowly returns to gravity and the accumulated tension above can gradually release. It is a very soft, deep, quiet and gentle way of practising yoga which begins to work a powerful magic, once one starts to allow the body and the breath to simply 'be', without force, without struggle. It is a surrender to gravity, which in return brings lightness, liberation and balance to the whole body.

Many contemporary yoga teachers mistakenly place great emphasis on the postures themselves, without this sort of awareness of their relationship to gravity or the way they are animated by the breath. Therefore, they lose connection with the forces of power which affect the mechanical and emotional balance of the body. This means that the practitioner gets tied up in details of the posture itself, with no frame of reference to the rest of nature. Some styles of yoga may even involve using force to get the body into tortuous positions for which it is not yet flexible enough. It is possible for this approach to result in physical injury and it can be painful and unenjoyable.

By contrast, the new way of yoga is very feminine. It is pleasurable and easy to do and extremely gentle and kind to the body. It is never forceful or painful, so it is completely safe and harmless and it is therefore especially suitable for pregnancy. The new way of yoga involves focusing your concentration on the wave, the ripple of the breath through your body while you are actually practising the postures. This gives them life and movement and invests them with a profound power to transform your body and your experience of life.

We do yoga for the fun of it. To twist, stretch and move around, is pleasant and enjoyable, a body holiday. There is the unexpected delight in meeting earth and sky at the same moment! (Gravity).

VANDA SCARAVELLI
(Awakening the Spine, p.58)

HOLISTIC PREGNANCY

This book is an invitation to prepare for birth and motherhood with yoga. It may seem strange that a woman needs to 'prepare' for birth and mothering. After all, these are completely natural, instinctive and biological functions. Our bodies are ideally designed and adapted to carry, give birth to and nourish our young just like any other mammal and yet, unlike other mammals, we appear to be the only species which has such difficulty in fulfilling our instinctive potential.

This has not always been the case. Throughout the ages, in cultures and traditions all over the world, the power of women to give birth and nurture their young was honoured and deeply respected as central to life. However, with the development of our modern industrialized lifestyle, the power of women as birthgivers has been steadily degraded and replaced by the science of obstetrics.

Today only a small percentage of women in the so-called 'civilized' West manage to give birth naturally. The art of breastfeeding has declined so much that it is hardly in evidence any more. Somehow we have become alienated from our natural habitat and also, at the same time, from many of our instinctive capabilities. Therefore, we need effective means such as yoga to help us to rekindle our power to give birth and to fulfil our biological potential as mothers.

When BIRTH became OBSTETRICS

The domination of childbirth by obstetrics began with the invention of forceps in the seventeenth century in France. Since then women in the West have gradually lost control over their bodies, as the power of birth has fallen more and more into the hands of the medical profession. While we are fortunate to have the back-up of modern obstetrics when there are problems, birth in the Western world is still seen mainly as a medical event.

This approach leads to a huge increase in the need for drugs and interventions and an escalation in the number of surgical and instrumental births. This has become obvious in every country which has adopted the medical model of birth. There is now widespread international concern about the damaging side effects and the unknown long term effects and consequences of routine obstetric intervention.

The failure of routine obstetrics to improve upon normal birth is now being widely recognized, as the statistics worsen in the places where obstetrics is most deeply entrenched. For example, in the USA today, one in four babies is born by caesarean section and most of those born vaginally are assisted by chemical or mechanical interventions. By contrast, birth outcomes are best in countries such as Holland, where 30% of women give birth at home, or in small homelike birthing centres all over the world where intervention is minimal, or in countries like Sweden where midwives are the primary attendants at births. In Japan, too, there are still a small number of midwives who observe the old skills and traditional

We need effective means such as yoga to help us to rekindle our power to give birth and to fulfil our biological potential as mothers.

practices, where the birthing mother goes to stay at the home of the midwife for her labour and birth and early postpartum days. Their perinatal statistics are amongst the best in the world and contrast favourably with the newer obstetric maternity hospitals in Japan where a higher rate of complications is noted.

This is telling us that, after all is said and done, women and their bodies, with the help of their midwives, know best how to birth their babies and that it is time to explore new ways to regain trust and confidence in our own instinctive potential.

The IMPORTANCE of PREGNANCY

If more women are to give birth naturally in the future, it is essential first to recognize that the birth is the consequence of what happens throughout the pregnancy. Sadly, the importance of pregnancy is still greatly underestimated in our society.

Most contemporary women have grown up as girls with a negative mental conditioning about birthing and breastfeeding. They expect birth to be a medical event and approach it with fear. The process of surrender of the mother's power and control over her birth begins as soon as the pregnancy is confirmed, if not earlier. Responsibility is handed over to the doctor and the woman is usually steered in the direction of the nearest hospital. Then the emphasis throughout the pregnancy is usually focused on medical antenatal care and testing for problems or abnormalities. While this in itself may be useful and necessary, it is not sufficient and undermines the woman's trust and confidence in her own body and her own power.

The emotional, spiritual, and physical aspects of pregnancy are vitally important and should not be neglected. The potential for self-empowerment, change, healing and transformation, which is so great during these months, needs to be positively enhanced and encouraged. Women in pregnancy should not be expected to face the challenge of birthing without any adequate physical or emotional preparation.

Today there is a lot of concern for the environment and for healing and restoring the damage done to our planet and yet most people fail to realize that the first ecological situation for human life is the mother's womb and the continuing relationship between mother and baby throughout the impressionable and vulnerable phase of infancy. Before we can begin to find solutions for the ecological crisis at large, nothing less than a revolution is needed in our attitudes towards conception, pregnancy, birth and motherhood. We need to find new ways to enhance rather than undermine women's confidence in their own power to be mothers.

The re-emergence of the feminine principle or the change of consciousness often called 'The New Age', to which Marija Gimbutas refers in the quote on p. 16, must involve a new and more holistic approach to pregnancy and an honouring of its importance both for the future of the individual in utero and for our society at large.

The emotional, spiritual, and physical aspects of pregnancy are vitally important and should not be neglected. The potential for self-empowerment, change, healing and transformation, which is so great during these months, needs to be positively enhanced and encouraged.

19

RECLAIMING the FEMININE
POWER of BIRTH and MOTHERING

Throughout this century, alongside the development of high-tech obstetrics, there has been a global movement to rediscover and to reclaim the normal physiology of birth and breastfeeding. It began with the recognition that the more deeply a woman in labour can relax, the easier it is likely to be for her to cope with the intensity of the experience without drugs. Various relaxation methods have been taught to mothers during pregnancy, mostly involving the ability to focus on breathing techniques. This was helpful to thousands of women but somehow not effective enough. In this book we explore a way to learn to relax both the body and the mind in pregnancy with the help of yoga, which is deeper and more successful in liberating the mother's instinctive potential.

This work with self-empowerment in pregnancy needs to be accompanied by the availability of a conducive atmosphere for the birth, in which the mother will be free to be instinctive and to put what she has learned and discovered in her pregnancy into practice. At the present time we are in a transitional phase in which most women are expected to give birth in a hospital environment designed for an obstetrically managed birth. At the same time there is a greater understanding of the needs of human mothers in labour, which has been leading to some fundamental improvements in the birthing environment. Many obstetric units are attempting to provide a more intimate private and home-like atmosphere for mothers, as the realization is dawning that this is most conducive to the physiological processes of labour and birth. It is now more widely understood that the hormones which the mother's body produces, which stimulate and regulate the birth process, are secreted more efficiently in a familiar, homely and comfortable place of her own choosing. Slowly people are realizing that the human mother is a mammal, that she needs privacy and seclusion in order to feel safe enough to give birth physiologically, just like all the other mammals.

The training and education of midwives is changing radically to incorporate this new awareness and there is much greater recognition of the importance of a well-established, trusting and personal relationship between the mother and her midwife.

It is also becoming common knowledge that nature's elements have an important part to play in helping a mother to give birth. For example, the natural upright positions which are instinctive and most comfortable during labour and birth allow the force of gravity to aid the baby's progress through the birth canal, and to make uterine contractions more efficient and effective. Midwives are realizing that labour usually progresses better when the mother is disturbed as little as possible and has the freedom to move and to express herself without inhibition. A pool of warm water in the birthing environment provides a powerful means of assisting the mother to relax deeply and allow her instincts to take over. More hospitals and midwives are now realizing that making a birth pool available is a harmless and effective way to increase the chances of a physiological birth and reduce the need for painkilling drugs or other interventions.

You will need to focus on what is essential and have faith in yourself.

As ideas such as these are steadily gaining ground we can begin to enjoy a new atmosphere in the labour room and look forward to better provision for women who choose to give birth naturally. With the gradual discarding of the unnecessary routines and procedures which disturb and disrupt the mother's instinctive powers we can anticipate an increase in the number of physiological births in the future. At the same time we have the reassurance of the benefit of modern obstetric help as a safety net in the background when there are difficulties or complications.

However, it is important, if you are hoping to have a natural birth during this time of change and transition, to look for a midwife or maternity care setting in which this approach is encouraged and supported. In some places there may be several acceptable options to choose from, while in others the obstetric approach may still be deeply entrenched and choice may be limited. For some women it may be very difficult, if not impossible, to find a suitable midwife or a conducive birthing environment locally. In this case, good positive preparation is crucial. If you are to gain the trust and confidence you need to make the most of what is available, while remaining in control of your body and your birth, you will need to focus on what is essential and have faith in yourself, and your own power, despite the lack of ideal facilities.

Many women do manage to be quietly but firmly assertive in these circumstances, trusting their own instincts so deeply that they are able to go ahead and give birth physiologically in a setting more suited to the medical model of birthing. In fact it is the courage and determination of these pioneering women that has inspired the transformation we are witnessing today. The power of their example has initiated the change in consciousness and practice which occurs when birth attendants trained in obstetrics begin to witness the miracle of physiological birth.

CHAPTER ONE

WHY DO YOU NEED

YOGA

IN

PREGNANCY?

When you begin to practise yoga regularly you have taken a very important step towards positive living. You have made a conscious choice to devote some of your time to nurturing yourself, both in body and in soul. This is helpful at any time of your life, but especially when you are pregnant and your body is providing the very first surroundings, or the primal environment, for your growing child.

This is a crucial stage of your baby's development in which all the essential human functions, both physical and emotional, are developing. Your baby's personality is forming at the same time as his or her physical body, and communication takes place between you and your baby on many levels at once. Throughout these nine months your baby is an active partner in your pregnancy, sharing the dynamic flow of your living energy and depending on all your internal body processes.

Physically, all your life support systems are working for two. At the same time there is a communication taking place on a subconscious, emotional or psychic level, which is completely natural and instinctive. Your baby learns throughout the pregnancy from the richness and variety of his or her experiences in the womb. The sound of your voice, your movements, thoughts and feelings, even your dreams, influence your baby and are part of your baby's world.

This powerful psychophysical bond begins at conception and continues throughout your pregnancy. It is the beginning of the so-called 'bonding' which occurs immediately after the birth when you hold your baby in your arms, feel each other's naked skin and gaze into each other's eyes for the very first time. These bonds are present and forming throughout your pregnancy, long before birth, and are the foundation of the relationship you will share for a lifetime.

Your BABY before BIRTH

By the time your baby is born, he or she will have a whole array of sensual abilities. Inside your body, your womb is a world which is alive with sounds, pulses and rhythms. All of your baby's senses – seeing, hearing, tasting and being touched – are beginning to work.

Throughout the nine months your baby is rehearsing, preparing for life outside the womb. Movements begin at around seven or eight weeks as your baby stretches and exercises his or her arms and legs. You will become aware of them during the fourth or fifth month of your pregnancy. Your partner will be able to feel them from the outside soon after that. These movements strengthen your baby's body and stimulate all the nerve pathways to the brain, enhancing the baby's development.

Your baby floats and is rocked by the amniotic fluid and practises essential activities such as swallowing and breathing, yawning, grasping the umbilical cord and even smiling or grimacing. Patterns of sleep and wakefulness develop which you will become more aware of towards the end of your pregnancy.

By the time your baby is born, he or she will have a whole array of sensual abilities. Inside your body, your womb is a world which is alive with sounds, pulses and rhythms. All of your baby's senses – seeing, hearing, tasting and being touched – are beginning to work.

Sensitivity to touch or skin feeling is the first sense to develop in the womb. From very early in pregnancy your baby feels the warm sensations of the amniotic fluid on the skin and the smooth, velvety surface of the membranes lining the womb. He or she is massaged by your movements and stimulated by your hands as you unconsciously touch your belly hundreds of times a day in the latter part of your pregnancy. Your baby can feel your partner's touch when your belly is being stroked or massaged in the weeks approaching the birth.

Hearing is very well developed during pregnancy and your baby hears a symphony of sounds and vibrations inside the womb. These include your heart beating, the sound of your voice, the air whooshing through your lungs and the blood pulsing through your blood vessels. Your baby also hears sounds from outside the womb and is aware of the voices and the presence of other members of your family.

Studies have shown that unborn babies are even aware of light changes (when, for example, you are out sunbathing) and are preparing for seeing in the latter part of pregnancy; they also respond to different taste sensations with pleasure or displeasure.

Throughout pregnancy you and your baby are deeply connected. You interact on every level as your baby responds to your actions and your feelings. Your body rhythms are naturally synchronized. As you are adapting to being pregnant, your baby is tuning in to the flow of your daily habits and is already learning to be a member of your family.

HONOURING your PREGNANCY

We can now be sure that the foundation of good physical health begins in the primal period in the womb, long before the birth. Important developments in psychology in this century have shown us that this primal phase, from conception to the end of infancy, is also a vital stage in our emotional development. We have discovered that people have an inner remembrance of experiences going back to intrauterine life, birth and infancy. This is not the mental remembering we do as adults, but more of an imprinting on the psyche, a resonance in our cells from our earliest experiences which remains with us and can affect us throughout our lives. Since a baby is so deeply sensitive and impressionable at this time, it is important that his or her primal life experience is as positive as circumstances will allow. When a baby is consciously nurtured throughout the whole primal period, from conception to the end of infancy, the result is usually a healthy, robust and psychologically secure and happy child.

The nurturing of the prenatal and newborn child is the pregnant mother's responsibility. We are the real experts in providing this first environment and essential nurturing for human life. We are genetically programmed both physically and emotionally and our bodies are designed for the purpose. Even when we are fortunate to be

As you begin to feel more in tune, more in harmony with yourself and the natural forces of the environment, your body and soul will be nourished by their life-giving energy and you will pass all of this on to your baby.

helped and supported in this by our partners and families, primarily this nurturing is our work. While this responsibility may seem awesome, it is deeply instinctive. Given the right encouragement and circumstances, we do it quite naturally, without thinking.

Of course, the fact that this work is our responsibility does not mean that we should try to be perfect, or feel guilty about our faults and weaknesses. There is no such thing as a perfect mother. The so-called 'negative' elements or imperfections which are in everyone are part and parcel of normal life. So long as they are not overwhelming, they prepare your unborn child for reality. But it does mean that you have the choice to be creative and to influence your pregnancy and early mothering positively and to make the most of the transformative potential of these months.

The first step is to honour your pregnancy and the essential work you are doing at this time, by giving yourself and your baby the time and attention you both need. An easy way to do this, along with all the other commitments in your life, is to make some space to practise a little yoga every day. This will help you to focus more deeply on your pregnancy. You will feel more in touch with your inner self, more connected to nature, and you will begin to discover that the power to give birth and to nurture your baby lies within yourself. You will also find this very helpful after the birth.

When you practise yoga in pregnancy, its benefits extend to your baby too. As yoga brings your mind, your awareness, into your body, it also awakens your awareness of your baby inside and deepens your inner connection with your child. As you begin to feel more in tune, more in harmony with yourself and the natural forces of the environment, your body and soul will be nourished by their life-giving energy and you will pass all of this on to your baby.

The BENEFITS of YOGA in PREGNANCY

Yoga has many benefits during the whole childbearing year. In pregnancy perhaps the greatest is that it helps you to focus on your pregnancy in a deeper way. This creates the space and time you need to integrate the process of change which is taking place and to gradually adjust your priorities and your lifestyle.

FOCUSING on your PREGNANCY

By bringing your mind, your awareness, into your body, by becoming aware of how you are standing, sitting or lying down and how your body simply contacts the floor, your attention is drawn inwards. This inner awareness gives you a new perception of yourself which is in balance, in harmony with the rest of nature.

For many of us these days, life is complex and stressful. It's easy to be so distracted by 'busyness' that we neglect ourselves and forget that we are connected to nature and her power to nourish and heal us and restore our energy. Pregnancy or, better still, pre-conception, is a wonderful time to learn how to turn your attention inwards and to benefit from the limitless sources of energy which are available to you, as soon as you make space to breathe and relax.

As your thoughts turn to the well-being and development of your child, you are bound to become more aware of your own state of health and to give more attention to the way you feel both physically and emotionally. Pregnancy slows you down and awakens the instinctive and intuitive side of your nature. As the months go by you will feel an increasing need to spend some of your time relaxing and focusing on the miracle which is taking place in your body. There is a profound change of consciousness in pregnancy which deepens as you get closer to the birth of your baby. You are likely to become less intellectual or 'cerebral' and more inclined to be centred on your body, your baby and your feelings. While it is possible and even healthy to work or to be active while you are pregnant, you may also feel a need to retreat and to rest more, in addition to building up your strength and vitality for the birth.

Setting aside some time each day for yoga will give you this space to focus more deeply on your pregnancy. This is especially important if you are working or have a busy or stressful life or a demanding family to look after. No matter how busy you are, yoga will help you to cope with your life in a more relaxed and focused way. It has a miraculous way of making more space and more energy available.

ENERGY

Pregnancy should be a time of great vitality when your body is filled with creative energy and life force. Much of the exhaustion and tiredness women complain about in pregnancy and postnatally is avoidable. Exhaustion may be caused by insufficient rest, poor nutrition or suppressed emotions. However, to a greater degree than we realize, low energy is the result of simply misusing our bodies.

When your body is well balanced, it functions in harmony with the life force, your skeleton supports your body and your muscles can enjoy their work of moving your bones without stress. When your posture is out of balance, your muscles have to compensate and act as supporters, so they contract and stiffen and you end up carrying the burden of a lot of unnecessary tension. You become blocked and resistant to the vitalizing forces from the earth and the air which nourish your system. It's like being separated or cut off from nature. This creates havoc throughout your whole body. The cumulative effect on your nervous system results in fatigue, which is never completely relieved by sleep. So of course, the added work of nourishing a baby is going to result in exhaustion.

When you begin to practise yoga, the effect on your energy level can be dramatic. As your posture becomes more balanced, the circulation of blood and fluids improves and your breathing flows more easily. Your body then relaxes, becomes more at ease and more in tune with nature. As your energy is awakened and flows more freely, this in turn allows you to feel more open-hearted and loving and to pass on this energy and nourishment to your baby.

INFLUENCING your BODY POSITIVELY

Yoga has the power to help you to bring your whole being into balance. During pregnancy it can provide you with a deeply effective way to influence your mind and body positively and to empower yourself for birth and motherhood.

Your body is very 'intelligent' when you are pregnant and very responsive to change. Improvement can be more rapid than at any other stage in your life. This is a perfect time to give yourself some attention and to increase your health and vitality and improve your way of life.

Our modern lifestyle, especially in an urban environment, often prevents us from exercising or using our body as nature intended, so that our full potential in terms of energy and movement is rarely called upon. This can result in our bodies becoming structurally weakened and out of balance. Neglected muscles gradually become stiff and joints lose their full mobility when their full potential to extend is not used.

For example, most of us have forgotten how to squat. This position is meant to be a resting position which our bodies can assume with ease for a length of time. A toddler squats naturally and begins to stand and to walk from this position. And yet most of us, by the time we are adults, find squatting uncomfortable and may even have difficulty sitting in a relaxed way on the ground.

Yoga is an ideal form of exercise for the childbearing year, since it encourages relaxation, flexibility and strength in a completely gentle and non-strenuous way. It brings your body into balance posturally as a mechanical structure and helps to release some of the accumulated tension and stiffness in your muscles and joints. It is a way of re-educating your body to regain comfort, innocence and freedom and to change the postural habits of a lifetime which create stress and imbalance. The physical benefits of yoga can transform your experience of pregnancy from a time of weakness, discomfort and indisposition to one in which you feel healthy and strong. Problems such as tiredness, back pain, nausea, anxiety, headaches and many other common complaints of pregnancy may be eased by practising yoga and often they may disappear altogether (see Appendix, p. 195).

YOGA and EMOTIONS

Yoga exercises the mind as well as the body. When yoga is practised in a gentle and mindful way, it will also benefit you emotionally. As you learn to observe the ebb and flow of your breathing and the release of tension in your body, you will find that your attention turns inwards and allows you to experience and become more aware of your feelings. You become more familiar with your thoughts and more in touch with your emotions and understand more clearly how they are expressed by your body. Yoga quietens your mind, allowing you to feel more peaceful within yourself. Sometimes we become so caught up in our thinking and our minds that we more or less live in our heads and carry our bodies around with us without really fully occupying them. The ability to focus on breathing for a while calms the mind and reduces anxiety, allowing us to feel somehow more present in our bodies and, thus, calmer emotionally.

Yoga can also bring about emotional healing. From the beginning of our lives our bodies express our feelings. When we are happy we feel relaxed, light, loose and comfortable. When we are unhappy, frightened, angry or anxious, our bodies tense up to protect us from emotional pain. We store memories in our bodies from the time we are conceived until the present moment, so that over the years emotional stress becomes 'embodied' as a kind of defensive armour. For example, suppressed feelings of grief may result in stiff or rounded shoulders. This physical tightness deadens the feelings of sadness which become deeply buried. When a person in this state takes up yoga, the muscular tension will gradually begin to release. As her posture changes and the rounded shoulders open out, the original feelings of grief will surface too, providing a new opportunity for them to be re-experienced, understood and released. In this way, if the need is there, yoga can be a very helpful tool for emotional self-healing, helping you to free yourself of any emotional blocks, suppressed or unresolved feelings. As both emotional and muscular tensions unravel, you will find yourself feeling more harmonious and in tune with life. Your full potential and creativity will awaken.

The additional weight in the pelvic area as your baby grows gives you a feeling of being physically 'grounded' when you are pregnant. This is increased when you practise yoga and leads in turn to a feeling of greater emotional stability, calmness and equilibrium.

Pregnancy can be a natural state of ecstasy and celebration. There are many peaceful and blissful times to be enjoyed during these months. Yoga can help you to make the most of the sense of contentment, well-being and fulfilment which women can experience when they are pregnant. Its benefits will continue in the many pleasurable hours you will spend with your baby after the birth.

Pregnancy can be a natural state of ecstasy and celebration. There are many peaceful and blissful times to be enjoyed during these months.

PREPARING for BIRTH

In most traditional societies women were encouraged in pregnancy to build up their strength and improve their fitness in readiness for the birth. By all accounts, they also, on the whole, gave birth much more easily than we do. I am convinced that modern women do need to prepare both physically and emotionally for birthing – and that it can make all the difference.

Giving birth is, amongst other things, a tremendous physical exertion and it is just as important to approach it at your physical best as it would be if you were to enter an athletic event or go on a trekking expedition. It is also a great emotional challenge, a time when you are experiencing the important life transition from woman to mother. Throughout the childbearing years you will be experiencing change and facing new and unknown experiences.

It is as important to address your emotions and feelings as it is to prepare physically for birth and mothering.

Yoga is an ideal exercise system to use as preparation for birth because it is deeply effective and yet completely effortless and non-strenuous. It prepares your body for birth and mothering and, at the same time, works on a psychological level and has a meditational quality which connects you to the sources of energy which empower you to create and give birth to a new life.

Your INSTINCTS and INTUITION

Your body already has all the knowledge and power you need to give birth and to nurture your baby. This knowledge is instinctive. It is in your genes and it has been there since you yourself were conceived. You can trust its wisdom, even though what will happen at the time is unknown and unpredictable.

Practising yoga while you are pregnant is an effective way to discover and learn how to liberate these instincts and to overcome any inhibitions which could prevent you from using your instinctive potential when you are giving birth. Yoga will help you to relax and to trust and have confidence in the power of your body to go through the natural processes which occur during birthing, even if you start out feeling apprehensive and fearful.

With practice you will begin to feel from the inside that if all goes well, you have the ability to do it! You will develop an authentic sense of being at one with yourself, which allows you to experience your birth from a position of inner power, whether it is straightforward or complicated, difficult or easy. Yoga will enable you to be in tune with the source of primordial knowledge and wisdom within yourself.

The majority of women are perfectly capable, in the right circumstances, of giving birth naturally without help. But it is important, even if you are hoping to do so, to remain openminded so that you can accept the safety net of medical care should the need arise, as it does in a small percentage of births. Accepting help from a position of clarity and autonomy, when it is really necessary, is never disempowering, it is wise.

Pregnant women are incredibly intuitive. When you are carrying a new life inside you, your intellectual and rational side may quieten for a while, but your animal instincts, your intuitive and visionary powers awaken. Dreams become more vivid and easier to remember and you may feel very creative and inspired to make things with your hands, paint or draw, cook inventively or rearrange and decorate your house.

These heightened intuitive powers will help you to sense what is right and not right for you. They will guide you in choosing just the right environment and the right helpers for the birth of your baby – especially towards the end of your pregnancy when the 'nesting instinct' is strongest. They will also help you to make the best decisions for yourself in labour.

Generally when you follow what your intuition is telling you, what your heart desires and your gut feelings, you are unlikely to go wrong. This inner guidance will stand you in good stead in every situation in life as well as during your birth. The inner connection you gain from practising yoga helps you to access your intuition and give it time to rise up into your conscious awareness. When you can feel and trust this inner wisdom and you know that it will guide you through any difficulty, then you can look forward to the challenge of giving birth without fear.

COPING with your LABOUR

The sensations you will experience in the hours of labour as your body opens to give birth are very powerful. They will take you to limits of endurance which you didn't realize that you had. There are extremes of both pain and pleasure, ecstatic highs and deep dark lows involved in the extraordinary inner journey which brings your baby to birth.

The processes of birth are involuntary. They happen without your conscious control. Contractions of the uterus which occur in labour are stimulated by the release of a hormone called oxytocin by your brain. As the contractions strengthen, your body adapts physiologically to the increase in intensity.

Your brain also produces floods of hormones called endorphins which are natural relaxants and pain relievers. They help to bring about the change of consciousness needed as the birth draws closer. Your 'thinking mind' quietens and the primitive or instinctive part of your brain takes over. During pregnancy, endorphin secretion increases in preparation for birth. This is enhanced by your yoga and breathing practice which stimulates the release of endorphins, thus preparing your body's physiological responses to pain in labour.

The very best way to cope with the hours of labour is to accept whatever the experience brings you and to surrender to this involuntary process. The art of getting through labour is to relax and trust your body, to let go of your mind and let your instincts take over. With this attitude you can look forward to it just as you would to a journey full of unexpected events. Then with a little patience and perseverance you will soon be holding your newborn baby in your arms.

Yoga is a wonderful preparation for this. It teaches you to make space between your thoughts to focus on what you are feeling in your body and this is precisely the same kind of surrender and letting go which you need to do in labour. Then you can relax deeply and accept and yield to the process which is taking place rather than resist and fight it. This reduces pain and makes it easier to cope. So throughout your pregnancy you are slowly cultivating a really effective way to relax and enhance your ability to accept the power of birth.

When you can feel and trust this inner wisdom and you know that it will guide you through any difficulty, then you can look forward to the challenge of giving birth without fear.

The HELP of the BREATH

Yoga teaches you to let your breathing flow naturally and normally, and to be aware of its rhythm. By closing your eyes and focusing on the alternating cycle of inhalation and exhalation, your attention is drawn within to your own inner feeling 'centre'. You will also be learning to become conscious of your body's relationship with gravity and discovering the way in which your breathing allows you to connect with this awareness.

When you become practised in this, you develop an increased feeling of physical and psychological stability – a feeling that you have both feet firmly on the ground, so to speak; that you are 'grounded'.

Then it is not necessary to learn any special breathing techniques for labour and birth, when breathing should be free and spontaneous. In fact, having to memorize such techniques can be distracting and prevent you from fully letting yourself go.

However, to be able to concentrate on the 'breath' – the source of all life – can help you to get through the most difficult times in your labour. Knowing how to focus your awareness on your breathing without disturbing its natural rhythm will stand you in good stead if you feel a need to centre yourself, or if you feel overwhelmed by the intensity of the sensations when you are in labour. Many women find this deeply effective as a way to stay calm and grounded through the most stormy and turbulent contractions.

When you practise the yoga positions you learn to breathe and release the sensations of stiffness as your muscles lengthen and stretch. This is good practice for breathing through contractions in labour to dissolve and release the pain. Also, some of the pain in labour may be associated with stiffness caused by tight muscles in the pelvic area. Working through and releasing some of this tension during pregnancy may also help to reduce the pain you will experience during labour and birth.

While this is true, it is important not to have any illusions that breathing will take away the pain of labour. However, it can certainly help you in a powerful way to release some of it and not to tense up, resist or fight against it. It also has a miraculous way of transforming your perception of the pain so that it becomes tolerable and acceptable.

Finally, it can also be said that breathing comfortably without pushing or holding the breath is also important for your baby, who is depending on you for his or her supply of oxygen throughout labour.

DEVELOPING COMFORT and
EASE in BIRTHING POSITIONS

Many of the yoga positions we use in pregnancy are very similar to positions women instinctively assume in labour, especially those which involve opening and releasing in the pelvis. They widen the pelvic diameters, helping to position the baby properly, and also prepare you psychologically to open and release while you are giving birth. Regular practice of the pelvic exercises helps you to develop ease in positions such as squatting and kneeling which are natural during labour and birth and which allow gravity to assist your baby's passage through the birth canal. While you are doing yoga in pregnancy your body automatically absorbs this knowledge, so that without needing to think about it at the time, you will move freely and spontaneously in labour.

Informing your body in this way through practical experience is more powerful than any ideas you can remember mentally. You will be gradually re-educating your body to be instinctive and to naturally use positions such as squatting, which bring your body into harmony with gravity. In fact, since giving birth involves using your body to make the most of the help of gravity, the new yoga, with its emphasis on grounding, is ideal and effective preparation.

DISCOVERING your INNER POWER

This is a truly remarkable time in your life. You are going through an incredible transformation. You are carrying a child and you have already begun the experience of motherhood. Inside you is a little person who is one of the most important people in your life. It is your challenge to love and guide this person through life to the best of your ability. As a mother of four, I can tell you that you are in for an amazing adventure, in which you are going to learn a lot about yourself. Children are great teachers. You have a unique opportunity for self-development and spiritual evolution. You are already being called upon to be a strong and healthy parent. You need to be fully in possession of your power and energy.

This is easier said than done. For most of us there are all sorts of physical and emotional blocks and barriers which prevent us from having this sense of our own inner power. Generally the best we can do is to cultivate a habit of self-awareness and then work in the best way we can to free ourselves from the obstacles which stand in our way. In my experience, yoga is one of the best helpers I have come across. Over the past fifteen years yoga has helped me through the path of personal liberation, together with a great deal of conscious focus on my inner psychological world. I have learnt and am still learning what makes me tick. I've worked through my own childhood from the time of my conception and tried to understand the patterns I have inherited from the past and the psychological matrix which motivates my behaviour and seen how it has been reflected in my body and in my relationships. My children are a wonderful mirror and a powerful stimulus for self-improvement.

Yoga is always a great friend and helper. I have had the pleasure to witness this in the hundreds of women I have inspired to use it while they are becoming mothers. Besides all the benefits it brings you in pregnancy, it also helps in a profound way to prepare you for giving birth. It won't guarantee that you have an easy birth or that the transition into motherhood will be without difficulties, but it will empower you to make the most of your own inner resources now while you are pregnant as well as during the birth and postnatally.

CHAPTER TWO

CHANGE

AND

TRANSFORMATION

The beginning of pregnancy sets in motion a dramatic process of change in your life. You are going through one of the most important transitions in your life – the initiation from womanhood to motherhood. You are discovering, perhaps for the first time, your instinctive ability to create, birth and nurture a child.

This is to be a challenging and exciting time during which you will experience an incredible transformation in your body, along with a tremendous psychological adjustment. The birth of a new baby also means that a new family will be born. It is going to bring personal change as well as some inevitable alterations in your relationships, occupation and lifestyle.

When you first discover that you are pregnant the amazing miracle taking place in your body will be your secret and will not yet be outwardly obvious. In the weeks that follow, as you share the news with others, you will begin to feel and look pregnant. Then a gradual adaptation slowly unfolds on every level of your being – body, mind and spirit.

This chapter will outline some of the changes you can expect to experience, starting with the marvellous physical adaptation your body makes to nourish and give birth to your child, and then exploring the way you might feel emotionally.

How your BODY CHANGES

Your body is miraculous. Made for bearing, giving birth and feeding a child, it has a natural ability to adapt to the needs of your growing baby.

Understanding how and why your body changes will help you to welcome and enjoy the transformation you are experiencing. It will also increase your awareness of how wonderfully you are already protecting and nourishing your baby, and enhance your sense of connection with the natural forces which are creating new life inside your body.

How HORMONES affect your BODY

The changes which occur when you become pregnant are set in motion by special chemical messengers called hormones. These are secreted by various glands in your body. The main gland at work during the menstrual cycle and also during pregnancy and birth is the primitive part of the brain called the hypothalamus which contains the pituitary gland. (It is called 'primitive' because it is the first part of the brain to develop in the unborn child.) It controls all the involuntary processes of your body, including labour and birth. The hormones produced by your brain work in an interdependent way with other hormones secreted by your endocrine glands and also by the placenta and by your baby.

Hormones play a dynamic role in maintaining the right conditions to sustain and nourish your growing baby, and to prepare the uterus for birth. They also stimulate the onset of contractions in labour and the expulsive reflexes of the birth itself. Later, they regulate breastfeeding and the production of breastmilk throughout the infancy of your child.

During pregnancy, hormone secretion changes considerably from the outset. This is responsible for the physical and emotional changes which you may experience in the early weeks. As soon as your baby implants in the lining of your womb, the placenta and the embryo produce the hormones oestrogen and progesterone to maintain the pregnancy. These hormones have a very important role to play. They soften and relax the smooth muscle tissue of your whole body, helping to adapt to the increased needs of the pregnancy. This softening effect enables the uterus to grow and expand to accommodate the pregnancy, and also affects the fluid balance and circulatory system of the entire body, enhancing the 'transport system' to and from the uterus.

During the pregnancy the level of oestrogen and progesterone is about 100 times higher than usual. After the birth the levels of these hormones drop rapidly to help the body tissues to return to their prepregnant stage. As a result of this fall, the pituitary hormone called prolactin is produced to stimulate the production of breast-milk. This hormone is secreted by the pituitary gland in the brain throughout pregnancy, rising to a high level during breastfeeding.

Throughout pregnancy the placenta also produces a hormone called relaxin. This is a special pregnancy hormone which softens the connective tissues and ligaments of your body. This allows the spinal and pelvic joints to become more mobile, and the strong ligaments which support your uterus to increase in laxity and expand as it grows in pregnancy. Practising yoga will help you to make the most of this natural increase in joint mobility and tissue softening so that your body becomes more supple faster than it would do normally.

Endorphins are morphine-like hormones secreted by the primitive part of the brain. They are the body's natural painkillers and tranquillizers. Their production is increased during physical activity, exercise, lovemaking, dancing or singing. They are responsible for a sense of well-being and they affect your perception of pain and pleasure.

During pregnancy the level of endorphin secretion rises and continues to do so during labour, as a natural physiological response to the increasing intensity of the contractions, reaching peak levels by the end of labour. We can thank the increased level of endorphins for the general sense of well-being which is common in pregnancy, and for acting as natural painkillers and relaxants during labour. The secretion of endorphins is enhanced when you do yoga, thus directly influencing your enjoyment of pregnancy as well as preparing you for the onset of labour (see p. 174).

Your adrenal glands produce an increased level of cortisone during pregnancy, sometimes helping to improve allergic conditions such as eczema or asthma. The adrenal glands also produce adrenalin and noradrenalin. These work together with the endorphins to regulate and maintain all the involuntary functions of your body such as circulation, breathing, digestion and elimination, including the work of the uterus. Like endorphins, they also affect and are affected by your moods and emotions. For example, fear and anxiety produce adrenalin (the 'fight or flight' hormone). In labour the secretion of adrenalin would inhibit contractions, but in the moments before birth adrenalin helps to stimulate the onset of the involuntary expulsive contractions of the uterus, which allow you to give birth.

Your brain also secretes the hormone oxytocin which stimulates your uterus to contract and maintains efficient contractions in labour, when the level of oxytocin secretion increases. This hormone will also have an important role to play later on in stimulating the reflex which causes your milk to eject when you are breastfeeding. Oxytocin is an important hormone in many physiological events of your sexual life, including orgasm, so it is called the 'hormone of love' (Michel Odent, *The Nature of Birth and Breastfeeding*). It also has a vital role to play in the emotional bonding and attachment between you and your baby after birth.

Your baby also produces hormones. At the end of pregnancy, when his or her lungs are mature and ready to breathe air, your baby releases certain hormones into the amniotic fluid. These are absorbed by your body and stimulate you to produce the hormones called prostaglandins which soften your cervix and initiate labour. Your baby also produces hormones while you are in labour.

So, to conclude, even from this very simple explanation, we can see how the complex balance of hormone secretion changes and increases throughout the childbearing year, accounting for the enormous physical and emotional upheaval you experience.

FLUID BALANCE

Your body is made up of about 70 per cent fluid. In pregnancy, due to hormone secretion, the muscular walls of the blood and lymph vessels relax and soften. As a result, the entire fluid content of your body tissues, cells and blood increases dramatically, so that by the end of your pregnancy you could be carrying an extra 7 litres (about 12 pints). About half of the weight gain in pregnancy is made up by this extra fluid which will be lost after the birth. It is distributed all over your body in your bloodstream, soft tissue, muscles and organs and helps fluids to circulate more freely through your body to accommodate the pregnancy. It also makes your body tissues more pliable to aid the passage of your baby during the birth. Some goes to make up the increased blood flow to the placenta and to make up the protective amniotic fluid in which the baby floats in the womb.

Yoga helps to circulate and distribute this additional fluid around your body, and to prevent swelling or oedema.

CIRCULATION

Soon after you have missed your first period, your heart begins to work harder to pump more blood into your circulation to meet the needs of your growing baby. While your heart rate remains the same, the pumping power of your heart increases. This accounts for the breathlessness some women experience in pregnancy (see Appendix – Breathlessness, p 200).

Your own organs need more blood, and the growing baby and placenta will eventually need approximately one quarter of the blood pumped into your circulation. To provide for this increased need the extra fluid in your body gradually increases the volume of your blood so that, by the end of pregnancy, the additional blood volume is just over 9 pints (5.2 litres).

Your blood is made up in part of red blood cells. These contain a substance called haemoglobin which has the vital task of carrying oxygen from your lungs to all your body cells as well as the placenta. It also contains iron, and one third of your iron reserves will be used by your baby. In pregnancy the oxygen-carrying capacity of your blood is increased by a rise in the number of red blood cells. Although the overall haemoglobin content of your blood is greater in pregnancy, the general increase in fluid dilutes the concentration by up to 20 per cent. This means that when your blood is tested, the haemoglobin count may be lower than usual. This is quite normal and is called 'physiological anaemia of pregnancy'. It does not affect the oxygen-carrying capacity of the blood.

The relaxation of the muscular walls of your blood vessels due to hormone secretion ensures that your blood travels faster around your body to carry oxygen and nutrients to your baby. It can also result in softening of the valves in the larger veins in some women, causing varicosities in the legs, anus or vulva (see Appendix – Varicosities, p. 216). Yoga and pelvic floor exercises help to enhance circulation and can help to improve varicosities.

Yoga and pelvic floor exercises help to enhance circulation and can help to improve varicosities.

BLOOD PRESSURE

Blood pressure is a measurement of the pressure that the blood exerts on the walls of the arteries. It usually remains fairly constant throughout pregnancy. In mid-pregnancy, softening of the arterial walls may result in a lowering of blood pressure. This may rise again towards the end of pregnancy.

Your blood pressure can be temporarily affected by posture. For example, if you stand for too long the blood may pool in the lower half of your body causing a feeling of queasiness or faintness (see Appendix – Low Blood Pressure, p. 207 – and the caution on p. 150).

While you are pregnant or in labour, blood pressure can drop when you lie down on your back. This is caused by pressure from the weight of the heavy uterus on the large artery called the aorta and the inferior vena cava, the largest vein of the body. The aorta carries oxygenated blood from your heart directly into your circulation, while the inferior vena cava returns deoxygenated blood from the lower part of the body back to the heart. These two large blood vessels run along the inside of the spine and are compressed by the additional weight when you lie on your back, which can reduce blood flow to the uterus and back to the heart. As a result, a few women find reclining on the back, especially in late pregnancy, uncomfortable. This is a sign that it is time to concentrate on using other positions (see Appendix – Supine Hypotension, p. 215).

As a precaution, it is wise for all women to stop lying on their back in the last six weeks of pregnancy. If you tend to roll onto your back in your sleep there is usually no need for concern as you are unlikely to do anything instinctively that does not suit your body, but it is wise to try to sleep on your side.

DIGESTION

Your digestion is also affected by the hormonal softening of the smooth muscle which forms the wall of the digestive tract. This means that muscle tone is reduced and food passes more slowly from the oesophagus through the stomach and the small and large intestines to the rectum. In pregnancy your stomach empties much more slowly. In some women, the slower emptying of the large intestine may cause constipation. Heartburn can be caused by softening of the muscular valve between the oesophagus and the stomach, so that partially digested, acidic food may leak back up into the oesophagus, causing a burning sensation in the chest. Sometimes nausea or 'morning sickness' is caused by hormonal changes and may cease after the third month when your body has adapted to being pregnant.

GENITAL AREA

Regular practise of pelvic floor exercises helps to ensure good muscle tone.

During pregnancy a general softening of the tissues of the genital area may be noticeable due to hormonal secretions. The blood and fluid supply to the area increases so that the labia and clitoris become fuller and softer and often much more sensitive. Sometimes the increased blood flow can result in enlarged veins in the vulval area (see Appendix – Varicosities, p. 216). The softening of the vulva and perineum in pregnancy ensures that they will be capable of expanding and stretching as your baby's head and body are being born.

The glands inside the cervix become more active so that there is an increase in the normal vaginal discharge. This is usually quite watery and whitish, or pale yellow, with a mild inoffensive odour.

Regular practise of pelvic floor exercises helps to ensure good muscle tone of both the pelvic floor and the blood vessels and will prevent or improve any varicosities. Visualization of the baby's head emerging as these tissues open and release is useful preparation for the birth (see p. 140).

This part of your body is self-lubricating and does not require any special attention during pregnancy. It is advisable to wear loose, comfortable cotton underwear, avoiding synthetic fibres.

How your UTERUS CHANGES

Your uterus is the principal organ involved in pregnancy and childbirth. In its non-pregnant state, it is a small, hollow, muscular organ which resembles an upside-down pear situated in the pelvis.

During the forty weeks of pregnancy the uterus undergoes an enormous increase in size to accommodate your growing baby. By the time you reach full term it will have expanded to occupy most of the abdominal cavity to reach just below your lower ribs. The top part of the uterus is called the fundus, while the cervix is the hollow passage or opening about 1.5" long, which leads into the vagina. During pregnancy it remains closed and is sealed by a plug of mucus to protect and contain your baby. The uterus is well supplied with blood vessels from two huge arteries to ensure adequate nourishment for the baby and placenta throughout your pregnancy.

Your uterus has three layers of muscle and its fibres are made of what is known as smooth muscle. This is like the muscles of the digestive tract or the blood vessels, in that it does not come under your conscious control but is regulated by the autonomic nervous system so that its function is completely involuntary. The uterus prepares for the birth with an increase in the contractile muscle tissue. By the end of pregnancy it is mature and ready to expel your baby.

During labour the powerful muscular walls of your uterus will contract at regular intervals, gradually opening at the base. By the end of labour the entrance to the womb, or cervix, will have opened wide enough for your baby's head to pass through. Then your uterus will contract strongly to expel the baby down the birth canal and out of your body during birth.

After the birth the uterus contracts vigorously, especially when your baby breastfeeds. Within a few hours it retracts back into the pelvis and then within a few weeks returns to more or less the same size as it was before pregnancy.

Your BODY and your BABY

Your baby's life begins from the moment of conception. Deep inside your body, at the entrance to the fallopian tube which leads to the uterus, egg and sperm fuse to form the first cell of your baby's body. This cell multiplies rapidly into a cluster as it wafts down the delicate fallopian tube towards the uterus. The journey takes about a week.

When the cell cluster arrives in the womb, it lands on the soft, blood-rich inner lining and implantation takes place. Tiny blood vessels penetrate the womb lining to form the first link with your bloodstream which will sustain your baby throughout the pregnancy.

Although you may not be aware of it, pregnancy begins to affect your body as soon as implantation has occurred when your baby is just 7–8 days old. The cells which are forming your baby's body continue to multiply rapidly so that, within weeks, some will begin to form the placenta, some will form the baby's body and some the surrounding membranes and cord.

The FIRST SIGNS of PREGNANCY

In the first twelve weeks of pregnancy the changes in your body occur internally. While a miracle is taking place inside you, there may be no obvious outward sign until around the end of the third month, when you may begin to notice your waistline beginning to disappear and your belly becoming rounder.

You will probably find from early pregnancy that you need to urinate more often. This is caused in part by the increased pressure on the bladder from the growing uterus and also by the general rise in fluid volume in your body. This will continue throughout your pregnancy. At night, more frequent urination helps to eliminate fluid accumulated in the tissues during the day. Your kidneys work as filters which take fluid waste products from your blood to be excreted as urine. In pregnancy they work harder, eliminating extra waste from your own organs as well as waste products in your blood-stream from your baby. The increase in fluid and blood volume ensures that your kidneys can cope with the extra workload.

You may very well sense changes in the breasts as the first sign that you are pregnant, and these can occur within days of conception, especially if this is your first pregnancy. The breasts may respond to the hormonal changes by enlarging as they begin to prepare for breastfeeding. They may become fuller and feel warm, tender, tingling and more sensitive. The nipples may enlarge and lengthen with a visible darkening of the areola – the skin around the nipple. Around the areola, little glands which produce natural lubricating oils appear. They keep the nipples soft and supple in preparation for your baby's sucking. The general increase in your blood supply (see p. 39) may result in more prominent veins in the breasts during pregnancy which will return to normal after breastfeeding. During pregnancy the number of milk-producing cells and milk ducts in your breasts will also increase. During these early weeks your body will already be working hard to support the pregnancy, using up a lot of your energy. This is why unusual tiredness is so common at this stage.

All your vital life systems will be adapting from the start to nourish and sustain your baby. You may also begin to feel vibrant with a joyful sense of the new life growing inside your body.

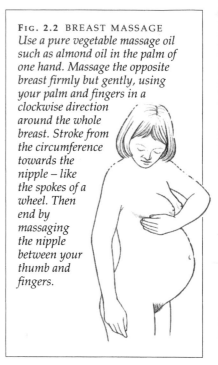

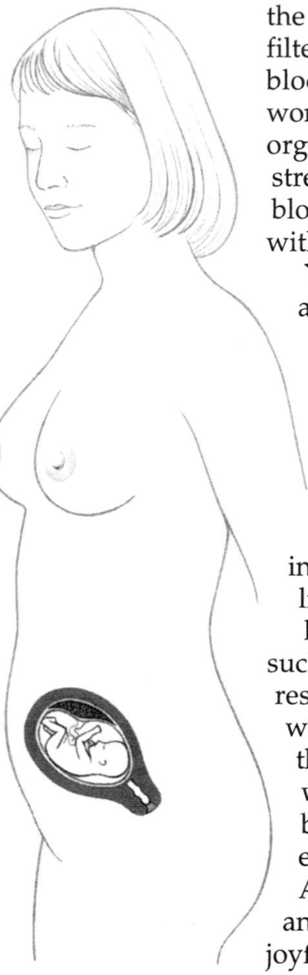

FIG. 2.2 BREAST MASSAGE
Use a pure vegetable massage oil such as almond oil in the palm of one hand. Massage the opposite breast firmly but gently, using your palm and fingers in a clockwise direction around the whole breast. Stroke from the circumference towards the nipple – like the spokes of a wheel. Then end by massaging the nipple between your thumb and fingers.

TAKING CARE of your BREASTS in PREGNANCY

Due to the increased size and weight of the breasts, it is sensible to wear a well-fitted cotton bra for support most of the time while you are pregnant. However, it is a good idea to sometimes go without a bra and to expose your breasts to the air or mild sunshine occasionally. It is not necessary to wear a bra at night.

Around three weeks before your baby is due to be born is a good time to invest in some special nursing bras to use while you are breastfeeding.

When bathing, never use soap on your breasts as this removes the

FIG. 2.1
EARLY PREGNANCY
At about week 12 your baby and the placenta have already formed inside the uterus and your body has begun the marvellous adaptation to pregnancy.

natural lubricants they produce. A gentle massage with a pure vegetable oil after bathing is beneficial.

Yoga postures which release the spine, shoulders and rib cage and improve posture will help to ensure adequate support for the extra weight of your breasts during pregnancy and breastfeeding.

MID PREGNANCY

Around the end of the third month you will have made the adjustment to the early changes and things should feel more settled. Although they do occasionally persist, discomforts such as nausea or tiredness usually disappear and a new feeling of being more comfortable and at ease with the pregnancy can arise. Most women enjoy this part of pregnancy and it may be a good idea, if possible, to consider a holiday or some time out in a natural environment as this is the best time of your pregnancy to travel.

Now is the time you are going to be increasingly aware of the presence of your baby inside your body. Some time between the sixteenth and twentieth weeks you will begin to feel the first fluttering of life inside you, as your baby moves and exercises in the womb. Then, in the weeks and months that follow, your uterus will expand into the abdominal cavity as your baby develops and your belly increases in size.

Throughout pregnancy you will be providing all the ingredients your growing baby needs. You will be keeping a consistent internal body temperature as well as breathing, eating and excreting for your baby. Your bloodstream will carry a continual flow of oxygen and nutrients to the placenta and eliminate waste products by transporting them to your organs of elimination. This is why it is important to look after yourself and to create the time and space to make the most of your pregnancy.

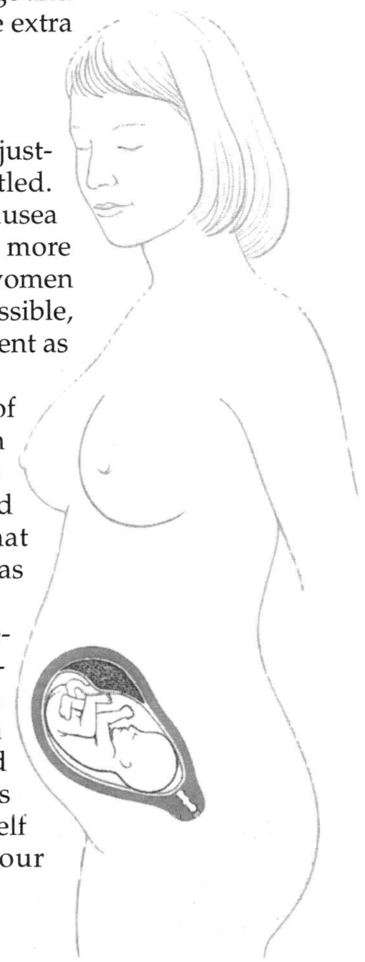

LATE PREGNANCY

By the end of pregnancy the top of your uterus will lie just under your ribs and your body will be full and majestic.

Some women feel wonderful throughout late pregnancy, but often the last few weeks can be a bit uncomfortable. Around the thirty-sixth week you are likely to feel fullest with your baby's head reaching right down to the pelvic rim while the feet reach all the way up to your rib cage. You are also carrying approximately 20 lb more weight. Not surprisingly, many women feel breathless and may have difficulty sleeping and digesting. Pain in the rib cage or in the area of the pubic bone or a feeling of heaviness and pressure in the lower abdomen and pelvis are common.

You may notice an enlargement of the breasts in late pregnancy. Sensitivity of the nipples increases in preparation for the stimulation from the baby's sucking which will regulate the milk supply.

Some (but not all) women notice signs of an amber or yellowish fluid emerging from the tiny openings in the nipples during

FIG. 2.3
MID PREGNANCY
Your baby develops rapidly during this phase and you become increasingly aware of his or her movements in the womb. This is an enjoyable time for most women. As your belly enlarges visibly, feelings are heightened and dreams may become more vivid.

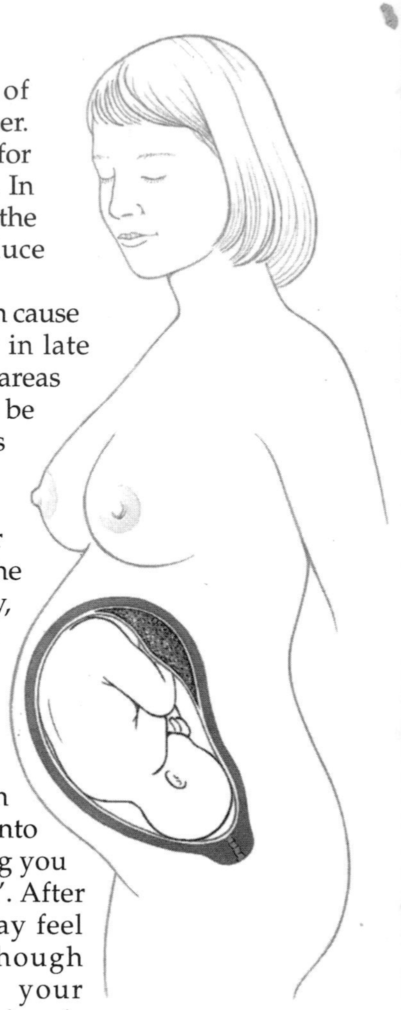

pregnancy. This usually occurs towards the end of pregnancy although in some women it can occur earlier. This fluid is called colostrum and it is the perfect food for your baby during the first two or three days after birth. In some women colostrum may not be evident until after the birth and this is not significant. Your body will produce colostrum when your baby begins to breastfeed.

Hormonal softening of the tissues in late pregnancy can cause excess fluid to collect in the lower parts of the body in late pregnancy, resulting in some swelling (oedema) in such areas as the feet, ankles and hands in some women. This can be uncomfortable, but there is no need for concern unless the oedema is accompanied by high blood pressure and protein in the urine (see Appendix – Oedema, p. 208).

Within the last six weeks of your pregnancy your baby's head may 'engage' or descend into the brim of the pelvis. This tends to happen earlier in a first pregnancy, but in some women it may not occur until around the due date. Sometimes stronger contractions can be felt for a time when the baby's head engages which may be mistaken for early labour. However, some women are not aware of this happening at all. A visible lowering of the abdomen can sometimes be noticed in some women as the baby drops when the head engages and settles into position for the birth, giving you a bit more 'breathing space'. After this has happened you may feel more comfortable, although increased pressure on your bladder from the baby's head may result in a need to urinate more frequently.

Your uterus contracts involuntarily throughout your life. During this later part of your pregnancy you will probably be able to feel these contractions as the whole uterus hardens from time to time. These are known as Braxton Hicks contractions and are usually painless, lasting for 10–15 minutes before the muscle fibres soften again and relax. They are quite different to real labour contractions. As the day of birth approaches you may be aware of an increase of muscular activity in the uterus from time to time as a kind of rehearsal for labour.

Sometimes the final days of pregnancy can drag by very slowly,

FIG. 2.4 BELLY MASSAGE
After bathing, use a pure vegetable oil or aromatherapy anti-stretch mark oil to massage your belly. Pour plenty of oil into one hand, then rub your palms together and stroke the oil into your belly with a clockwise circular movement. This helps to keep your skin supple and well lubricated and, at the same time, it is an opportunity to be aware of the presence of your baby inside. Towards the end of your pregnancy your baby can probably feel the caress of your hands through your abdomen. Continue for several minutes and then proceed to massage your thighs and hips and the rest of your body. Alternatively, your partner may enjoy massaging you sometimes, and this is especially helpful before sleeping at night. This can be done as you lie on your side with your partner sitting or kneeling comfortably behind you.

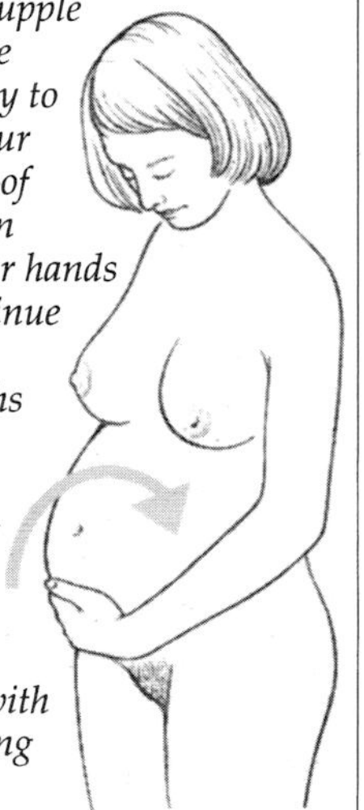

FIG. 2.5
LATE PREGNANCY
As you near the end of your pregnancy your uterus extends up to just below your ribs and your baby occupies most of the space available. Approaching the birth, your energy and awareness need to be focused inwards on your baby and your body. You will need to rest more and to become quieter and more meditative.

especially if you have passed your estimated due date. Many women feel weary and cumbersome, and long for labour to start. Some women, on the other hand, enjoy these last days of being pregnant and luxuriate in the sense of peace and calm which can pervade the period just before birth.

A 'nesting instinct' is common as you prepare your home for the arrival of your baby, and spurts of energy as well as a desire to sleep a lot are common. This is a good time to follow what your body is telling you and to sleep or rest whenever you feel the need.

What to EXPECT after the BIRTH

As soon as your baby is born, hormonal changes prepare your body for breastfeeding and the fluid balance of your body changes. Any oedema from late pregnancy will soon disappear. It can take a week or two for the soft tissues of the genital area to recover, especially if you have torn or had stitches, or are troubled with haemorrhoids or varicosities. Your abdomen will take some time to shrink back to its former shape and size, and it is bound to appear saggy and distended in the early weeks.

A 'nesting instinct' is common as you prepare your home for the arrival of your baby, and spurts of energy as well as a desire to sleep a lot are common.

When your baby breastfeeds, the sucking motions stimulate nerve endings in the nipples and trigger the release of the hormone oxytocin from the pituitary gland in your brain. This has the dual function of stimulating the muscular walls of the milk-producing cells in your breasts to contract to eject the milk, at the same time as stimulating contractions of the uterus. These are called after pains and can be felt as your uterus contracts. So as your baby feeds, your body is being helped to return to normal. At first these after pains may be quite crampy and painful, but they soon become milder until you do not feel them any more. In time your baby's feeding will give you a feeling of pleasure and well-being.

The inner lining of your uterus which provided the blood-rich bed for the baby's placenta will be gradually shed in the weeks after the birth. This is called lochia and is like a protracted, diminishing period.

Your breasts undergo a dramatic change after the birth. In the first day or two they produce the nutritious colostrum or first food for your baby (see p. 43). Then, on the second or third day, the milk comes in and this usually causes the breasts to become engorged. You can expect them to feel very hot, swollen and uncomfortable for a period of twenty-four hours or so. Then things will settle down and the milk supply will begin to regulate itself. There may be some discomfort such as nipple soreness but, in time, this will go.

Your body will continue to produce breastmilk as long as your baby continues to feed. The amount of milk your breasts produce depends on the growing needs of your baby and can continue as long as you wish to breastfeed.

Since the milk-producing hormone prolactin suppresses ovulation, you may not menstruate for some months as your hormones maintain the right conditions for breastfeeding. But, you cannot rely on this for contraception as the onset of ovulation is unpredictable.

EMOTIONS

Pregnancy is a time when feelings, desires, dreams, intuition and inner vision are heightened. From the early stages, as your hormonal balance changes, you may experience your emotions very strongly.

It may surprise you how rapidly your moods change so that you laugh and cry more easily, or become angry or irritable without much provocation. Having such intense feelings can be frightening but if you can learn to accept them you will discover that you have a wonderful opportunity of becoming more aware of your self. It can be much easier to do this when you are pregnant than it normally is because your emotions arise so easily.

This is a time to respect your feelings and senses. Change is taking place on a deep unconscious level and, at times, the little child within you may be calling out for attention. Whether the emotions you experience are sad or happy, are related to the past or the present, the process of being open to feel and express them will lead to greater understanding of yourself and make way for the mature, responsible and loving adult you will need to be as a mother.

Allowing your emotions to surface and to flow abundantly without fear while you are pregnant will enable you to become openhearted and ready to love your baby. This is a wonderful time to heal and purify yourself; to let go of negative patterns of behaviour and thought and to make way for good loving communication.

BECOMING a MOTHER

As you begin to be aware of the first signs of change in your body, you may feel delighted to have a baby growing inside you, or perhaps the pregnancy will have come as a surprise or even a shock.

Women react differently to the start of pregnancy. Some do not even quite realize at first that they are pregnant, while others are aware of the very moment of conception. Some feel tired, nauseous or apprehensive while others enjoy a radiant sense of health and well-being. No matter what your circumstances, getting used to being pregnant is a gradual process. Even though you may have longed to have a child, the responsibility may seem daunting at first, as you contemplate the inevitable and long term commitment involved in parenting. You will need to consider how you really feel deep down about becoming a mother and how having a baby is going to affect your daily life, your career, your relationships with your partner and other family members, and your freedom in general. On the other hand, your body is fulfilling a deep biological need and the growing awareness of a new life stirring within you is bound to be thrilling as well as challenging. Whether you planned the pregnancy or not, you are likely to feel a mixture of emotions, with joyful anticipation balanced by some fears and doubts. This is to be expected when such a huge change is taking place in your life.

Allowing your emotions to surface and to flow abundantly without fear while you are pregnant will enable you to become openhearted and ready to love your baby.

Deep down, whether consciously or not, you have chosen to become a mother. Some people believe that the pregnancy may also, in part, be initiated by the soul of your baby who has chosen you in particular to be his or her mother. Ultimately it is a great responsibility but also a great privilege to be pregnant. During the nine months in the womb your baby is in a state of complete innocence. Like a highly evolved being or a Buddha, your baby is pure, intelligent, sensitive and loving. If you can fully accept and tune into this, you will find that your baby has a lot to teach you and is already enriching your life in unexpected ways.

As you learn to communicate inwardly with your unborn child and to be aware of his or her presence and responses, you will be more than compensated for the considerable challenges which are part of the ongoing adventure of motherhood. Some women sail through the transition into parenting effortlessly but most have quite a profound adjustment to make in accepting the new responsibilities, the change in priorities and values which are involved.

After the birth your life will need to be centred around your baby's needs for a considerable length of time and your baby will be completely dependent on you. Undoubtedly you are bound to feel some conflict and anxiety as you contemplate these realities. However, this is balanced by the tremendously positive feelings which arise from the joy of creating, nurturing and relating to your newborn child.

Your FEELINGS about your BODY

As we have seen, your body goes through a remarkable process of change when you become a mother. It is natural to expect to have intense feelings about this, as well as some anxiety about whether you are likely to recover and return to your previous shape in the end. Some women regain their figures amazingly quickly after childbirth. However, sometimes the return to 'normal' is a slow but steady process. This is more common with second or subsequent babies.

Provided you eat a healthy wholefood diet and exercise sensibly during your pregnancy and after the birth, your figure will eventually return to virtually its prepregnant shape, although sometimes some change is inevitable. It is unwise to diet, thus depriving yourself of important nutrition. This will only make you feel depleted and low in energy. It is best if you can enjoy the glowing fullness and sensuality which are normal in early motherhood and accept this as nature's way of ensuring that you are able to nourish your baby. There is no point in feeling pressurized to live up to any fashionable ideals of how a woman's body should look. You may find that you feel more comfortable with your body after having a child and appreciate how wonderfully it is serving you and your baby.

Some women feel entirely positive about their bodies in pregnancy. They enjoy a feeling of radiant health and energy accompanied by a glowing complexion and shining hair. However, for others it may be quite difficult to feel positive, especially if pregnancy is

*A*s *you learn to communicate inwardly with your unborn child and to be aware of his or her presence and responses, you will be more than compensated for the considerable challenges which are part of the ongoing adventure of motherhood.*

47

accompanied by nausea, tiredness, stretch marks, indigestion or other discomforts. Most of these problems can be helped by restoring balance in the body through specific exercise, massage, diet, or natural therapies (see Appendix, p. 195).

The biggest adjustment may come at the beginning of your pregnancy as you first notice your waistline disappearing and your breasts and belly enlarging. On the other hand, the early changes may be exciting and fascinating while the fullness at the end may be more difficult to accept. Most women feel dismayed soon after the birth when they first view their saggy belly in the mirror but, miraculously, it will return to normal during the early postnatal months.

It is realistic to expect to have a variety of emotional reactions to your changing body during your childbearing year. You may enjoy the fruitful rounded form of your pregnant shape or, on the other hand, it may be difficult at times to reconcile your new body image with the way you perceived yourself before pregnancy. These feelings are also likely to be affected by the way your partner or close associates feel and react to your changing appearance now you are pregnant.

Certainly resting, exercising and eating sensibly can make all the difference to the way you feel and transform your perception of your pregnant self. It is helpful if you are able to let go of any conditioned or fashionable expectations of the ideal female body and develop a positive attitude towards its marvellous ability to create and nurture your baby. This is a wonderful time to enjoy your body and to perceive its beauty from the inside out, to ask for nourishment and accept it. True beauty is an external reflection of an inner sense of well-being and contentment. This arises very naturally from the deeper consciousness and enjoyment of your body which you will discover when you practise yoga.

PARENTING ALONE

If you are having a baby alone it is especially important for you to have all the help and support you can get.

It may be your preferred choice to be a single parent. If, however, you find yourself unexpectedly alone, you may feel vulnerable, unprotected and unsupported at times, especially if the father of your baby is unable or unwilling to meet the challenge of fatherhood. Such feelings are likely to arise at times, even if you have chosen deliberately to be a single parent.

Whatever your circumstances, there are going to be times when facing the challenges of pregnancy, birth and parenting alone are not going to be easy without the love and support of a partner. Nevertheless, many women do go through this experience alone and manage very well, deriving great joy and satisfaction from the arrival of a baby and the start of a single parent family.

It may help to anticipate some of the likely difficulties and to try to look for some positive solutions ahead of time. Loneliness and having to manage on your own at those moments when you feel you cannot cope will probably be the biggest problem, so it is especially important to have a network of possible helpers, whether they are friends with whom you can share childcare, family or professional helpers, and to try to establish these links ahead of time if possible.

If you choose your place of birth carefully, finding very support-ive and personal care, it will help. A personal connection with your midwife is especially important if you will be alone in labour. You can try asking to be introduced to one or two midwives who may attend your birth, explaining that you are having your baby alone and would welcome this support. It is also possible in some areas to arrange for an independent midwife to look after you, and this is well worthwhile if you can afford the extra expense of private care.

Having a birth partner with you for emotional support and help in labour can be a great comfort. You might consider asking a friend, family member or antenatal teacher to accompany you at the time, and possibly to come with you to some birth preparation classes too.

Finances may be a problem when parenting a baby alone and careful planning in advance about how you are going to cope with the expense involved is important. There are special organizations (see p. 219) which offer help and advice to single parents on a broad range of issues which include information about entitlement to Social Security and maternity benefits, as well as other problems.

If you are going to have to work after the birth it will bring you peace of mind to investigate the choices of childcare in your area ahead of time.

Looking after yourself when you are involved in the intensity of being alone with a new baby is something that will need determined planning. It is vital to arrange a little bit of time and freedom to pamper and care for yourself so that responding constantly to your baby's needs does not become overwhelming. You need to take little bits of time out in the early days in order to refresh yourself and stay sane. You also need to plan the practicalities of your everyday life well in order to make sure you feed yourself well and get enough rest and relaxation.

Keeping up your yoga in the brief snatches of time when your baby is content and does not need you will help you enormously to feel nurtured. Your baby needs a lot of physical contact and care while breastfeeding and being carried. This means that your body is 'giving' constantly to another. When you are alone and no one is cuddling you, attention to your body through regular practice of a few postures and some breathing and relaxation helps to replenish all the energy you are giving out.

The occasional body massage by a professional masseur is a wonderful way to pamper yourself, and is more of a necessity than a luxury if you are the sole carer of a baby.

Some other interest or source of stimulation is going to be impor-tant so it is wise to think ahead about how you are going to nourish, amuse and entertain yourself in the early weeks and months of parenting. Your relationship with your baby will be your priority but this need not mean a complete denial of your own needs, as it

It is vital to arrange a little bit of time and freedom to pamper and care for yourself so that responding constantly to your baby's needs does not become overwhelming.

may easily do if you do not plan ahead to give a bit of attention to yourself.

Above all, give yourself space for your feelings and, if possible, cultivate a friendship or relationship where you can share them with another person – or else keep a journal. Allow yourself to feel and express emotions such as anger, hurt, bitterness and resentment, as well as the joy, forgiveness and gratitude that are bound to be there as well.

Contact with other mothers at regular weekly postnatal excercise classes or baby massage groups can be an invaluable source of support at this time, so try to find out what is available before the birth and then make the effort to get there soon after your baby is born. Spending time with other women who are going through a similar experience is vital. Your baby's health and happiness do depend on you. Naturally, this is true of all mothers, but the responsibility may seem daunting if you are alone and become isolated. Of course, it is helpful to have two people involved in parenting a baby but it is also quite possible for one parent to manage extremely well with some careful planning and the right kind of support.

PREGNANT AGAIN

If this is your second or a subsequent baby you are bound to wonder whether you have the capacity to love another child and will also be thinking about the practical implications of introducing a new baby into your family and how this is likely to affect your other child or children and your relationship with your partner.

In some ways you have the advantage of your previous experience to make things more familiar and easier this time around. Or perhaps there were difficulties last time which need to be resolved so that you can approach this experience afresh, perhaps in a different way.

If another pregnancy is a surprise or has come sooner than expected, accepting the reality that another baby is on the way may involve quite an adjustment.

Early pregnancy may be different this time around, especially if you are looking after another child or children at the same time and have less time to devote to yourself. Physical changes may happen more quickly and may be more difficult to cope with than before. Other people's reactions may be different too.

Finding time to look after yourself is the key to enjoying another pregnancy, even if you have to consciously organize this to ensure that it happens. Your diet and rest are very important. The time you spend doing a little yoga each day can make you feel nurtured and create a special space in which you can concentrate on this pregnancy and find the inner calm and relaxation you need.

It is a matter of knowing what is most important and making yourself one of your priorities. Then somehow you will probably find that everything else does get done and everyone else gets attended to. Eventually a new order and harmony will evolve which includes your new baby.

INNER WORK

CLEARING the PAST

Growth and transformation require us to release the old and embrace the new. Putting your past in perspective will allow you to become a more independent and whole human being. Every one of us has a 'personal agenda' made up of our past experiences. Some of these may be particularly relevant to our ability to give birth and mother a baby. From the moment we are conceived ourselves, everything that happens to us is part of who we become. Experiences in our childhood or even further back in infancy, birth or intrauterine life can affect what happens to us in the present. Most people have an unconscious tendency to repeat patterns from the past in present relationships. Emotional self-awareness helps us to put the past into perspective and to discover the freedom to release and change these patterns. In this way we learn to discover and rely on our own inner sources of wisdom and security.

As we become mature adults we learn to understand and come to terms with our previous emotional history, to get to know ourselves more deeply. Pregnancy can be a very good time to continue or to begin this process, and to clear any unresolved issues or tensions resulting from held back, misunderstood or blocked emotions.

In pregnancy you are going through an important life change, perhaps the biggest since your adolescence. You are facing a new phase in your personal life and new challenges. Your emotional equilibrium is also affected by hormonal changes (see p. 36). It is not surprising that many women find that deepseated memories from the past surface more easily in pregnancy, both consciously and also in dreams. The irrational moods of pregnancy are much more understandable when we think of them as an emotional cleansing or releasing which is natural at this time and is helping you to prepare for motherhood.

Not everyone needs to do so consciously, but it can be very helpful to undertake a good look at your own birth, infancy, childhood and adolescence, and your relationship with your parents. You may be fortunate to have had a smooth and happy childhood and satisfactory relationships with your parents. This will add to your confidence and give you a good basis for your own parenting. It is always useful to look at family attitudes to sexuality, birth and breastfeeding and think about any differences you would like to introduce now you are becoming a parent and are creating your own family.

For some of us, life has had its share of difficulties, or even tragic and traumatic experiences, resulting in painful feelings which may be held inside for many years. Perhaps there has been the loss of a loved family member, for example.

Whether your relationships with your parents were satisfactory or not, you will need to go through a process of emotional separation from them before you can function independently as an adult yourself. This will be an ongoing challenge throughout your experience as a parent, but it is very helpful to begin to be conscious of these issues now. In this way you will be able later to recognize inherited patterns and have the choice whether or not to introduce them into your own parenting.

As you are exploring any past or present issues which are affecting you, you will also discover many of the good things from your past from which you can draw pleasure and comfort. Even though very few of us have a perfect childhood there is usually a wellspring of the love and nourishment you did receive which, you will find, has prepared you for becoming a parent yourself in ways you did not realize. You may discover a new closeness to your parents now you are pregnant, especially after you have understood the inner emotional ties from childhood.

The process of exploration does take time but once feelings have been fully expressed and released you are likely to feel a profound sense of relief and inner peace. Understanding, compassion and forgiveness often follow this inner work leaving you free to be yourself and enjoy your life and the loving relationships within your present family.

PAINFUL FEELINGS

The process of exploration does take time but once feelings have been fully expressed and released you are likely to feel a profound sense of relief and inner peace.

Sometimes women are afraid to experience painful feelings during pregnancy in case they harm or disturb the baby. However, if these feelings do exist inside you already, it can only be an advantage and a relief to both of you to release them. This will clear the way for the enjoyable and loving feelings from the present to predominate. Having a baby involves a rich texture of emotions which may, at times, reach extremes of ecstatic happiness and bliss as well as pain or deep sorrow. Like anything truly worthwhile, there are going to be lows as well as highs.

The best way to deal with such intense emotions is to be completely honest and allow yourself to experience your feelings as they arise, whether painful or pleasurable.

Sometimes the obstacle in a difficult birth is an emotional resistance or block which could have been dealt with during pregnancy. Occasionally, repressed feelings surface during the labour itself and this can be frightening and more difficult to deal with than if they had been addressed prior to or during pregnancy. Likewise, a postnatal depression may be the result of unresolved emotional issues and could have been avoided by attention to emotional matters earlier on. This all-important aspect of pregnancy is often overlooked and neglected in antenatal care or classes, and that is why you may need to make a point of giving yourself and your feelings the attention you need.

Anything from the past or present which you are unhappy or fearful about can be explored. Sometimes feelings around a previous miscarriage or termination of pregnancy may not have been fully resolved. Often the depth of feeling about these experiences is not understood and results in the suppression of grief or fearful memories. A previous birth experience may need clearing. Perhaps there are problems of communication with your partner or other family members in your present situation. Financial stresses, problems at work, housing difficulties or other practical problems affecting yourself or your loved ones are all possible sources of emotional pain in the here-and-now. Isolation and loneliness or, on the other hand, not enough space and seclusion for yourself can affect the way you feel in your daily life.

Occasionally there is a death in the family when a woman is pregnant. It can be especially difficult to reconcile the seemingly contradictory emotions which accompany illness, mourning and grief with the optimism of an impending birth. It is possible, although complex, to give time to all these feelings as they arise. What is most important is to take your feelings seriously and to give them space.

Honesty, openness and the ability to let go are essential when you face the powerful challenges of giving birth and mothering. The months of pregnancy give you a wonderful opportunity to learn to cultivate them. You can do this in many ways. The simplest is to talk to a friend or your partner, or perhaps meditating alone, going for long walks, inviting your feelings to emerge or keeping a dream journal will be best for you. Your midwife, doctor or antenatal teacher may be a good person to talk to. Sometimes it is very helpful and fruitful to see a therapist or a professional counsellor for a while, especially if your dreams are disturbing or recurrent.

It is wise to seek professional help if you feel overwhelmed, depressed or in need of guidance. Whatever you do, it is important to release your emotions fully, to cry away grief, to feel and express anger in a safe way, to let go of hatred, fear, disgust or jealousy, especially if such feelings have been held inside from the past.

RELATIONSHIPS

If you will be sharing the experience of parenting with your husband or partner you will need to consider how the arrival of a baby is going to affect your relationship. Your partner will also be going through an important psychological change and facing new responsibilities and commitments, even though this may not be very well understood or recognized by others. It is important from early on to consider his feelings and to make a special effort to understand and share them.

Your relationship is certainly one of the most important factors in a successful pregnancy and birth. It is also the basis of a secure foundation for a happy family life. Your partner may choose to be deeply involved in the pregnancy, birth and care of your baby or may prefer to keep more of a distance. Perhaps work considerations will determine his participation. However you decide to organize the tasks of parenting, good communication between you is vital.

People often do not realize how challenging and intense the first months and years after the birth of a baby can be. It is easy to get so caught up in daily life with your baby, and the work of keeping the household running, that communication may suffer.

Honesty, openness and the ability to let go are essential when you face the powerful challenges of giving birth and mothering.

Sometimes fulfilling the needs of your baby can be so demanding that both you and your partner may end up feeling unnurtured and neglected. It is essential to plan to spend time together enjoying some pleasant activity without your baby on a regular basis. This will probably need to be organized in advance at a time when your baby is likely to be asleep or content to be left for a short while with someone else. Schedule these 'meetings' into your life just as you would a business appointment, to be sure that they happen regularly.

It is also vital to be open with one another and to share your feelings regularly, taking time to both talk and listen. Do remember to let your partner know regularly what you appreciate about him. We all need to feel appreciated and to know that we are not being taken for granted. If you have any complaints to make, try to do so in a gentle way without accusation, following it with your recommendation as to how you would like things to change. If there is a serious conflict which you are unable to resolve, then some professional guidance can be very beneficial and helps to avoid a crisis later on.

Sexuality may be affected in pregnancy or after the birth. Some women feel an increase in libido in pregnancy while others experience a decrease. Sexual intercourse in pregnancy is completely safe as long as you choose positions which do not squash the baby. Normal sexuality can continue until the birth, provided your membranes have not broken.

It is common for women to take several months before they are interested in resuming genital intercourse postnatally, although the opposite may be true for some. The breastfeeding hormone prolactin suppresses ovulation and can also affect a woman's libido for a time. One cannot rely on prolactin for contraception, though, because the onset of ovulation is unpredictable. Many women feel, after a day of feeding and carrying a baby, that they have no energy left to share and simply need to rest. In this case, a lovely massage with a suitable aromatherapy oil can work wonders.

Sometimes, fear of another pregnancy may be an inhibiting factor and this may be eased by seeking advice about contraception. Understandably, if you are going through a period of low sexual libido, this may be frustrating for your partner who is likely to feel confused and rejected, or even jealous of the baby if he does not know that a lack of interest in sex is a common phenomenon both in pregnancy and postnatally and will not last for ever. He needs to be reassured of your affection in other ways and given the opportunity to express his feelings. There are many other ways you can give pleasure and show affection to your partner and this is a very good time to learn the art of giving a relaxing body massage.

After the birth you will probably be absorbed with your new baby for a few months. Often this starts from the very first moments after the birth, like love at first sight, but sometimes it is a slow process which gradually unfolds as the love between you grows deeper in the weeks and months after birth. However your relationship develops, it is going to be very absorbing in the early stages. The intensity of this is comparable with the first months after two lovers meet, when they are entranced with each other and seek to spend as much time together as possible. This is exactly what nature intends. Then this new love matures and other relationships begin to have more meaning for your baby as he or she becomes more interested in the world. It is important, while enjoying your relationship with your baby, to keep a healthy balance in the time and attention you give to the other members of your family, including your partner.

Above all, the key to successful relating with anyone is to know that your primary relationship is always with yourself. If you are aware of this and working on your personal inner world, then you are in a good position to relate to others. Relationships are very much a matter of communication from your own inner centre with that of another person. The meditative awareness yoga brings you – of sitting quietly and focusing on your own inner centre – is very helpful in finding a good basis from which to relate to others. The standing postures and those which improve your sense of balance are also very helpful in restoring your equilibrium and improving communication with other people. In this way you can learn to avoid projecting your own moods on to another person and let go of any poor habits of communication, such as accusing or blaming, demanding or expecting, which you may have acquired in the past.

It is essential to know yourself first and then to respond to others appropriately. When we lose the sense of coming from our own centre it is so easy to forget about this and to fall into abusive or childish behaviour, or to transgress the personal space of the other by assuming we know how they feel or think. Having said that, it does take two to make a relationship and you do need the cooperation of the other person for good communication to be possible.

APPROACHING BIRTH

Towards the end of your pregnancy you are likely to have a mixture of feelings about facing the unknown of giving birth. You may look forward to it with excitement or with a calm acceptance, but you may also at times experience some anxiety, fear or the occasional panic.

Sleep is often disrupted in the last weeks when it becomes more difficult to be comfortable in bed for long periods and frequent visits to the toilet are inevitable. You may very well find yourself lying awake in the middle of the night, wondering how you are going to cope with your labour or whether the baby will be all right. You are bound to wonder whether you have the strength and endurance to go through such a powerful experience. Dreams become more vivid in very late pregnancy and many women have bizarre and unusual birth dreams as a natural way of releasing unconscious fears and anxieties. Sometimes dreams recur – as if to draw your attention to some deep, unconscious feeling.

Fears of having a complicated birth, an abnormal baby or even fears of dying (although, in reality, this is highly unlikely) can occur.

The meditative awareness yoga brings you – of sitting quietly and focusing on your own inner centre – is very helpful in finding a good basis from which to relate to others.

It is quite common to have these feelings. They usually dissipate as the time of birth draws near and your body prepares hormonally for the birth. It is helpful to acknowledge these perfectly valid emotions and to express them to someone who is likely to be understanding. It is also very useful to attend a birth preparation course so that you can learn about the physiological processes of birth and the obstetric back-up procedures which are likely to be used if a problem or difficulties should arise.

With accurate information you will be empowered to make the appropriate choices and decisions so that the birth can be a positive experience whatever happens. Making sure that you are fully aware of your options locally when selecting your birth place and birth attendants will help you to choose a situation in which you will feel safe and relaxed.

Familiarize yourself with the birth place ahead of time and try to get to know the midwife or team of midwives who are going to be with you when you give birth, as this will add greatly to your peace of mind. The confidence and trust in your body and the awareness of your breathing which you will acquire during your yoga practice will also stand you in good stead. If there is one available locally, joining a pregnancy yoga class is an enjoyable way to get help and encouragement with your practice and also to meet other women with whom you can share common feelings and experiences.

LOOKING BEYOND the BIRTH

While you are pregnant it is helpful to try to think beyond the birth and to have realistic expectations about what the twenty-four hour job of mothering a baby will really be like. As well as being one of the most enjoyable and rewarding tasks of your life, it is also going to be intense and demanding.

Most women underestimate the sheer hard work, dedication and patience involved in caring for a baby. You are going to need to be available day and night, or to make sure that someone else is. There is bound to be a considerable loss of freedom and change in your usual activities and rhythms, and possibly the loss of an interesting career or second income. If your circumstances allow, the easiest way to cope with this may be to devote yourself to full-time mothering during the years of infancy. This will help to provide a secure and healthy foundation for your child's development and is also likely to be very satisfying.

Alternatively, you may want or have to share the care of your child with your partner or another suitable person – especially if you plan to return to work. This can work successfully, but depends on establishing a really good basis to your own relationship with your baby now, while you have the time. A sensible approach under the circumstances is to make the most of being pregnant and the early weeks and months with your child, giving yourself time to settle your baby before thinking ahead if possible. This way you can be present to the task, devoting yourself wholeheartedly to the joys of mother-hood as they unfold, and coming to terms with the difficulties. With a secure foundation, you will then be in a position later on to plan your life according to your needs and those of your baby.

New friendships with mothers of young children or other pregnant women with whom you can share experiences will help you to learn about what to expect in a pleasurable way. Caring for and nurturing a baby is partly instinctive and partly a learned experi-ence. It is important to seek and establish friendships with other mothers actively, especially if you have not had much contact with babies and small children before.

It is normal to have mixed feelings about mothering and to be a little apprehensive about your ability to love and care for your baby. You are bound to learn as you go along, by trial and error. You will soon discover that all that is needed to be a 'good enough' parent is to respond as best you can to what your baby is telling you. Like any other relationship, good and appropriate communication is the key to success and this is not difficult to achieve if you are ready to be open and to learn from your mistakes and experiences.

Most women have very strong protective and maternal feelings for their babies. These usually flower spontaneously during pregnancy and soon after the birth, although it may take some time before you are fully aware of them. It is very unusual for a mother not to have this instinctive love for her baby and professional help or therapy is needed if this is the case. Maternal instinct arises normally as part of the natural physiological process which unfolds during the transition from pregnancy to birth and then into breastfeeding and mothering. The trust you develop in your body in pregnancy, helped by your yoga practice, enhances this continuum. You can also trust your baby to lead the way and to teach you most of what you need to know.

It is helpful to bear in mind that there is no such thing as a perfect mother. Every woman is different and our lives and circumstances vary. Babies are usually very adaptable. So long as they are deeply loved and understood, and their primal needs for food, affection, closeness and warmth are met, they generally settle in to life with equanimity.

Occasionally a baby may have difficulty settling and the demands of a fretful baby can be very stressful. However, things usually settle by the end of the third month. Sometimes a difficult start is unavoid-able, but may be less likely if you have devoted time to yourself during your pregnancy and have, thus, been responsive and sensi-tive to your baby's presence long before the birth. This enhances the instinctive connection between you and leads to greater ease of communication after the birth.

It is important to be realistic and anticipate that mothering will have its difficult times. But the fulfilment and happiness you will feel in those unique and wonderful moments when your baby spontaneously smiles or gazes up at you, returning your love, will make all the hard work involved worthwhile.

The fulfilment and happiness you will feel in those unique and wonderful moments when your baby spontaneously smiles or gazes up at you, returning your love, will make all the hard work involved worthwhile.

CHAPTER THREE

BREATHING

Your breath flows and ripples rhythmically in and out of your body from the first moments after you are born for the rest of your life. When you sit quietly and focus your awareness on this internal rhythm, your breathing has the power to bring your mind, body, emotions and spirit into harmony. Through breathing you are connected to the earth and also to the sky. You become open to receive the infinite nourishment which is offered to you by nature. Breathing allows you to release tension, to cleanse and purify your body with every exhalation, and to nourish and invigorate yourself and your baby with every inhalation.

'Your health and well-being, in fact your whole life, depend upon your breathing, but there is a world of difference between breathing merely to stay alive and really breathing to live.' These are the words of Sandra Sabatini, one of my teachers who, during a workshop in London, was encouraging each student, while breathing, 'to give a lot of love to your lungs'.

In this chapter, you will learn to pay attention to your breathing. With its help you can gradually dissolve stiffness in your body, releasing and letting go of the effects of stress so that you return to a state of inner freedom and relaxation. This does not mean that you need to learn any special techniques to control your breathing. On the contrary, it means learning to create the space for the natural flow of the breath to occur on its own, spontaneously, without getting in its way. Breathing is not a matter of doing anything but more an 'undoing' so that the natural rhythm of exhaling and inhaling can flow freely as it is meant to do.

In yoga, the word pranayama is used to describe the practice of breathing awareness. Prana means 'air', but it also has the meaning of a subtle life force or energy which we absorb along with the vital oxygen our bodies need when we breathe. This prana comes to us from the ground as well as from the air and nourishes us in the same way that plants and animals are constantly nourished by the earth's energy. When we are breathing freely, we too are open to receive this nourishment.

Of course, when you are pregnant you are breathing not only for yourself but also for your baby. This makes it even more relevant to make the most of the opportunity to be mindful of your breathing so that your baby has plenty of oxygen and is bathed in the energizing and vitalizing prana you are taking in for yourself.

Your health and well-being, in fact your whole life, depend upon your breathing, but there is a world of difference between breathing merely to stay alive and really breathing to live.

SANDRA SABATINI

YOGA and BREATHING

Breathing lies at the very heart of your yoga practice. If you were to practise yoga without mindfulness of the breath the yoga postures would be static and lifeless and very little change would happen in your body.

It is the breath that puts your body in contact with gravity while you are actually practising the postures. Then your muscles learn to move and release according to and in harmony with this pull, rather than against it. This allows the release of tension so that lightness or space becomes possible in your body where, before, it felt heavy and constricted.

Breathing makes the postures simple and easy to do. It gradually cleanses your body of tightness and stiffness, allowing your muscles to lengthen and relax and your joints to become more mobile. Instead of being painful, strenuous and difficult, the postures soon become pleasurable, when you know how to be aware of your breathing. At first this may seem unfamiliar, but it does not take long to begin to feel these effects and to understand how the breath works in the same way in every position.

With regular practice this kind of awareness will grow. You will feel that a miracle, a transformation is taking place. You will feel more alive, with a sense of a new lightness in your body accompanied by a more joyful and harmonious state of being.

What INFLUENCES your BREATHING

Breathing takes place automatically. However, it is also influenced by your emotions and body movements. You do have a degree of voluntary control over your breathing, although you would find it very difficult to stop breathing altogether. Most of the time you are unaware of the continual ebb and flow of the breath.

You might be asking 'Why, since it takes place automatically, do we need to pay any special attention to our breathing?' It may surprise you to learn that imbalance in breathing, like postural imbalance, is very common, although it is not always obvious. Many of us do not even realize that we are not breathing to the best of our capacity. Most people have a habit of shallow breathing which only uses part of the space available in their lungs, and have forgotten how to breathe deeply. You need only to watch a baby or a small child to remember what it is to breathe in a relaxed and effective way.

Your breathing is related to the way you use your body and also to the way you feel. Poor postural habits in which the shoulders are stiff, the chest cavity is restricted or the spine and pelvis are out of alignment will affect your capacity to breathe normally. In fact, physical stiffness is invariably accompanied by poor breathing and vice versa. We can begin to break this vicious circle by, first of all, becoming mindful of our breathing.

What HAPPENS when you BREATHE

Before you progress to the actual breathing exercises, you will need to know what happens, in physiological terms, when you breathe. Understanding the mechanical processes involved enables you to be more aware of your breathing.

When you inhale, air containing oxygen enters your body and passes through the windpipe and the bronchial passages until it enters the tiny air sacs in the lungs. There, oxygen is absorbed into your bloodstream and is carried to your heart, to be pumped around to reach every cell of your body. Exchange of gases takes place through the cell walls and the waste carbon dioxide is carried back along the same route to the lungs for exhalation.

When you are pregnant, the presence of your baby in the uterus is like having another organ to supply with oxygen and from which to eliminate carbon dioxide. It is helpful to understand that your baby has his or her own separate blood circulation. Nutrients and oxygen are passed in the form of molecules from your bloodstream to that of your baby through the fine blood vessels in the placenta. The action of your baby's heart beating pumps the oxygenated blood from the placenta through the umbilical cord, to reach every part of your baby's body. Exchange of gases takes place through the cell walls and then blood carrying waste products and carbon dioxide is pumped through the cord back to the placenta for elimination through your bloodstream.

This constant flow of blood to and from the placenta continues until soon after the birth when your baby will begin to breathe air through his or her own lungs independently, and the placental circulation will slow down and stop.

The MECHANISMS INVOLVED in BREATHING

The main participants in the rhythmic bellows-like movements of your breathing are the muscles surrounding the rib cage. These include the diaphragm and the intercostal muscles between the ribs. Your rib cage itself protects your heart and lungs.

The lungs are the main organs involved in breathing. They are like two large sponges which hang suspended from above on either side of your heart in the chest cavity. They are protected by the twelve pairs of ribs which make up the expandable bony rib cage, the thoracic spine at the back and the sternum in the front.

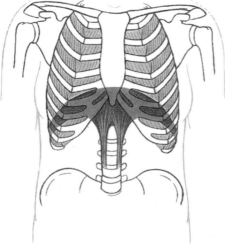

FIG. 3.1
THE MUSCLES
INVOLVED
IN BREATHING

The lungs are very simple organs and are very sensitive, their function depending on having the unconstricted space within the rib cage to expand and contract as you breathe. In pregnancy, the lungs expand to cope with the increased flow of oxygen. Towards the end, the growing uterus presses up into the floor of the chest cavity, reducing the room for expansion. As a result, you may notice a flaring of the ribs and a general increase in the size of your rib cage which will return to normal after the birth.

The DIAPHRAGM

While most of us assume that the lungs are responsible for inhalation and exhalation of air it is, in fact, the diaphragm that controls the breathing process. The muscular diaphragm is one of the most important parts of your anatomy and plays a key role when you breathe. It is shaped like a dome and forms both a floor to the thoracic cage and a ceiling for the whole abdominal cavity. The heart and lungs rest above it, while the liver, stomach and spleen are immediately below its undersurface.

Throughout your life, the rhythmic movements of the diaphragm can be felt. This is what we call our basic breathing rhythm. When you breathe, the diaphragm moves up and down. When you breathe out the diaphragm relaxes and rests, and when you inhale it contracts and goes into action. Since the exhalation is longer than the inhalation and is followed by a pause, the diaphragm rests for more than half the cycle of each breath. In this way it is able to keep working throughout your life.

The rhythmic movements of the diaphragm continually massage the organs which lie above and below it, which stimulates their healthy function. This means that your breathing rhythm influences your circulation, digestion and other organic functions.

The diaphragm also has a close relationship with your skeleton and its movements. Its muscle fibres attach to your lower ribs in the front and at the sides. Its roots (called the crura) at the back run down the inside surface (front) of your spine almost as far down as the hip bones. The slanting shape of the back of the diaphragm means that the lungs that lie above it are longer at the back than at the front. It is unique in that it is involved in every living function in your daily life, both conscious and unconscious, whether physical, structural or psychological.

BREATHING IN

When you inhale, the diaphragm muscle contracts, including the crura or lower fibres at the back. This has the effect of pulling down and lowering the surface of the diaphragm, rather like pulling down on the strings of a parachute, so that the chest cavity around the lungs is lengthened. At the same time, the intercostal muscles between the ribs contract, lifting the ribs and the sternum. Thus, the diameter of the chest from the front to back also increases. The muscles of the thoracic spine also lengthen so that the ribs can expand at the back. So your chest cavity enlarges in all dimensions. As this is happening your lungs expand so that a vacuum is created inside them. Then air rushes into the spongy air sacs of the lungs to equalize the pressure with that of the atmosphere. Acting like sponges, the lungs absorb the incoming air, filling up the expanded chest cavity.

This means that you never need to make an effort to breathe in or 'pull in' the inhalation. If you are attentive to your posture, then the rib cage will expand of its own accord to make plenty of space for the incoming breath to flow effortlessly into your lungs.

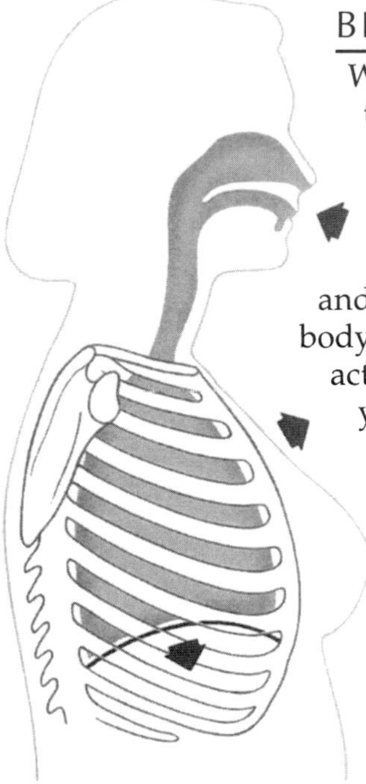

BREATHING OUT

When the diaphragm relaxes, the intercostal muscles relax too so that the whole chest cavity shortens and the ribs and sternum descend, pressing down on the lungs. This increases inside pressure and the air in the sacs is expelled through your nose or mouth.

Like the inhalation, if your posture is well balanced and your mind is relaxed, the exhalation will leave your body without effort. You do not need to try to breathe out actively or to control or lengthen the exhalation. Rather, you will learn how to let your outbreath leave voluntarily, taking with it everything your body needs to get rid of, cleansing, releasing and purifying your whole system. Then, when outbreath leaves the lungs empty, the inhalation which follows will be full and satisfactory.

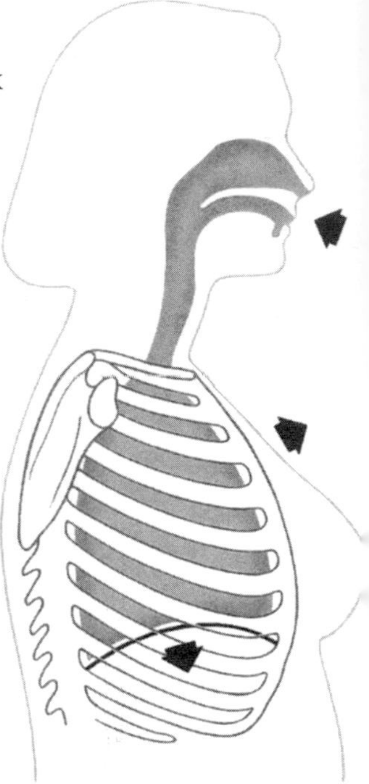

BREATHING and EMOTIONS

You may find, when you begin to practise mindful breathing, that along with the release of muscular tension there is also a need sometimes to release or express your feelings. Especially in pregnancy, there is a natural tendency for emotions to surface more readily than usual. It is like a natural cleansing process which helps to prepare you for birth and motherhood.

Generally, when we breathe freely, the diaphragm moves without restriction and we experience health and pleasure. But, when it is tight or restricted, the result is a limitation of feelings, breathing potential and energetic flow. When people habitually hold the diaphragm tight, they may be unconsciously trying to stifle unwanted feelings. A tight diaphragm divides and separates the body, preventing us from feeling whole and our feelings from flowing. A restricted diaphragm is like a personal defence against painful feelings but it will also reduce our sensations of pleasure and joy.

When feelings are held down or suppressed for many years, the diaphragm can become rigid and act like a lid. These feelings may be of intense rage or grief, for example, which may have collected over years of having to control assertive or expressive emotions. When this is the case, breathing is bound to be shallow and restricted to a degree and the postural problems resulting from the holding pattern in the diaphragm and interrelated muscles may also be present. In this way, the body expresses our emotional states. Most people are unaware that they are holding down all these feelings and may simply have become used to a somewhat depressed or low level of energy and feeling. Most of us experience this to a degree, which can be more or less intense depending on the circumstances. When a person with a tense diaphragm begins to practise yoga and

FIG. 3.2
HOW THE
DIAPHRAGM
MOVES
(a) Inhalation. When you breathe in, the diaphragm contracts and moves down, lengthening the chest cavity as the lungs fill with fresh air.

(b) Exhalation. Breathing out, the diaphragm relaxes and moves up, shortening the chest cavity so that the stale air is relaxed out of your lungs and leaves through your nose or mouth.

learns to allow the breath to flow freely, the tightness will begin to loosen and the held-down emotions are likely to surface. Blocked energy and emotion will gradually release with continued breathing practice as the diaphragm regains its flexibility.

The feelings that come up can sometimes be very intense at first, especially if they have been held down for a long time, and it may occasionally be necessary to seek the help of a sympathetic therapist. While initially the floods of releasing emotion can be like an avalanche, over time they will lessen in intensity until, finally, they are spent and you will be relieved of the struggle to contain them and free to enjoy a new sense of wholeness and well-being (see p. 46). You will be able to free yourself of waste products both physical and emotional and benefit fully from the flow of energizing prana or life force which you take in when you breathe.

Sometimes women express anxiety to me about releasing such deep feelings while they are pregnant. They are usually concerned that it will disturb or upset the baby. I am sure that this is not the case. On the contrary, when the blocked emotions release, the diaphragm will relax and make more space both physically and emotionally for the baby, as well as bringing all the benefits of better breathing.

In fact, I am sure that it is generally best to deal with these issues sooner rather than later and this way you can avoid being confronted with them during your labour and birth, or later when you are busy mothering your baby. Sometimes blocked emotions can be the cause of difficulties during the birth when you are going to need to surrender to the power of the contractions and breathe without holding back. Learning to let go of your feelings will help you to let go when you are giving birth. Facing and overcoming your fears now will only help you be without fear in labour. Similarly, some breastfeeding difficulties can be emotional in origin so it can only be helpful to allow your emotions to surface now if they need to.

So if you find yourself tearful or full of emotions welling up during or after your breathing or yoga practice, then try to trust the wisdom of your body and allow yourself to keep breathing and experience and express your feelings. Sometimes women experience intense feelings of fear as strong suppressed emotions come up for the first time. This may manifest in physical sensations such as faintness, nausea, shiveriness or fatigue. If this happens I would advise you to cover yourself with a warm blanket and curl up and lie down on your side with your head resting on a comfortable pillow. Let the flood of feelings flow through you and allow yourself to cry if you feel the need. The presence of a calm, sympathetic and understanding person may help you to be less frightened of your feelings, but if you are alone at the time, remember that these are only feelings which have been inside you for a long time and there is nothing to be afraid of. Feel how Mother Earth is supporting your body and try to let go and not to think too much about what is happening. Usually, after such a release, you will feel relieved. It is as if the earth acts like a sponge, absorbing tension as soon as it leaves your body, leaving

So if you find yourself tearful or full of emotions welling up during or after your breathing or yoga practice, then try to trust the wisdom of your body and allow yourself to keep breathing and experience and express your feelings.

you calm and comforted. Then understanding and insight may follow so that you are able to come to terms with the sources of these feelings in yourself and get to know yourself a little better.

This may continue to happen for a while when you practise breathing. Let it take as long as it needs to take without being impatient. Over time, things will change and you will be able to sit and breathe tranquilly and feel emotionally calm.

DEVELOPING AWARENESS of the BREATH

In the section that follows, some exercises are suggested to help you to develop awareness of your breathing.

These should not be confused with breathing techniques that are sometimes taught for labour and birth. There have been many such breathing methods in the past: Lamaze breathing, Erna Wright breathing and psychoprophylaxis are all names of such techniques. These were invented by experts in an era when women laboured and gave birth mainly in reclining positions. They were used as a way to overcome the pain of contractions without recourse to drugs. I am sure many women found them helpful to a degree. However, when a woman is free to be active, to move and use her body in harmony with gravity and to express herself without control or inhibition in labour, techniques such as this seem ineffectual and can even be a distraction. Some techniques involving very light, shallow breathing over the peak of the contraction may cause hyperventilation (faintness due to an abnormal loss of carbon dioxide from 'overbreathing'). If you are trying mentally to remember different levels or kinds of breathing in labour, it can prevent you from fully surrendering to what is happening in your body. It is important to let go of mental processes in labour and let your instincts take over. For these reasons, such techniques are now becoming obsolete.

It is important to let go of mental processes in labour and let your instincts take over.

While the exercises suggested in this chapter are not intended as specific breathing techniques to be used for labour, practising them regularly in pregnancy will effectively empower you to cope better with your birth. During labour and while giving birth it is best to breathe spontaneously, but many women find it very helpful to focus on the rhythm of the breath and, if necessary, to emphasize the exhalations. Exhaling helps you to release and relax and to counteract the tendency to tense up and hold the inhalation as a reaction to the pain. Developing awareness of your breathing in pregnancy will enable you to do this without imposing any control or limitations on yourself in labour. It will help you to go with the work of the contractions rather than against it. As the contractions become stronger and more intense, many women need to be noisy and to express sounds with the exhalation. This is a natural mechanism for releasing pain. The 'sound breathing' (on p. 72) is a good way to learn to release any inhibitions you may have about making a noise and will also help you breathe more fully.

The breathing exercises will not alter the natural flow of your breathing, but help you to make space for this rhythm to occur freely without any inhibition. They can be used at any time during your pregnancy, during labour and birth, or after your baby is born.

Spending a few minutes being mindful of your breathing will help you to calm and centre yourself when you feel emotionally upset, nervous or anxious and will also enhance the quiet blissful times you share with your baby both before and after the birth.

Breathing during your yoga practice is of the essence. Miracles can begin to happen from breathing in a mindful way when you practise the postures. As your spine lengthens and comes to life and your breathing mechanisms become better coordinated, muscular releases will occur throughout your body as a result. If you practise regularly you will really be able to let go gradually of stiffness and tension. With this release you will start to feel a wonderful sense of wholeness, a strong awareness of your own centre and your connection with the earth. This kind of quiet breathing practice has profound power. It is the most effective technique to restore physical well-being, emotional energy and a sense of interpersonal connectedness. If you learn only this from this book, you will have learned a great deal.

BREATHING EXERCISES

You need to find some time for practising breathing when you are not likely to be disturbed for about half an hour and have not eaten a big meal beforehand. First thing in the morning, last thing at night or before or after your yoga practice are times which may be suitable. Find a comfortable place to sit and make sure you have socks and a shawl or blanket handy if it is cool.

Since breathing exercises are best done with the eyes closed, it may help you to read the instructions very slowly out loud beforehand while recording them on to a tape so that you can relax and listen while you practise. Alternatively, someone else might read the instructions to you as you practise.

It is important to progress very slowly indeed, taking your time to complete and absorb each step without rushing.

At all times, allow your natural breathing rhythm to flow and do not interrupt or hold the exhalation or the inhalation in order to follow the instructions. Rather, keep going and use the suggestions according to your own rhythm, whenever it feels appropriate.

The SEQUENCE

The first exercise, 'Simple Breathing Awareness', is the most important, so start your practice by concentrating on this one only until it feels completely comfortable and familiar, and you are able to use this awareness easily when you are practising the yoga positions. It may take several sessions before you begin to 'understand' it fully.

Sometimes you can vary your practice by adding one of the other breathing exercises which follow at the end of your practice session.

PREPARING YOURSELF

This breathing teaches the perfect sitting posture, just as the perfect sitting posture teaches us to breathe.

MARY STEWART

Before you begin your breathing practice, you need to find a completely comfortable way to sit. It is important that your pelvis rests evenly on the floor with the two sitting bones placed firmly on the ground. Some support for your lower back is needed, so that your spine can then find its balance. There are a number of alternatives, so select the sitting position which feels most comfortable for you and change position whenever you feel the need.

You can sit up against a wall or a corner with your lower back in contact with the surface so that the base of your spine is supported. If you are practising with a friend, your partner or in a group, it may be enjoyable to sit back-to-back. The support should be just a light touch in the lower back so that you are not leaning on your partner or against the wall, and your spine finds its own balance. Alternatively, sit away from the wall with the edge of a small cushion, a folded blanket or a rolled yoga mat placed just under your buttocks. Then choose a comfortable position for your legs. You can sit with your legs stretched out or else cross them or sit in the half-lotus or full lotus position if it is comfortable.

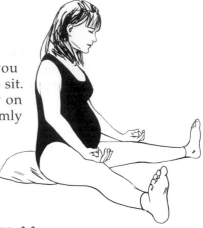

FIG. 3.3
SITTING WITH LEGS APART
This is a comfortable and stable position for breathing practice, and can be used for any of the breathing exercises. Sit on the edge of a small cushion or with your lower back supported by a wall. Spread your legs comfortably apart with your knees facing up towards the ceiling. Extend your heels so that each foot rests on the centre of the heel and then relax them. Let your arms hang loosely by your sides and place your hands softly on your thighs or knees, palms up. Enjoy the feeling of being grounded by the pull of gravity in the pelvis and legs, right down to the heels.

FIG. 3.4
HALF LOTUS POSITION
The half lotus position can be used for breathing practice, if it feels comfortable. Support your lower back and spine by sitting against a wall, or alternatively sit on the edge of a small cushion. This position may be used for any of the breathing exercises

Now that you are sitting comfortably, you need to relax. Before you start, close your eyes and feel the way your body contacts the floor. Bring your awareness to your breathing without doing anything special. As you exhale, allow your body to relax downwards, so that you are sitting well in your pelvis. Feel your lower back release down towards the floor, as if you have a long, heavy tail. Relax your legs, thighs and hips, and let them be soft and heavy. Let the muscles of the abdomen and pelvic floor release. Then, with this stable base, turn your attention to your upper body.

Circle your shoulders backwards a few times to release and loosen them and to open your chest. The top half of your body, well supported by the stable base, should feel relaxed and free. Place your hands on your knees with your arms relaxing downwards, elbows dropping away from your shoulders, so that you can breathe freely into your chest. Your chest needs to feel open and unconstricted.

Now focus on your head and let it find its own point of balance on the top of the spine by making some very tiny movements up and down and from side to side, and feeling your whole spine lengthen from the base as you breathe. Release your jaw. Let your head tilt forward so that your chin moves slightly downward towards your chest, allowing the muscles at the back of your neck to gently lengthen and release. Breathe comfortably and relax your eyes, allowing the eyelids to be long and heavy, resting serenely on top of the eye balls. Relax and release the little muscles of the face. Have a feeling of relaxation and release spread across your brow.

Now you are ready to start your breathing practice. Progress to one of the following exercises and continue without a pause.

FIG. 3.5
LOTUS POSITION
The full lotus position is ideal for breathing practice for those who can do it without any discomfort in the hips, knees or ankles. The base of the spine is naturally supported by the triangular shape of the legs and pelvis, enabling the rest of the spine to lengthen effortlessly. It can be used for all the breathing exercises, including the Alternate Nostril Breathing shown here.

1. SIMPLE BREATHING AWARENESS

Start by simply observing the flow, the rhythm of your breathing and do nothing. Let the air simply leave your body through your nostrils when you exhale. At the end of the exhalation, allow the new air to come passively into your lungs. Go on like this for between one and two minutes, breathing normally in your own natural rhythm, allowing your breathing to become quiet and settled.

● Continue like this, breathing very gently, very comfortably, and at the same time become aware of the ground, the pull of gravity underneath your body.

● Each time you exhale, feel your lower back release downwards and your hips drop down on to the floor as if you have imaginary roots going down into the earth. This subtle downward release is caused by the natural pull of gravity on your body from the waist down each time you exhale.

● At the end of the exhalation, be still and observe the little pause which occurs just after the lungs have emptied and before the fresh air comes in.

● Now, as you begin to feel like inhaling, keep your awareness of the grounded pelvis and let the air come into your lungs very quietly and passively of its own accord, while your shoulders remain relaxed. Feel your lungs expand ready to welcome and receive the inhalation so that you are aware of the ground and of your lungs at the same time.

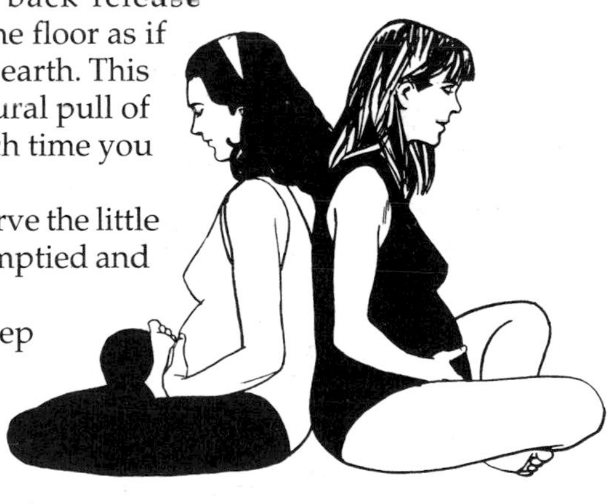

● Then exhale again, feeling the breath descend down the spine like a ripple going down towards the earth, and so on.

● Continue like this for up to five or ten minutes, or longer, as you wish. As you are breathing, try to be aware at all times of the contact your body is making with the floor. Have a sense of letting your

FIG. 3.6
BACK-TO-BACK
The base of the spine can be well supported sitting back to back with a partner. Make sure that your lower back (sacrum) is touching your partner's. You can simply cross your legs or use the legs-wide or the half lotus position. This position is useful in a yoga class where there is not enough wall space. It may be used for all the breathing exercises, including Awareness of the Centre, as shown here.

pelvis be on the ground, so you are not doing anything. Simply allow gravity to be active, pulling your pelvis down, while you do nothing. Each exhalation roots the pelvis and the base of the spine more deeply on to the ground. With the beginning of the inhalations, you begin to feel a lengthening all along your spine between the top of your pelvic bones and your rib cage, making more space in your trunk for your baby. It is as if your upper body grows naturally out of the 'grounded' pelvis like a plant grows out of its roots towards the light.

With a little regular practice, you will begin to feel the 'wave' of the breath rhythmically caressing your spine. Without any special effort on your part, your exhalations will go further down into the roots and your inhalations will rise higher to fill the whole of your lungs. You will begin to sense the ripple of muscular release which occurs along the length of your spine when you breathe. As your lower body begins to feel more connected with gravity, more 'grounded', your upper body will lighten and become looser and your spine will become more alive and flexible.

You will slowly begin to feel how your spine naturally lengthens in two directions as you breathe – down towards the roots, towards gravity, as you exhale and up towards your head, towards the sky, as you let the inhalation enter. After a while your chest and shoulders begin to feel lighter, more open and the prana from the air will be able to spread down into your arms until it reaches your fingertips. As the sense of 'rootedness' increases in the base of your spine, your head will feel lighter, more balanced, and your mind will become calm and receptive. In time, sitting and breathing like this will feel delightfully comfortable, increasing your vitality and joy in life.

CAUTION: Always remember that breathing is not a technique, it is an involuntary rhythm. Be careful not to push down the exhalations into the roots or pull in the inhalations. Above all, DO NOT TRY! Just let your breathing happen normally and deepen naturally over time. If you overbreathe or alter the normal quiet rhythm you may feel faint or uncomfortable.

When you are very familiar with Simple Breathing Awareness, you are ready to include the following exercises in your practice. Take your time to explore them, one by one, and then use them as you please.

You can follow Simple Breathing Awareness with another exercise at the end of the session or practise them each on a separate occasion if you prefer. After doing any of the breathing exercises which follow always end with a few minutes of Simple Breathing Awareness.

2. THE CYCLE OF THE BREATH

This exercise helps to regularize your breathing rhythm.

● Focus your awareness on the cycle of your breathing. Without disturbing the natural rhythm, notice each time you inhale and exhale, breathing in and out through your nose

● Notice that the cycle of the breath has three phases. First there is the exhalation. When you reach the end of the exhalation there is a pause, then the breath comes in. Continue in this way – exhale, pause and then feel the inhalation coming in – and repeat a few times.

● Now try counting slowly to yourself as you breathe. Exhale to the count of eight; pause to the count of four; then inhale to the count of four. Continue in this way for up to three minutes until you feel you have had enough, and then return to your normal breathing and open your eyes. If eight and four is not comfortable, try six and three, or ten and five.

3. INTERVAL BREATHING

This exercise will help you to use the whole of your lung capacity.

● Think of your lungs as having three parts – a base, a middle section and a top section.

● First we will work with the exhalation. When you exhale, start emptying your lungs slowly from the top downwards. Pause for just an instant between each part of the lungs. First the top section – pause. Then the middle section – pause. Then the base – pause. Sense your connection with gravity in the pelvis and the hips. Then inhale passively as you did in Simple Breathing. Continue like this for five or six cycles of the breath.

● Now we will work with the inhalation, breathing in from the base upwards. Think of water slowly filling a glass. Feel the air filling the base of the lungs and pause. Then the middle – pause. Then, without tensing your shoulders, feel it fill the top part of your lungs, right up to your collar bones – pause. And then exhale as in Simple Breathing, feeling the pelvis and hips grounded and the spine lengthen from this stable base. Continue for five or six cycles of the breath.

The length of the pauses and the breathing intervals should be more or less the same, lasting about one second each. Each pause is a moment of complete stillness and silence before the movement of breathing continues. During the pauses it is helpful to have a feeling of dropping your hips down on to the floor.

4. ALTERNATE NOSTRIL BREATHING

In the words 'hatha yoga', Ha means sun and refers to the right nostril (positive force), whereas Tha means moon and refers to the left nostril (negative force). This breathing brings the left and right, male and female, positive and negative, into balance and activates the energy, invigorating the whole internal environment of the body. It clears blocks and removes impurities from the system. It is lovely to do first thing in the morning.

It is very important here that your fingers touch your nose extremely lightly. Just close each nostril very gently. If you push the nostril you can disturb your balanced sitting or create stiffness in the neck and shoulders.

● Place the thumb of your right hand beside your right nostril and the middle finger of the same hand beside the left nostril. Now you are going to breathe in and out alternately through each nostril.

In the words 'hatha yoga', Ha means sun and refers to the right nostril (positive force), whereas Tha means moon and refers to the left nostril (negative force).

● Begin by closing your right nostril with your thumb, keeping your left nostril open. Inhale through the left nostril.

● Now close the left nostril with your middle finger, release your thumb and exhale through your right nostril, keeping the left closed. Inhale again through the right.

● Now close the right nostril and exhale through the left, then inhale through the left. Close the left, and exhale and inhale through the right.

● Continue in this way for a few minutes, calmly letting each part of the breath take as much time as it needs to take, until the left and right nostrils are equally clear.

5. AWARENESS OF THE CENTRE

This exercise helps you to breathe abdominally with your diaphragm and increase your awareness of the centre of gravity in the lower abdomen and the root of the spine.

● Place both hands gently, palms down, on your lower belly just above the pubic bone so that they cradle your baby. The lower abdomen is the power centre of your body – the Chinese call it the Tantien – and is thus the best place for your growing baby to be.

● Now focus your awareness on your breathing, inhaling and exhaling through your nose. Pay special attention to the exhalations. Notice the point at which each exhalation starts. Let the breath out slowly, breathing out until you reach the end of the breath. Pause in the empty space and then, slowly, feel the breath return of its own accord. Feel the lungs absorb the breath like two sponges.

● Continue until you have a sense of the exhalation being long and slow followed by the inbreath coming in passively without any special effort on your part.

● Continue breathing like this, but now focus your awareness on the spot in the centre of your belly behind your hands. When you exhale, feel the breath empty from just behind your hands as if it were drawing your baby closer to your spine. Pause. Now feel the inhalation coming in so that your belly expands softly into your hands.

● Continue in this way, keeping the rest of your body, especially your shoulders, completely relaxed. Allow yourself to feel this gently fluctuating rhythm in the belly as you breathe. Away from your hands as you exhale, take your time to breathe in – then towards your hands as you inhale. Now you are breathing deeply like a baby!

● Continue for a few minutes longer, and then slowly open your eyes.

In the last month of your pregnancy you may prefer exhaling through your mouth and inhaling through your nose. This is good practice for labour when the natural tendency is to exhale through the mouth.

6. SOUND BREATHING

This breathing exercise is wonderful practice for labour and birth and also helps you to extend your breathing to its natural limits and, thus, overcome any habits of partial breathing. It will enable you to feel 'grounded' and centred through the stormiest contractions in labour.

Awareness of the Centre helps you to breathe abdominally with your diaphragm and increase your awareness of the centre of gravity in the lower abdomen and the root of the spine.

● Place your hands on your knees and bring your awareness to your breathing. Notice the inhalation and the exhalation.

● Now, keeping your teeth softly in contact, begin to make a hissing sound (sssssssssss) with the exhalation. Continue to the end of the breath and relax and pause. Let the breath come in slowly. Continue in this way for several more breaths. This exercise helps to relax and release the diaphragm.

● Try making the sound 'oooooo' (as in 'shoe') when you exhale. Feel the sound coming from deep down in your abdomen. Take the sound to the very end of the breath. Pause and let the breath return slowly. Continue for a few more cycles.

● Now try the sound 'aaaw' (as in 'jaw') for one or two cycles.

● Then try 'aaah' (as in 'far'). Then 'eeee' (as in 'bee'). Then 'eh' (as in 'yeh'). Then try combining all of these vowel sounds in one exhalation: ooooooo ..... aaaaaww ..... aaaaah ..... eeeeeee ..... ehhhhhh

● Finally, end with the sound 'OM'. Repeat the 'OM' several times, feeling the 'mmmmmmm' sound vibrating on your lips and all the way down your spine until the end of each exhalation.

● Spend a few moments in silence, breathing quietly before you open your eyes.

As practice for labour, you might like to try some sound breathing in different upright labour positions such as kneeling on all-fours or standing (see Chapter 6). Many women find releasing sounds enormously helpful in coping with intense or painful contractions. It is useful to practise sound breathing in labour positions from time to time throughout your pregnancy so that your body 'learns' to breathe spontaneously with sound for labour and birth. If you practise now you will do this instinctively at the time. Use the vowel sounds as practice for now, but feel free to express any sounds that come up spontaneously when you are actually in labour.

Before you start, feel the way your body contacts the floor. If you are kneeling on all-fours, then imagine that you have roots going into the floor through your hands and knees. Using the vowel sounds, send the exhalations down deep into the ground and then relax to receive the inhalations as if they are coming from the roots. Take in nourishment from the earth with the inhalations.

Try combining this with a slow circling of your hips so that the position and the movement coordinate with the natural rhythm of your breathing. You can do the same thing standing.

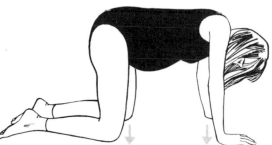

FIG. 3.7

HANDS AND KNEES

Kneel in the 'all-fours' position and place your wrists below your shoulders. Spread your fingers out wide like starfish and feel how your palms contact the floor. Position your knees underneath your hips and in line with your hands. Place your feet in line with your knees. Relax your neck and let your head hang down freely and close your eyes. Feel the ground underneath you and direct the exhalations down into the earth through your hands and knees, while gently rolling your hips. Inhale slowly, allowing yourself to receive fresh energy with each new breath, and then keep focusing on the exhalations, continuing for 4 or 5 cycles of the breath.

FIG. 3.8

STANDING

Stand with your feet comfortably apart and spread your toes, keeping your heels well grounded. Bend your knees slightly and place your hands at your sides or on your hips. Close your eyes and feel the ground underneath your feet. Direct your exhalations down through the soles of your feet like the roots of a tree. Relax to breathe in slowly, taking in nourishment as if it were coming from the ground with each new breath. Concentrate on the exhalations, and continue for 4 or 5 cycles of the breath.

CHAPTER FOUR

EVERYDAY

POSTURE

The way we stand, sit and move around is all a matter of balance. Balanced posture is beautiful, harmonious and poised, with a quiet strength. Maintaining a graceful posture can make all the difference to your comfort and health when you are pregnant. Throughout the coming months your body will have the additional task of carrying the increasing weight of your growing baby, uterus and its contents. By the time you reach the end of pregnancy this can amount to approximately 20 lb of extra weight! After the birth, the demands on your body change as a lot of time is spent carrying and feeding your baby. You will continue to carry your child, at least some of the time, until he or she is three years old or more.

Many women approach pregnancy unaware that they have postural 'bad habits' already well established and are then surprised to find that they experience various aches, pains and discomforts throughout the coming months, as the weight of the baby increases. The yoga postures in this book will begin to change these habits and bring your body into balance. If they are practised regularly, aches and pains should be eased within a few weeks and then slowly disappear, unless the additional help of an osteopath is needed (see Appendix – Osteopathy, p. 208; Pain, p. 209).

The first step to take is to develop awareness of your posture while standing, sitting and moving around. The yoga positions you will learn in the next chapter are based on this awareness of basic body positions from everyday life.

As you read this chapter, pause to try out the practical suggestions and then begin to put them into practice when you go about your daily activities as you discover how to use your body to your best advantage.

STANDING UPRIGHT

Millions of years ago our female ancestors, the apes, were quadrupeds and went about their lives on all-fours. Posturally this meant that the abdominal organs, including the uterus in pregnancy and the supporting muscles, all hung down from the horizontal spine. The pregnant mother's body weight was transmitted evenly through the four supports of the limbs to the ground. The abdominal organs were supported by the abdominal muscles from underneath.

In the course of evolution, our ancestors became bipeds and stood upright. This involved an enormous postural change. In the upright position the units of body weight

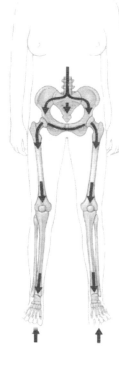

FIG. 4.1
DISTRIBUTION OF BODY WEIGHT WHEN STANDING
When standing upright your body weight is transferred through the pelvis to the legs and feet and, from there, to the ground. Rebounding energy from the ground enters your body through the soles of your feet, allowing the upper spine to extend towards the sky from a stable 'rooted' base.

are slung from the curved vertical column of the spine. Their weight accumulates and is concentrated on the narrow base of the pelvis and then distributed through only two supports of the legs to the ground. This means that the main supports for the weight of your trunk and abdominal organs are your pelvic bones and muscles.

The upright position gives us many advantages, including the free use of our arms and longer-ranging vision. However, without postural awareness, stress and strain can easily arise, especially with the extra weight of a pregnancy.

In HARMONY with GRAVITY

The first step towards graceful posture is to understand the dynamic relationship your body has with the earth. At every moment, your body is subject to the downward pull of gravity. Without it, you would be totally 'ungrounded' and float weightless like an astronaut in outer space. The lines of force which keep your body in balance in relation to gravity pass through your bones so the weight of your upper body is transferred by your spine to your pelvis and, from there, through your legs and feet to the ground.

Your centre of gravity is located around the base of your spine in your lower back and abdomen. In pregnancy, as the weight of your body increases, so does your awareness of the effect of gravity, especially in the last three months. Unless your body is in a balanced relationship to this force, stress and strain, fatigue and pain will ensue.

From a structural point of view, the human body can only function smoothly when its own centre of gravity is in harmony with that of the earth. This book will help you to discover this harmonious relationship between your body and the earth, firstly in the way you use your body in your daily life and then, also, when you practise yoga.

GETTING to know your SPINE

Your spine is the central supporting system of your body. Becoming aware of its relationship to gravity is the key to freeing your body of tension and stiffness so it is important to explore and understand the way it is formed and functions.

Your spine is made up of a column of bones called vertebrae, plus the sacrum and coccyx at the base. It is deep set and takes up about half of the diameter of your body. The front inner side of the spine is a smooth S-shaped curve, while the back surface is made up of the individual spines of the vertebrae which are the rounded points we can feel just under the skin. Between each of the vertebrae of your spine there is a little cushion, shaped a bit like a squashed golf ball, called an intervertebral disc. Their task is to absorb shock and prevent the bones from grinding against each other. They also protect the spine from the effects of compression caused by the pull of gravity in the upright position.

There is a central, circular canal passing through the vertebrae along the whole length

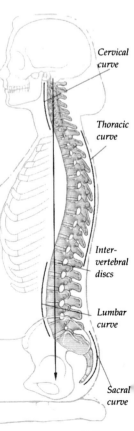

FIG. 4.2
THE SPINAL
CURVES

Cervical curve

Thoracic curve

Intervertebral discs

Lumbar curve

Sacral curve

of the spine which contains the spinal cord. This extends from the brain and, from it, nerves branch out all along its length to reach every part of the body, forming the intricate network of the nervous system. The nerves stemming from the lower part of the spine supply the pelvic basin and uterus. This is why massage of the lower back in pregnancy and in labour is such an effective way to relieve strain or discomfort in the pelvic area (see Chapter 6).

In order to become more familiar with your spine, try the following massage and visualization.

SPINAL MASSAGE and VISUALIZATION

Start by looking at the drawing of the spinal curves on p. 77. Then, working with a partner, position yourself comfortably. You could try the kneeling position on p. 124 with a beanbag or a pile of cushions to support your trunk. This is best done using a little massage oil, without clothes on.

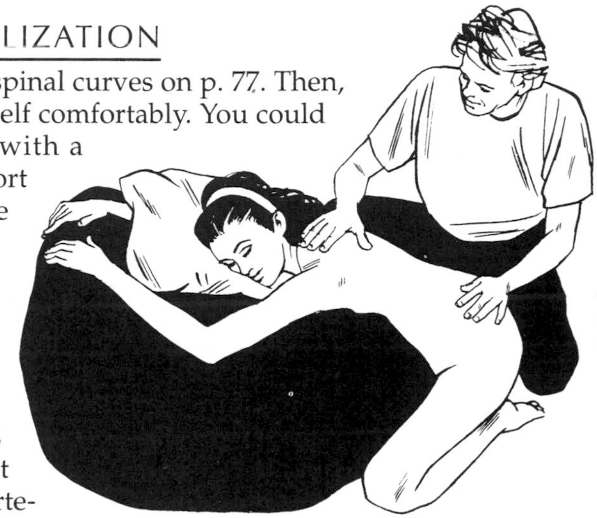

FIG. 4.3
SPINAL MASSAGE

Ask your partner to explore the outer parts of the spine from the top of the neck down to the tailbone. As he or she passes from one vertebrae to the next, relax and breathe.

Following your partner's hands as they work down the spine, sense the first vertebra in the neck and all the small vertebrae below it. Visualize the way the vertebrae continue through the upper back, the middle of the back, down to the large and heavy vertebrae in the lower back. Sense the thickness of these larger bones. Now visualize the curved wedge of the triangular sacrum forming the back wall of your pelvis, and the coccyx at its base.

Relax as your partner intuitively massages the muscles on either side of your spine from the neck to the tailbone, concentrating especially on the lower back. Then change with your partner and repeat.

The SPINAL CURVES

The unique extended S-shape of your spine is what allows it to function as the central support of your body, forming a series of graceful alternating convex and concave curves. These continuous curves create a dynamic equilibrium as they cross and recross the central axis (see p. 77).

The curves are named after the anatomical region in which they occur. The sacrum forms the base of the spine and the back wall of the pelvis. It is a concave curve made up of five fused vertebrae and the coccyx. In the lower back or lumbar region the spine becomes more convex and then continues into the long concave curve of the chest or thoracic spine. The cervical curve in the neck is convex.

The most flexible parts of your spine are the convex curves in the neck and the lower back. They make up the 'working curves' of the spine where movement occurs. The light bones of the neck allow the widest range of movement.

The neck supports your head and stabilizes the spine while the lower back allows you a range of movements which allow you to stand, sit, turn, bend forwards, backwards or to the side.

The concave curves of the chest and the pelvis are more stable since they support the rib cage and the pelvis. If you turn your upper body to look behind you, you will feel how the thoracic spine in the chest can rotate and has a degree of flexibility. But the sacral curve in the pelvis is completely inflexible to give your spine a strong stable base through which the weight of your trunk can be supported and transferred to your legs and feet.

In the yoga instructions, I will often refer to the sacrum and coccyx as the 'root' of the spine. The centre of gravity of the whole body is in the lower abdomen and the sacral part of the spine. It is the fulcrum or the point of balance of the body where our weight is transferred from the upper body to the legs and feet and thence to the ground.

Your body is posturally harmonious when your spinal curves are in balance with the weight and position of the loads of your head, chest, abdomen and pelvis. When a good balance is maintained, the heaviest parts of the body are drawn close to the central axis of the spine, creating a state of equilibrium. The movable parts of the spine are also the most vulnerable and will be the first to come under stress when an imbalance occurs. The point most vulnerable to stress lies between the last lumbar vertebra and the pelvis which bears the whole weight of the upper body. This is why lower back pain can be such a common problem in pregnancy.

The EFFECTS of PREGNANCY on the SPINAL CURVES

Your uterus is supported by the pelvic floor muscles from below (see p. 135) and six strong ligaments which run from the lower half of the uterus and attach to the bony pelvis in front, at the sides and to the sacral spine at the back. These ligaments increase in laxity in pregnancy so that the uterus can move by a couple of centimetres, up, down and sideways. While they are strong enough to hold the uterus in position, they depend upon the correct positioning and tilt of the pelvis to which they are attached.

As pregnancy advances, the uterus becomes heavier and its weight pulls on these ligaments. This has the effect of drawing the sacrum forward so that, towards the sixth or seventh month of pregnancy, the curve in the lower back is considerably exaggerated. This gradually affects the balance between the curves of the spine and the weight it supports.

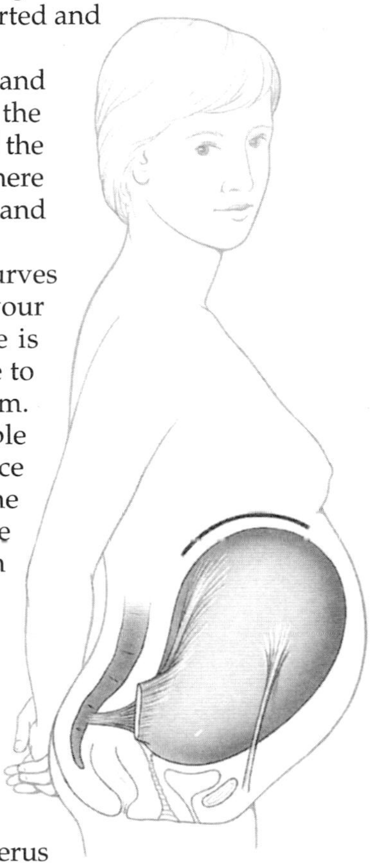

FIG. 4.4
THE LIGAMENTS SUPPORTING THE UTERUS AT FULL TERM
At full term the uterus is supported by strong ligaments which attach to the pelvic bones.

FIG. 4.5 (a)
THE EFFECTS OF
PREGNANCY ON
THE SPINAL
CURVES
Not pregnant

To compensate for the additional curve in the lumbar spine, all the spinal curves become exaggerated in pregnancy as your body seeks to find a new balance.

In a woman with a healthy spine and good posture prior to pregnancy, this adjustment will happen gradually without any special discomfort or stress. However, postural imbalances prior to pregnancy are more likely to become apparent and may be the cause of stress or discomfort.

If the pelvis is tilting too far forward, for example, it places excess strain on these ligaments and throws the weight of the uterus and baby forward on to the abdominal muscles, consequently pulling on the lower back. This may result in low back pain or sacroiliac pain. On the other hand, if it is tilting too far back, the baby is carried towards the back and the pressure increases on the lower spine which can result in chronic back pain (see Appendix – Pain, p. 209).

The emphasis placed on lengthening the lower back and grounding the root of the spine and the correct adjustment of the pelvic tilt which are encouraged by the yoga postures will help to ensure that the correct balance is maintained between the support of the bony pelvis and the strong but slightly elastic action of the uterine ligaments. This will help to support your baby during pregnancy and also to position your baby correctly for birth. The pelvic floor exercises (see p. 138) will ensure good support from the levator muscles below.

Paying attention to your everyday posture, combined with regular yoga practice, can achieve wonders in helping you to accommodate these changes with greater ease and maintain a graceful posture throughout your pregnancy.

FIG. 4.5 (b)
*Pregnant.
The spinal curves
are exaggerated as
the weight of the
uterus increases.*

DISCOVERING
Your CENTRE of GRAVITY

As we have seen, your lower back is the main weightbearing part of your body and it is also its centre of gravity. You will find that the instructions for each of the yoga postures will include awareness of the centre of gravity in the sacrum or lower back. This awareness is equally important in your everyday posture when you are pregnant and when you carry your baby after the birth.

In each yoga position, the instructions will suggest 'lengthening' or 'dropping' the lower back downwards. This is a very subtle release which does not involve any gross muscular movements because it occurs constantly as the force of gravity receives your body weight from the ground. It is more of a sense of release or 'letting go' of the weight of the body through the lower spine to follow its natural tendency to elongate in accordance with the pull of gravity. When the spine becomes 'grounded' in the base, it can then also lengthen and release upwards or sideways, rather as a tree with strong, deep roots can grow up higher and spread its branches towards the light.

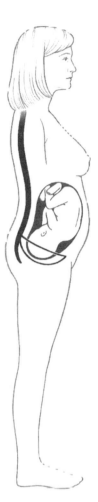

By continuing to allow gravity to be active in your daily practice, you will gradually be bringing the centre of gravity of your own body into balance and harmony with the earth's gravitational force. As the lower part of your spine finds its 'roots' through the sitting bones or in the feet, your upper body will become more free and lighter. The effect of the spine lengthening is that all the muscles that attach to the spine are able to release and the discs in between the vertebrae can expand and regenerate. This encourages further lengthening, so that a releasing process takes place throughout your upper body, making more space for your baby.

The length in the thoracic spine will also open out your ribs so that your chest cavity will lengthen and widen, and your breathing will improve.

When the base of your spine lengthens downwards you are able to 'carry' your pregnancy well. The curve in your lower back is free from tension and your pelvis is brought into alignment with your spine so that it rests directly under the abdomen and supports your baby from underneath – like an eggcup under an egg or a cone under an icecream. This means that you are holding your baby in position close to your spine, allowing your body weight (plus the weight of your uterus) to be transferred easily through your pelvis to your legs and feet, and then to discharge into the ground.

If, on the other hand, you were to arch your lower back inwards, the lumbar curve would be exaggerated and contracted while the base of the spine is pulled upwards. Your pelvis then tips its contents forwards and a kind of 'traffic jam' occurs in your lower back as all the weight of your upper body plus the pregnancy falls upon the point between the last lumbar vertebrae and the sacrum. Inevitably the result will be strain and backache. Your abdominal muscles will also be under strain from having to support too much of the weight of your belly as it is thrown forward.

Similarly, the lengthening of the spine upwards in the neck, which occurs as a result of the deepening of the roots, will also bring the weight of your head into balance with the central axis of your spine. As your posture becomes more balanced and centred in relation to gravity, you will be free to experience the joy and pleasure of carrying your baby with ease, both before and after birth.

POSTURE and BREATHING

Posture and breathing are mutually interdependent. We have already seen how lengthening the base of your spine makes more room in your chest cavity. It also has a direct influence on the diaphragm, which is the main muscle involved in breathing (see p. 62). The roots of the diaphragm muscle are closely associated with the muscles of your lower back as well as the deep iliopsoas muscles in the pelvis, which are responsible for holding your pelvis in the right position since they all attach to the same part of the spine. When the pelvis tilts too far forward it is out of alignment and the resulting strain in

FIG. 4.6 (a)
BALANCED
POSTURE
When posture is graceful and well balanced, the lower back lengthens downwards so that the uterus is supported securely from beneath by the pelvis. The heavy root of the spine is grounded by the pull of gravity and the body weight falls through the hips, legs and feet to the ground.

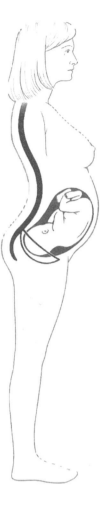

FIG. 4.6 (b)
UNBALANCED
POSTURE
With an exaggerated curve in the lower back, the pelvis tilts forward and the weight of the uterus and baby is thrown forward on to the abdominal muscles. Posture is unbalanced, often resulting in stress and pain in the lower back and hip joints. The lower spine is ungrounded and shortens so that normal weight transference to the ground is disturbed.

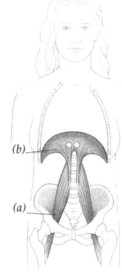

FIG. 4.7
THE RELATIONSHIP
BETWEEN THE
ILIOPSOAS
MUSCLES AND THE
DIAPHRAGM
*The deep iliopsoas
muscles of the
pelvis (a) and the
diaphragm (b)
attach to the same
part of the spine so
that breathing and
posture are closely
connected.*

the lower back will affect the closely associated deep iliopsoas muscles as well as the roots or crura of the diaphragm, limiting its ability to contract. This explains why an exaggerated curve in the lower back is very likely to be accompanied by tension in the diaphragm and shallow breathing as well as pain in the lower back or sacroiliac joints.

So a well-balanced relationship between the pelvis and lumbar spine is crucial for harmonious breathing and, of course, this is most important as you go about your everyday life. The next part of this chapter will explore how you can acquire good postural habits when going about your usual activities in pregnancy.

STANDING and WALKING

To understand how to stand and walk in a balanced way you need to begin with your feet. Your feet are made up of a series of arches which transmit your entire body weight from the legs through the centre of the ankle bones to the ground.

They are a very important part of your anatomy. When the feet are unbalanced the whole body is 'ungrounded' and unsupported and subject to stress. You will notice that in every yoga position, as well as in the guidance for your everyday posture, precise instructions are given about the position and balance of the feet. It is important when standing still for any length of time to keep your weight evenly distributed on both feet, rather than to stand with your weight on one leg only.

Besides exaggerated arching of the lower back, a common postural problem, especially in pregnancy, is to turn the feet outwards. This leads to the ungainly 'pregnancy waddle' in the later months. Even worse, the inner arches of the feet tend to collapse and the body weight loses its support system. This results in a pulling forward of the body weight on to the head of the large femoral bones of the legs which, in turn, pulls the pelvis forward and stresses the spine. So a bad habit of standing and walking with 'turned out' feet can easily lead to pain in the sacroiliac joints and backache.

Try this: walk around the room in your normal way and notice how you position your feet. Now try to walk with your feet really parallel, without any 'turn out'. Start each step with your heel and place your foot consciously, keeping your knees slightly bent and your lower back 'long'. Try to walk like this whenever you can until it becomes a habit and feels more natural.

LOOKING AFTER your FEET

Your feet are a vital part of the structural balance of your whole body. They work in coordination with the spine and pelvis. Learning to walk and stand well on your feet will help to bring your body into balance from the base up.

Most people have damaged feet through wearing tight and narrow shoes so that the feet become compressed and lose the ability to

FIG. 4.8 (a)
POSITIONING THE
FEET CORRECTLY
*When the feet are
parallel the heels
spread. The legs
align with the hips
and the lower back
widens allowing
normal weight
transfer through
the pelvis to the
ground.*

FIG. 4.8 (b)
*With feet turned
out, the heels are
turned inwards
affecting the normal
alignment with the
hips and narrowing
the lower back. Pain
can result in the
lower back,
sacroiliac joints,
hips or knees, as
weight transfer
is disturbed
and stress
accumulates.*

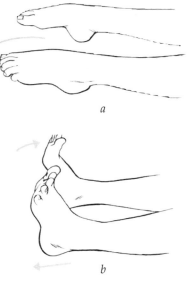

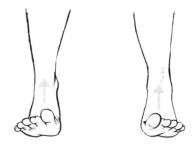

'spread'. Toes suffer from this cramping effect so that they are squashed together and may have lost their ability to move independently. Wearing high heels, which throw the weight on to the front of the foot, is also highly damaging to the whole postural balance of the body.

It is wise to give up wearing high heels completely. Try to find soft, comfortable, flat shoes which allow plenty of space for your toes. Even a small heel has a profound effect on your posture and throws you off balance. Some shoe shops specialize in shoes and sandals which are designed to be both foot-shaped and fashionable. At home or out of doors, take advantage of the opportunity to walk around bare foot as much as possible.

Wear cotton socks or tights so that your feet can 'breathe', and open sandals in warm weather. Try to become conscious of the way you position your feet when standing and walking. Walk for at least one hour every day but when you do not need to stand, get your feet up and rest them!

Regular massage of the feet is wonderful in pregnancy. You can massage your own feet, but it is a marvellously relaxing treat to have your feet massaged by a friend, partner or a professional masseur.

Here are some simple foot exercises you can do whenever you remember. They will help to keep your ankles flexible and to stretch the back of your heels. They also stimulate the circulation of fluids to and from the feet and legs.

FIG. 4.9(a/b)
FOOT EXERCISES
(a) and (b) Sit comfortably on the floor, using some support for your lower back if necessary. Point the toes of both feet as far forward as you can, and then extend your heels. Continue, alternating these movements for a minute or so, and then relax. Then try pointing the left foot while extending the right heel, and keep changing simultaneously.

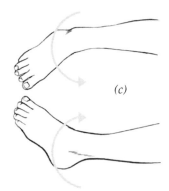

FIG. 4.9 (c/d)
With your legs spread comfortably apart, make circles with your ankles, first inwards up to ten times, and then outwards up to ten times, and then relax.

(d)

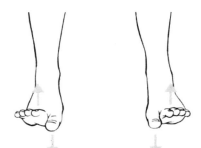

FIG. 4.9 (e)
Stand up with your feet about 12" apart and parallel. Lift all your toes up off the floor, spreading them out wide, and then relax them. Repeat 5 or 6 times.

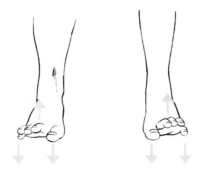

FIG. 4.9 (f)
Press down the base of your big toes. Keep them down and lift all the others. Hold for a few seconds and relax. Repeat 5 or 6 times. Then try keeping all the others down and lifting only the big toes.

FIG. 4.9 (g)
Finally, try keeping the big toes and little toes down while lifting the three middle toes, and then relax (to strengthen the arches of the feet see the Thai Goddess exercise on p. 143).

BASIC STANDING

To get a good sense of the right way to stand, try the following exercise. It may take a little time to do this at first, so stop and take a rest if you need to along the way. With practice, you will be able to do it in a few seconds. As with the Simple Breathing Awareness, you may find it helpful to record the instructions on to a tape and then play it back as you practise. If you are inclined to feel faint when standing still for any length of time, then sit or lie down and rest when you need to. Work through your whole body, focusing your awareness on each part in turn, beginning with your feet.

FEET

Stand up and position your feet so that they are about your hips' width (about 12") apart and parallel.

Turn the heels out and the big toes in towards the centre, until the outside edges of the feet form two parallel lines. This may feel a little 'pigeon-toed' until you get used to it.

Now close your eyes and feel the way your feet contact the floor, allowing your weight to sink down into your heels, and through them into the floor.

Rock a little back and forwards, until you feel your weight evenly balanced at the centre of each heel and between both legs.

Now press your big toes down into the floor and then stretch out, separate and spread your toes so that your feet widen as much as possible.

Stretch the little toes out and place them down firmly on the floor. If your little toes have no independent movement yet, then you may need to bend your knees and bend forwards to help them to open out with your hands, and then come up slowly.

The inner arch of the foot should be raised while the outer arch drops down on to the floor. Your body weight goes down through your heels and is held in balance by your feet between the widely spread big and little toes.

Now try to relax your toes and feet in this position so that it begins to feel natural to stand like this. Feel as if you have wide feet like someone who has never worn shoes. Do not worry if this is impossible at first. After a few months of practising yoga a transformation will begin to take place and your feet will begin to regain their natural grace and flexibility.

Now relax and focus on your breathing for a moment or two. Exhale 'through your heels' and feel the breath move down into the floor like the roots of a tree. Then feel the inhalations come slowly into your body, like a tree takes in moisture through the roots.

KNEES

Now bring your awareness to your knees. Keep them straight, but do not 'lock' them so that the energy can flow through them freely. Beware mainly of the back of your knees, feeling the creases 'open' and release.

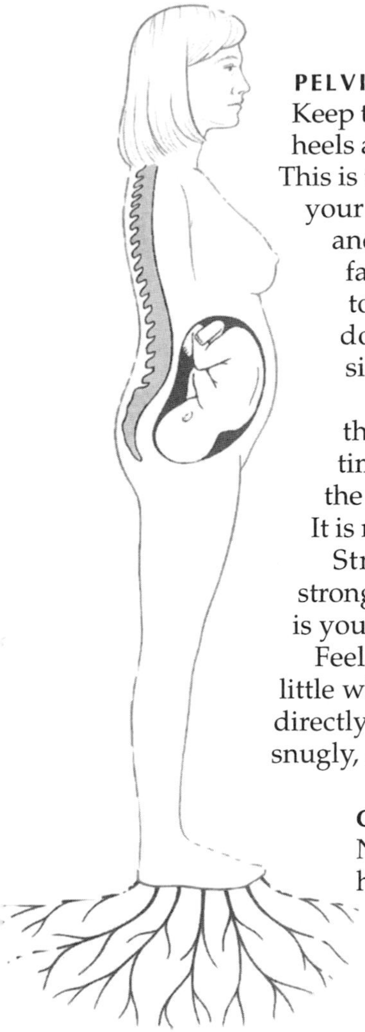

PELVIS

Keep the 'grounded' feeling of your weight going down into your heels and bring your awareness to the bony basin of your pelvis. This is the main supporting structure of your body. The weight of your head, shoulders and trunk accumulates through the spine and is concentrated in the last lumbar vertebra. From there it falls on to the sacrum. Remember how this is ideally shaped to transmit the weight through the bony arch of the pelvis down to legs and feet when you stand, and through the sitting bones into the floor or chair when you sit.

Focus on the back wall of the pelvis which is formed by the lower part of the spine – the sacrum. Breathe out a few times and allow the sacrum to release and elongate towards the floor so that the base of the spine lengthens downwards. It is rather like having a long, heavy tail dropping downwards.

Stroke down your lower back with your hands to get a stronger sense of this downward lengthening of your spine. This is your centre of gravity.

Feel how the pubic bone in front naturally tends to lift up a little when your lower back lengthens, so that your pelvis comes directly under your belly. Feel how you are carrying your baby snugly, close to your spine.

CHEST

Now that your centre of gravity in the lower back is in harmony with the earth's downward force, your lower body, from the waist down, is 'grounded'. Stand and breathe for a moment and feel this sense of connection with the earth in your body. Feel how your body weight drops down your lower back through your legs and heels. As you exhale, have a sense of the breath going down into the earth like roots, through your heels.

With this same grounded feeling, your upper body is well supported and free to release. The lengthening of your lower back allows your ribs and sternum to expand and your upper back to feel longer and wider when you inhale.

Be aware of the air coming into your lungs when you inhale, as if it were coming from the ground, from the roots, just like a tree absorbs moisture from the earth. Feel the air filling your lungs from the base upwards, until the breath reaches the top part of your lungs just under your collar bones, but keep your shoulders relaxed and down.

Continue breathing comfortably with your awareness focused for a few seconds more on the sensations of the air entering and leaving

Fig. 4.10
STANDING
• *Feet parallel with toes spread out wide and heels well grounded like the roots of a tree.*
• *The back wall of the knees opens.*
• *The lower back gently lengthens towards the ground.*
• *The pelvis supports the belly from underneath.*
• *The baby is held comfortably close to your spine.*
• *From the pelvis downwards, your body is attracted towards the ground by gravity.*
• *The upper spine lengthens from the waist up towards the sky as if growing from the roots.*
• *The shoulders hang loose and free.*
• *Arms hang softly with heavy elbows and wrists.*
• *The back of the neck lengthens, with the chin slightly down towards the chest.*
• *The head balances on top of the spine.*

your lungs. Be aware of the space between the top rim of the pelvis and the lower rim of your rib cage, and feel this gently lengthen as you breathe, making more space for your baby.

SHOULDERS

Keep the awareness of length in the lower back and weight going down through the heels and, at the same time, have a sense of how your shoulders hang suspended from the neck on top of your rib cage – rather like a heavy coat on a coat hanger. Shrug or circle them backwards a few times and feel them release and relax.

ARMS

Let the arms hang by your sides, like two heavy pendulums. Keep your hands soft and loose, with the palms open. Feel that the tension leaves the upper part of your body through your elbows and your wrists.

NECK AND HEAD

Stay aware of the length in the lower back and the weight going down into your heels, and focus your attention on your head and neck. Your head weighs between 10–15 lb and sits evenly balanced on the top vertebra of the spine in the neck, known as the atlas bone.

Try nodding your head very gently, making tiny movements up and down, from side to side and front to back. You will get a sense of the way your head balances on top of the vertebrae of the neck. When you make the tiny nodding movements, you can sense the movement of the small delicate muscles in the nape of your neck which keep your head balanced on your spine (the suboccipital muscles). Now tip your head forward slightly so that your chin moves down a little towards your chest. Breathe deeply and feel the gentle releasing and lengthening of all the muscles at the back of the neck and upper back as the suboccipitals release.

Before you change your position, breathe and enjoy a feeling of balance through your whole body – your pelvis, legs and feet well 'grounded', with a light loose feeling from the waist up.

SITTING

When sitting, the same principles apply as when you stand, only now the weight of your trunk drops down through the sitting bones into the chair or floor.

Always try to make sure that the base of your spine is grounded and lengthens downwards. Then the rest of your back will be supported from the base upwards. Always avoid slouching and make a point of bringing your lower back up against the back of the chair or a wall. If you are sitting on a couch or sitting up in bed, use enough cushions behind your back to support it upright rather than leaning back. When sitting in a chair, use the straightbacked variety whenever possible. If your feet do not touch the ground easily, then use a low footstool or a book so that your legs feel well supported.

If you are working long hours at a desk, using the right chair is especially important. The special kneeling stools which can be obtained from back shops give very good support to the spine. Try not to cross your legs as this blocks your circulation, which is already affected by the weight of the pregnancy. When working at a high surface in the kitchen, use a high stool to sit on rather than standing.

Sitting or kneeling correctly on the floor is in itself good exercise for pregnancy, so try to abandon the sofa and sit on the floor whenever you can. Many of the yoga positions can become part of your daily life and can be used as sitting positions around the home.

Squatting on a stool without strain is very helpful in pregnancy and can be used as a sitting position. Squat on a low stool or a pile of large books (see squatting exercise 12b, p.129). Lengthen your lower back downwards and spread your knees comfortably apart. Allow your trunk to lean forward slightly so that your spine and neck feel free. Place your feet flat on the floor with the heels down. Squatting regularly widens your pelvis and helps to position your baby and prepare your body for birth.

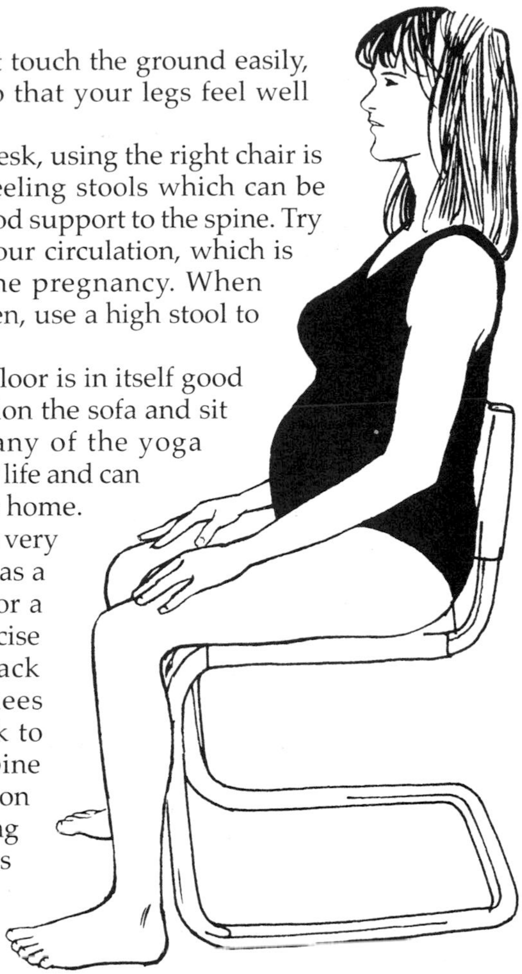

BENDING

When you bend over to lift a heavy object, to get something out of a bottom drawer or to do your housework, make sure that you lengthen your lower back downwards and that the bend takes place from your hip joints rather than your spine (see standing forward bend exercise 23, p.155). Bend your knees and squat down when lifting up an object or a small child from the floor so that your legs do the work rather than your spine.

Go down on to your knees rather than bending over too far or come on to your hands and knees if you need to wipe up a spill on the floor.

FIG. 4.11
SITTING
• *Feet comfortably apart, flat on the floor.*
• *Knees slightly apart.*
• *Sit well back in the chair to avoid slouching. Lower back lengthens towards the ground.*
• *The pelvis, legs and feet are pulled down by gravity.*
• *The upper spine lengthens towards the sky from a stable base.*
• *Shoulders and arms hang loosely.*
• *The neck lengthens and the head balances on top of the spine.*

GETTING UP from LYING DOWN

When you get up from lying in the bath, on the floor or in bed, never pull yourself forward to come up as this may strain your lower back and your abdominal muscles. Rather, roll over on to one side and then come up slowly into a sitting or kneeling position and from there, stand up.

RESTING and SLEEPING

In the months before and after birth it is important to spend time each day resting. A lot of your vital energy is being used to nourish your baby. A rest at midday is essential, and two 'mini' rests during the midmorning and midafternoon can make all the difference. If you are working a full day, this is especially important, so try to arrange a place to lie down at work.

As we go about our daily activities, gravity takes its toll on our bodies. The spinal curves become increasingly compressed the longer we are upright. During pregnancy, this compression is increased due to the additional weight you are carrying.

As we go about our daily activities, gravity takes its toll on our bodies.

When you rest or sleep or release your spine during your yoga practice, the spongy discs between your vertebrae literally soak up more body fluid which causes them to expand and become more elastic. Muscular releases occur so that the curves of the spine open out and the spine literally lengthens. This also makes more space for the spinal nerves as they emerge from the spinal cord, and invigorates the whole body. Relaxing and resting or practising some yoga for as little as twenty minutes can result in this 'rejuvenation'.

When you sleep, both body and mind are nourished and recover from the expenditure of energy during the day. Towards the end of pregnancy it may be difficult to make yourself comfortable at night and sleep may be interrupted by the need to empty your bladder. A warm bath using three or four drops of essential oil of camomile in the water will encourage restful sleep. It is wise to invest in some extra pillows in the later months to support your body comfortably when you sleep. Spinal massage before rest or relaxation is very helpful in late pregnancy if you have a willing masseur around. Use the breathing exercise on p. 69 or the relaxation on p. 171 when you first lie down to rest or sleep. If your sleep is erratic at night, then take every opportunity to rest during the day. There are various positions you can use when resting or sleeping.

LYING on your SIDE

This comfortable position is enhanced by the use of plenty of pillows. Place a small or a soft pillow under your head and one more between your knees so that your legs are supported. Turn your hips until you feel comfortable or extend the bottom leg. Your spine should be supported more or less in one straight line. Some women like to place an extra pillow under the belly too, for support. Hugging a pillow in your arms may help to support your shoulders.

KNEELING FORWARD over CUSHIONS

On a soft surface on the floor or on your bed, spread your knees comfortably apart with the toes pointing inward and kneel forward from the hips on to a beanbag or a big pile of comfortable cushions (see p. 78). Make sure that your spine feels free and your whole body is well supported, and then breathe deeply and relax.

RESTING on to a TABLE

When it is impossible to lie down, leaning forward with your arms placed on a desk or table is a good way to have a rest for a few minutes. Position your arms comfortably on the table and rest your head on your forearms. Spread your legs comfortably apart and keep your feet flat on the floor. Relax your neck and shoulders and breathe and release your spine.

POSTURE after BIRTH

Your lower back remains very vulnerable in the early weeks and months after the birth and it is important to avoid strain. In the first few weeks after the birth it is wise to arrange a changing table at a comfortable height so that you do not need to bend when dressing or changing your baby. You can use any table in the house for a few weeks as, later on, you will enjoy changing your baby on the bed or the floor, and the table becomes dangerous once the baby can roll over!

Your neck and shoulders are also subject to considerable strain when you are feeding and carrying your baby. Paying attention to releasing and relaxing them throughout the day will minimize stress.

BREASTFEEDING POSITIONS

You can breastfeed in a variety of positions – sitting upright on a straightbacked chair, sitting upright in bed, on a sofa with cushions behind your back, or lying on your side. Whatever position you are in, make sure you are really comfortable and no part of your body feels strained. When sitting to breastfeed follow all the advice given on p. 86 and use plenty of pillows if necessary and a footstool so both legs can relax. Hold your baby close to you in a well-supported position. Make sure that he or she is facing towards you 'belly to belly' with head, neck and back all in a straight line. The baby's mouth should be just below your nipple before you start. This will make it easiest for your baby to latch on to the breast without having to turn the head or strain. In the early weeks, it is helpful to place a pillow across your lap so that the baby is held at a comfortable height and you may want another cushion under your elbow.

MOVING AROUND with your BABY

You are going to spend a lot of time carrying your baby and, indeed, this is very important for his or her healthy development. It is a good idea to invest in a good baby carrier from the outset and get used to using it. Always pay attention to the way you walk and stand when your baby is in a front carrier as they can place strain on your lower back unless you are continually mindful of your posture (see p. 82). At around 5–6 months, a good backpack is better for your posture but remember to keep lengthening your lower back and to walk with parallel feet. If you invest in a stroller, check the height of the handles carefully so that you can push it without bending when you walk.

CHAPTER FIVE

PRACTISING
YOGA
IN
PREGNANCY?

Practising yoga is a deeply effective way to make the most of the transformative potential of your pregnancy and, at the same time, to empower yourself for labour, giving birth and mothering.

In Chapter 3 you began to understand the essence of yoga by learning to relax and observe the natural flow of your breathing. You have already started to discover the art of focusing your awareness on this basic rhythm so that within a few minutes, you can become inwardly concentrated or 'centred'.

At the same time you will have begun to notice the effect of gravity on your body while standing and sitting and to be aware of the centre of gravity in the base of your spine and lower abdomen.

Now it is time to introduce some simple yoga postures into your practice. While you are doing these postures you can apply what you have already learned, noticing the wave of your breathing and becoming aware of the work of gravity in each position.

When you try the postures for the first time you will notice that some are easy to do, while others reveal parts of your body which are tense or stiff. Gradually, through your breathing, you will begin to 'unwind' and to let go of the deep muscular tensions which may, at first, prevent you from relaxing into the posture with ease. It is very important to be aware that this is a slow process which cannot be forced. You will need to be very gentle with yourself and take your time. With perseverance you will begin to perceive your own inner centre and become increasingly aware in each position of how your body weight is drawn towards the earth. As your breathing naturally deepens without effort you will discover the invisible roots which connect you with gravity. You will become 'grounded'.

The word yoga means 'union'. It is like a marriage between your own inner centre and that of the earth itself, which is brought about when you practise yoga regularly. Then, when you become more deeply connected with the earth, the way will become clear for you to experience a sense of oneness or union which could be called spiritual. As you become more centred and grounded, you will find that you can live more harmoniously with yourself, your surroundings and your fellow beings. You will experience more energy, vitality, light and joy in your life.

But the lightness is felt first of all in your body, as the natural consequence of becoming aware of its connection with the earth. It comes to you like a gift, when your body finds its harmonious relationship to gravity, without any special effort on your part.

You cannot force or hurry this process or 'do' anything to make it happen. It is more a matter of letting go, of letting your body simply 'be'. The more you surrender to gravity and allow it to do its work, the more you make space for the light.

Doing this slow and gentle work as your pregnancy unfolds is very pleasurable. Your own intention to relax and energize yourself works in harmony with the natural tendency at this time towards greater fluidity, openness and flexibility. As your sense of your own

You will experience more energy, vitality, light and joy in your life.

'roots' deepens, a feeling of spiritual lightness, peace and calm will arise from within. You will become truly, deeply empowered.

To my mind, this is the everyday meaning of enlightenment. It is not only a mystical state reserved for yogis who can do all sorts of complicated postures and endure years of austere practices. It is the natural consequence of the daily awakening in our consciousness, which can occur easily in all of us when our body begins to come into balance with the earth. We soon learn that both heaven and earth can be found within ourselves.

There is no better time to discover this than now, when your body is filled with the vitality of a new life and awake with a special kind of instinctive intelligence which is unique to pregnancy.

How to START

When to START

Ideally, the earlier you start the better. Some women begin to practise yoga before they conceive and this can only be an advantage. Early pregnancy is a very good time to start, from as early as twelve weeks, provided your midwife or doctor agrees. If you have had any problems with conception, bleeding or miscarriage, then it may be wise to give the pregnancy time to settle and to begin at around sixteen weeks.

If, however, you are already well into your pregnancy when you discover this book, it is never too late to start. The last few months and weeks are very important and your body will respond rapidly to the postures as a result of the higher levels of pregnancy hormones you are secreting.

When to PRACTISE

You will find, as you get to know them, that many of the yoga postures become new 'body habits' which can be included in your daily life when you are relaxing at home. However, it is best to set aside 30–60 minutes each day for a more formal yoga practice, when you can relax and concentrate more deeply without any other distractions or disturbances.

The time of day depends on your own convenience. Never practise immediately after eating as you will need your energy for digestion. It is also best to avoid all but the most relaxing postures if you are very tired. Early morning is a good time to practise, but bear in mind that you will feel more stiff at this time and have a warm bath to loosen up before you start. It will be well worth the trouble. You will feel energized and centred throughout the day. In the afternoon or evening your body will be more flexible after moving around all day, and practice can be easier and very enjoyable.

If you have a very hectic or busy life you do need to slow down during pregnancy, and making time to practise yoga is even more important. However, you will need to be disciplined and determined to develop a habit of practising regularly. You will be surprised how setting aside this time will calm you and help to make room for everything else you need to do in a more centred and relaxed way. You will feel much better in yourself and you will also avoid running the risk of overdoing it and possibly developing unnecessary complications in your pregnancy as a result.

If daily practice is really impossible, then try to practise at least two or three times a week. If discipline is your problem, then it may help to join a local class or to use a practice tape at home (see Useful Addresses and Resources). Getting together with a pregnant friend or two is also a very enjoyable way to practise.

How to PRACTISE

The yoga postures can be practised throughout pregnancy, provided you follow the cautionary notes and instructions carefully. They all involve your body as a whole, but the essential exercises focus specifically on the pelvis in order to prepare your body for giving birth.

The order in which you choose to practise the postures comes with experience. Over the months of your pregnancy you will become very familiar with the postures and vary them daily according to your mood or needs at the time. I have arranged them in convenient groups for beginning your practice but feel free to change the order in any way you please thereafter.

The postures in Group 1 (Nos. 1–8) serve as a good warm-up, loosening the spine, hip joints, ankles and knees, while bringing you in touch with your centre and with gravity.

Group 2 (Nos. 9–13) are the essential basic postures for pregnancy which should be practised daily if possible. The remaining groups can be practised as suggested or in any order you prefer.

If you feel very tense in the neck and shoulders then it may help to begin with Group 4 (Nos. 18–20).

You can start your practice with a few of the standing postures in Group 5 (Nos. 21–27) if you feel energetic. However do not try to do all of them in one session!

Group 6 (Nos. 28–31) are advanced postures which should only be done if you have been learning yoga for a long time. If you usually practise these postures you may wish to continue doing them in pregnancy, although it is not essential to do so.

On days when you feel very tired, ten minutes of relaxation (Group 7) before you start may be helpful. Then, perhaps, you will enjoy practising some sitting postures very slowly to begin with.

You should always end your session with ten minutes or so of relaxation.

Varying the order will make your practice more interesting and allow you to use most of the postures within the week, as you are unlikely to manage to go through them all in each session unless you have plenty of time.

Not every position will suit your body. The cautionary notes will help you to determine whether you are ready to try a particular position or whether you should concentrate on others until your body becomes more flexible. Always listen to your own internal signals and do not ever push yourself or strain to do something your body is not yet ready for. This is the golden rule of practising yoga in the right way (see p. 17).

What to do in the POSTURE

Each posture starts with a description of the position and its benefits, followed by instructions on how to place your body. If there is any special caution or suggestion to note, you will find this at the beginning.

The length of time you should spend in each posture really depends on how you feel. Stop as soon as you have had enough. The times specified at the end of each exercise are general guidelines which are useful to follow in the beginning until the positions become more familiar. Then your body will tell you how long to continue in each posture when you practise.

The instructions are carefully graded so that you can begin slowly, going only as far as you can without straining. You will soon learn to find what I call 'your comfortable limit'. You will learn to tell the difference between the sensation of stiffness or tightness you reach within your comfortable limit and the sort of pain or tension which signals that you are straining too far. Gradually, over time, this limit will extend until you can do the full posture without straining. But you will need to be patient. It may take weeks, months or even years, depending on how deep the stiffness is and how much time you give to your practice.

Don't be in a hurry. Doing the full posture is not the main aim or the goal. At first, looking at the pictures of the full posture may seem somewhat daunting. However, you will soon be encouraged and inspired as you sense your body beginning to loosen and release, and you realize that each time you practise you are moving towards regaining your natural suppleness. All it takes is practice. You will start to feel the benefits from the beginning, and they will steadily increase the more you practise.

Of course, you will also have the added advantage of the increase in flexibility which is natural to pregnancy and this will aid your progress. What really matters is the sense of balance and awakening you experience during and after each session. The full posture will come to you as a gift in due course, as your body relaxes and becomes looser and more supple.

GROUNDING and CENTRING

Your awareness will be drawn in each posture to your centre of gravity in the lower back and abdomen and to the parts of your body which are making contact with the floor. You will learn how to align yourself with gravity in each position with the help of your breathing. The awareness of this connection with the earth should be retained as you follow the remaining instructions until you come

When you practise yoga, always remember that the 'intelligence' in each position comes from the earth. Keep your brain, your mind, focused on the ground and breathe, breathe, breathe!

SANDRA SABATINI

out of the posture. This is what I call 'grounding'. To find your centre you need only to sit quietly for a while and focus your awareness inwards on the rhythm of your breathing.

LENGTHENING the SPINE

Every posture includes a reminder to lengthen the lower part of the spine downwards. Sometimes I say 'ground' the root of the spine, or the sacrum or tailbone. The key to finding your centre in each posture is to gently lengthen your lower spine, bringing it down to earth.

It is very important to realize that this is a very subtle inner release which does not involve any tensing or gross muscular movements. The thought of lengthening the spine allows the natural curves to release and come into balance as you breathe so that your awareness of the root of the spine increases.

Over time, this sense of stability in the base, this connection with gravity, automatically encourages the upward release and lengthening of the whole spine all the way to the top of the neck. Freedom of the body comes from the ground. By grounding the heavy root of the spine, the whole column eventually releases. As the spine becomes free, the rest of the body relaxes. So start by focusing your awareness on the earth. Feel how the pull of gravity works through your body, lengthening the lower spine, and let the releasing process unfold.

These subtle muscular releases are set in motion by your breathing; the exhalations connecting you to your roots and the inhalations giving you a sense of growing from the ground. Then, like a kind of miracle, your body unwinds and relaxes as tension is released by this 'ripple' coming from the earth.

TIMING

The amount of time you want to spend in each posture is something you will discover with practice. Sometimes it is enjoyable to choose just a few postures and practise them very slowly, while on other occasions you may prefer to do more at a more vigorous pace. Use the suggested timings as a guide when you start and then follow your own feelings, bearing in mind that it is best not to spend more than ten minutes at a time in standing positions while you are pregnant.

What to WEAR

Wear loose, comfortable clothing made from natural fibres in which you can make any movement without restriction. It is important to remove socks or tights so that you can sense what you are doing with your bare feet. Keep a pair of socks and a warm cover handy for relaxation at the end when your body temperature will drop.

When it is warm or you are indoors beside a fire, it can be delightful to practise the postures unclothed, using an aromatherapy oil suitable for pregnancy to massage your skin as you go along (see Useful Addresses)

What you NEED

It is best to set aside a space within your home which you can use every day. It is helpful to have a free wall space or a protruding corner you can lean against to support your back if necessary.

The room should be comfortably warm and the floor surface carpeted, or else you will need a couple of folded blankets and a yoga mat to lie on. Some of the postures (for example, the standing poses) require a firm surface with a non-slip yoga mat.

You will also need a soft belt. You can invest in a special yoga belt which has an easily adjustable buckle, but an old tie or a fabric belt which you can knot will be adequate.

A low stool or a pile of large books may be needed for squatting and some of the forward bends call for a stool about the height of a piano stool, a chair or a table.

It is very helpful to have a selection of cushions and pillows. A large bulky one a small firm cushion or two and a bolster from a futon shop are very useful if you have stiffness in the knees or ankles. A beanbag or pile of large cushions is an essential aid during labour and will be useful for massage and relaxation while you are pregnant.

A tape recorder with an empty cassette is useful to have at hand as you might like to read some of the instructions into a tape and then follow them, especially for breathing exercises or relaxation when it is difficult to read at the same time.

Since you will be spending some of the most special hours of your pregnancy in this room, you can create a sanctuary for yourself by making the room beautiful. Choose your favourite colours and some visual images you enjoy looking at for the walls. Plants will thrive on the energy of this room and some flowers, candles or a fragrant essential oil burner, as well as some quiet or meditative music, will enhance the experience. (Essential oils are powerful and some should not be used in pregnancy, so make sure that you are advised by an expert on which oils are suitable for pregnancy, and how to use them.) In good weather it is wonderful to practise out of doors in a natural setting or in the sunshine.

GROUP 1: WARMING UP

1 BASIC SITTING FORWARD BEND

Paschimottanasana

This posture is the basis for all the sitting positions. By directing your awareness to the pull of gravity in the base of your spine, pelvis, hips, legs and feet, it enables you to discover a sense of connection to the earth from the waist down and consequently a feeling of lightness and freedom in the upper body.

START by sitting down on the floor with the base of your spine supported by a protruding corner or a wall, or else sit back-to-back with a partner with your lower backs touching. You may sit on the floor without support only if there is no sense of strain in your back.

● Stretch your legs out in front of you with your feet about 12" or your hips' width apart, resting upright on the back of the heels. Relax your legs so that the muscles are soft. If your feet tend to fall outwards, allow them to do so and then gently roll them back upright so that the knees point up at the ceiling and the feet rest upright on the back of the heels.

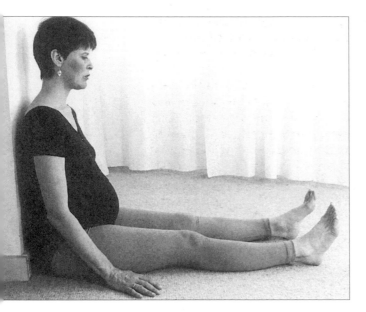

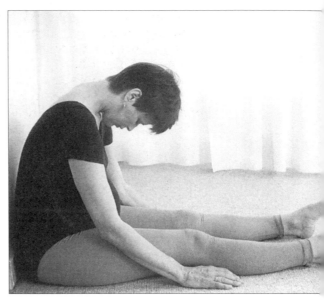

FIG. 5.1
BASIC SITTING
Against a wall

FIG. 5.2
BASIC SITTING
Leaning forward

LEANING FORWARD
● Now, lean forward slightly from your hips so that your hands touch the ground lightly beside your thighs and your spine relaxes (see Figure 5.2).
● Close and relax your eyes and loosen your jaw.
● Relax the back of your neck, allowing your head to release downwards slightly towards your chest.
● Become aware of your breathing and observe its natural rhythm without trying to control or change it in any way, and let your body settle down on to the floor.
● Become quiet and feel the contact your body makes with the ground, from the sitting bones and hips down the back of the legs to your heels.
● Continue to observe your breathing, becoming aware with each exhalation of the downward pull of gravity along the curve of your sacrum and through your sitting bones, hips, the back of the thighs, calves and heels.

COMING UP SLOWLY
● Now you are slowly going to return your upper body to an upright position with the help of your breathing.
● Breathe in a comfortable normal rhythm and feel your lower back releasing downwards, around the curve of the back of your pelvis

with the end of each exhalation. Feel the root of your spine slowly sliding down towards the pubic bone as your hips and pelvis become 'planted' into the ground.

● Each time you inhale, retain this rooted, grounded feeling in the pelvis. Imagine that the inbreath comes from the ground, as if through the roots, slowly up into your body. Feel the inhalations come slowly and spontaneously into the whole length of your lungs from the base up to the collar bones so that you feel as if you are growing and lengthening upwards without effort from the ground. You are like a plant growing towards the light, with the roots firmly planted in the earth.

● Continue like this for a minute or two. Gradually, with the help of gravity, your exhalations will bring your weight down more and more into the hips and the heavy root of your spine. The inhalations will allow your spine to lengthen slowly into the upright position as your lungs expand, like the leaf of a fern uncurling slowly from the base. Take your time so that it feels as if it is your breathing rather than your muscles that is bringing you up. It is like a 'ripple' coming slowly from the ground all the way up your spine.

● If you are using a wall or a partner for support, feel your spine lengthen from the base upwards, one vertebra at a time, until your upper back touches the surface as you return to an upright position (see Figure 5.1).

SITTING UPRIGHT

● Loosen your shoulders by circling them backwards a few times and then allow them to drop down, away from your ears. As the shoulders spread out, back and down, enjoy a feeling of lightness and openness in the chest.

● Let your arms hang loosely, with elbows down, and place your hands comfortably by your sides, or palms up on your thighs.

● Breathe comfortably for a moment or two and feel your weight continue to settle down into your hips and pelvis and come into harmony with gravity as if you have a long, heavy tail dropping down into the floor. Let your muscles relax so that your bones can rest on the ground.

● Keep the sense of being grounded in the pelvis, lengthen the back of your neck by releasing your chin forward slightly and relax your jaw.

● Breathe normally, feeling the wave of your breathing flowing through your body without 'pushing' or 'pulling' the breath in any way. Feel how your lungs quietly receive and welcome the inhalations.

● When you exhale, be aware of the air leaving your lungs through the nostrils and, all the while, keep your awareness of the grounded feeling in the pelvis. Stay in touch with the energy of the earth pulling your body downwards from below the waist, with a sense of lightness and length from the waist up.

● Continue for 1–3 minutes and then open your eyes.

2 HALF ANGLE POSE

Janu Sirsasana

This posture continues to centre and ground you while lengthening and releasing the back of the knees, the hamstring muscles in the back of the thighs, the calf muscles and Achilles tendons at the back of the legs. The gentle twisting movement at the end rotates and releases the spinal vertebrae in the upper back and neck. You will need a soft belt.

START in the basic sitting position (see Figure 5.1). Bend your right knee and draw the right foot in close to your body. Take care that you do not pull your right knee back too far and that your sitting bones remain parallel. Loop the belt around the ball of your left foot and hold it loosely at a comfortable distance with your right hand, making sure that your spine feels free and your arm and leg are not stiff and tense (see Figure 5.3a). If you prefer not to use a belt, simply relax your arms comfortably by your sides.

FIG. 5.3 (a)
HALF ANGLE POSE

● Focus on the pull of gravity underneath your body. Relax your thigh muscles so that they feel loose and heavy. Then feel the way your sitting bones and the backs of your legs contact the ground.
● Elongate your left heel gently so that the calf muscles stretch without becoming stiff and the Achilles tendon at the back of the heel lengthens gently along the floor.
● Breathe deeply and with each exhalation, feel your lower back, hips, sitting bones and the backs of your legs become more grounded while the upper body feels light and free as you inhale.
● Go on breathing and releasing the spine for about a minute and then continue with the twist on p. 101.

TWIST IN HALF ANGLE POSE

● Sitting upright, continue holding the belt (or your left leg) softly with your right hand, placing your left hand on the floor beside you (see Figures 5.3b and c). Avoid leaning back so that your spine remains vertical.

● Release both hips and the lower spine down towards the ground.

● Now slowly turn your trunk slightly towards the left, keeping your awareness in the grounded pelvis. Keep the right sitting bone and hip firmly down.

● Start the twisting movement slowly from the base of your spine. Feel it turn gently towards the left until your left shoulder turns, followed by your head. Keep your left arm and shoulder relaxed so that your chest feels free, and keep your jaw soft and your eyes relaxed.

● Focus your awareness on your breathing, retaining the grounded feeling in the both hips, and continue for about thirty seconds, then come slowly back to the centre.

● Change legs and repeat on the other side with the left leg bent and the right leg extended.

FIG. 5.3 (b)
TWIST IN HALF
ANGLE POSE
Back view

FIG. 5.3 (c)
TWIST IN HALF
ANGLE POSE
Front view

3 SITTING TWIST

Marichyasana – sage's pose

As you felt in the last exercise, your spine has the capacity to rotate to the left and to the right. Twisting movements maintain the flexibility of the intervertebral joints and help to release stiffness in the spine. They also stimulate the secretion of lubricating fluids in the joints so the effect is like 'oiling' your spine. These beneficial effects will occur in all the twisting postures.

CAUTION: Your spine has a natural capacity to rotate to either side. All twisting movements should be very soft and gentle. Allow the upright column of your spine to rotate naturally without turning to an extreme or leaning back.

START in the basic sitting position (see Figure 5.1), but away from the wall this time, with both legs extended. Breathe and ground yourself before you start by releasing your lower back and hips downwards and keep this awareness of the 'roots' throughout.

● Leaving your left leg on the floor, keep it soft and heavy, and gently extend the heel. Bend your right knee and place the right foot on the floor a comfortable distance away from your left knee and parallel to your left leg.

● As you exhale, lengthen your lower back downwards and feel both hips and sitting bones sink downwards. At the same time, very gently, allow your trunk to turn slightly towards the left, feeling your

FIG. 5.4 (a)
SITTING TWIST
With bent knee

spine rotate slowly from the base upwards, keeping the right hip down.

● Place your left hand on the floor beside you to help you keep your balance and bring your right arm over so that your hand holds the outside of the left thigh.

● Keep releasing your lower back downwards and be aware of the root of the spine becoming more grounded and lengthening with each exhalation.

● Breathe comfortably and release your spine, shoulders, neck, jaw and eyes, and allow your spine to turn gently. Let the rotation happen naturally, without trying to increase the twisting movement beyond the natural limit.

● Relax your shoulders and allow your left shoulder and arm to release backwards and down as you breathe, to relax and open your upper body.

● If it is easy for you, you can pass your right arm around the bent knee and bring it behind you, clasping your hands behind your back (see Figure 5.4b).

● Continue breathing and hold the posture for up to thirty seconds, and then come back slowly to the basic sitting position.

● Now extend your right leg and bend your left, and repeat the twist on the other side.

● Come back to the basic sitting position.

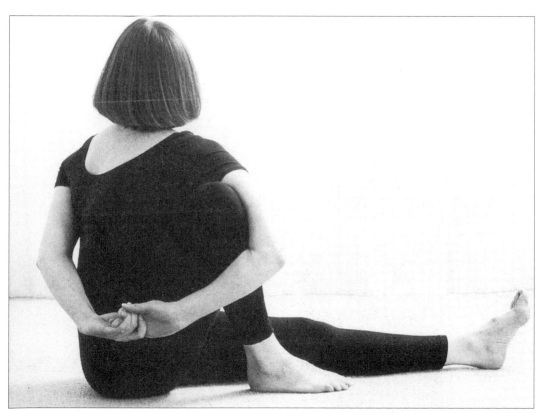

FIG. 5.4 (b)
SITTING TWIST
With clasped hands

FIG. 5.5 (a)
HALF LOTUS

4 HALF LOTUS

The lotus posture is the most stable sitting position and is very useful for meditation and breathing practice. It is very centring and gives very secure grounding in the pelvis and, therefore, support to the spine. It releases stiffness in the hip, knee and ankle joints, and should be approached gradually in stages, only attempting the full posture (see p. 107) when you are sufficiently supple. Practising the half lotus first and, eventually, the full lotus will improve the mobility of your hips and ankles and help to free your spine.

FIG. 5.5 (b)
HALF LOTUS
Leaning forward

CAUTION: The knees are the largest joints in the body and tend to stiffen very easily. If you are not used to sitting on the floor, you may experience some discomfort or pain in the knees and ankles at first in these postures. To avoid injury, never use force to exceed your comfortable limit. Allow it to extend gradually with practice.

START in the basic sitting position (see Figure 5.1) with your legs extended and your lower back touching the wall or a partner for support if necessary. Bend your left leg and place your left foot on the floor close to your body. Now lift up your right calf in your hands. Turn the ankle and the heel up towards you so that the sole of the foot faces upwards and place the right foot on the floor in front of the left foot. Feel your hip joints and sitting bones sink down firmly on to the floor (see Figure 5.5a).

LEANING FORWARD
● Lean slightly forward from your hips so that your pelvis remains well grounded and your hands touch the ground lightly in front of you (see Figure 5.5b).
● Relax your spine and lengthen the back of your neck by bringing your chin slightly down towards your chest.

COMING UP SLOWLY
● Using the breathing awareness you learnt in the basic sitting position on p. 97, allow your hips and the base of your spine to release downwards towards the ground with the exhalations as if you are planting roots into the earth.
● Feel the inhalations coming into the whole length of your lungs as if they are coming from the ground, allowing your spine to uncurl and lengthen slowly into the upright position from the roots. Take plenty of time, coming up little by little each time you inhale.

SITTING UPRIGHT

● Once you are upright, relax your shoulders and tilt your head slightly downward towards your chest to release the back of your neck.

● Place your hands on your knees with your palms up, enjoying the grounded feeling in your pelvis.

● Settle into the position for a minute or so, breathing comfortably, feeling your lower back and hips release downwards when you exhale and your upper body lengthen and lighten as your lungs expand to receive the inhalations.

5 TWIST in HALF LOTUS

This twist benefits from the stable base of the pelvis and the spine in this position, and encourages rotation of the vertebral column and lubrication of the intervertebral joints.

CAUTION: Twisting should never be forceful or unbalanced so leave out this twist if you are not completely at ease in the half lotus position, with both knees close to the floor, and concentrate instead on the sitting twist on p. 102 or the kneeling twist on p. 143. Take care when using the belt. Keep your elbows relaxed and hold the belt softly.

START in the half lotus position away from the wall with the right foot close to your body and the left foot in front. Lengthen your lower back downwards and have a sense of being well grounded in the hips and the pelvis.

● Take your belt and loop it around your left knee. Join the ends together and, holding them in your left hand, bring them behind your back.

● Put your right arm behind your back and pass the ends of the belt from your left into your right hand.

● Hold the belt loosely as far down as possible, without straining, and you will begin to feel your upper body slowly turn from the base of the spine towards the right.

● Breathe in a comfortable rhythm and follow the movement gently, looking round over your right shoulder, aware of the pelvis resting squarely on the ground and the root of the spine lengthening downwards.

● Keep releasing your lower back downwards and let your spine turn very slowly and gently from the base right up to the top of your neck.

● As you breathe, relax your neck and shoulders, your eyes and your jaw and hold for up to thirty seconds. Come back to the centre and then change legs and repeat on the other side.

FIG. 5.6 (a)
TWIST IN
HALF LOTUS
Front view

FIG. 5.6 (b)
TWIST IN HALF
LOTUS
Back view

6 HALF LOTUS FORWARD BEND

Ardha Padma Paschimottanasana

START in the basic sitting position (see Figure 5.1) with your lower back against a wall or partner if necessary. Focus on your breathing and ground your lower back, pelvis and hips.

● Keep your right leg extended and bend your left, holding the calf in both hands as you did in half lotus, turning the heel and sole of the left foot up towards you. Place the foot on the right thigh above the knee.

● Now bring the foot up the thigh towards the groin, going only as far as you can manage easily.

● If it is easy for you, then place the foot in or near to the crease at the top of your thigh, close to your belly.

● Loop the belt loosely around the ball of your right foot and sit evenly with both hips firmly down, breathing and feeling the contact your body is making with the ground. Keep releasing your lower back towards the ground and feel your spine lengthening from the roots as you breathe. Make sure that the back of your neck is lengthening and that your shoulders are relaxed.

● Breathe and relax in the posture for 30–60 seconds, and then repeat on the other side.

FIG. 5.7 (a)
HALF LOTUS
FORWARD BEND
*Half lotus with
one leg straight*

FIG. 5.7 (b)
HALF LOTUS
Using a belt

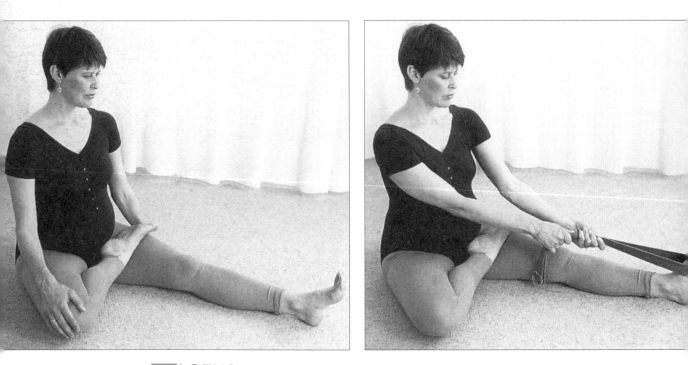

7 LOTUS

When you can do the half lotus posture with ease, then you can attempt the full lotus. This may not be possible without a lot of practice if your knees, hips or ankles are stiff. Never try to force this posture. It will become possible in time, as your flexibility increases.

In this posture, as your pelvis, hips, the base of the spine and your legs surrender to the downward pull of gravity, your body rediscovers its relationship to the earth, like a plant with roots. The sense of being grounded and centred in the pelvis increases as the roots deepen with your breathing. Then, from the top rim of your pelvis, the upper body lengthens and blossoms like a bouquet of flowers. Like a gift, energy and vitality will come to you from the ground, without effort.

START in the basic sitting position (see Figure 5.1). Keep your left leg extended and bend your right knee, holding the lower leg with both hands. Working gently with both hands, turn the ankle and the heel upwards so that the sole of the right foot turns towards your face. Place the right foot in the crease at the top of the left thigh. You can help the calf muscle to loosen with your hands and this will help the knee to release downwards.

FIG. 5.8
LOTUS
Full lotus position

Use your hands to help the right thigh muscles to release from the inside to the outside of the thigh so that the thigh feels grounded. Now complete the posture by doing the same thing with the left leg, placing the left foot on top of the right leg with the sole facing upwards (see Figure 5.8). Use your hands to help you to release the top of both thighs out and down. Let the hip joints and the sitting bones settle down on to the floor. Place your hands on your knees with the palms up. Make sure you feel comfortable or else change to half lotus (see p. 104). Lengthen and extend both your heels gently along the Achilles tendon.

LEANING FORWARD

● Be aware of the rhythm of your breathing, lengthening and releasing the root of the spine downwards. Feel the hip joints release into the floor as your weight settles into the pelvis.

● Bend slightly forward from your hips as you did in the half lotus position (see p. 104), relaxing your spine and the back of your neck. Touch the floor lightly with your hands.

COMING UP SLOWLY

● Focus on your breathing and plant the root of the spine downwards with the exhalations, slowly lengthening and uncurling into the upright position with the inhalations, and remembering to take your time, feeling the 'ripple' coming from the earth slowly up your spine, vertebra by vertebra.

SITTING UPRIGHT

● Once you are upright, become quiet and breathe normally and comfortably.

● Be conscious of the grounded, stable feeling in your pelvis.

● Release and lengthen the back of your neck by dropping your chin slightly downwards.

● Feel the pull of gravity increasing with the exhalations so that the base of your body is well grounded. When you inhale, feel your upper body lengthen above the stable pelvis. Have a sense of a gentle lengthening between the top rim of your pelvis and the lower rim of your rib cage as you breathe in, making more space for your baby. Feel each inbreath fill the length of your lungs from the base to the collar bones, without tensing your shoulders. You will begin to feel a pleasant sense of lightness and freedom in the upper back, shoulders and neck as your rib cage widens to receive the breath and your shoulders open out and relax.

● Focus on your breathing for up to two minutes and then change your legs around, starting with the left leg, and repeat.

8 COW POSE

Gomulkhasana

This posture is wonderful for releasing tension in the lower back, encouraging widening across the back wall of the pelvis. Since this part of your body bears most of the weight of your pregnancy, practising this position regularly can be very relieving, particularly if you have lower back or sacroiliac pain. In this position the hip joints rotate inwards in the opposite direction to most of the other sitting positions, making a useful contrast and helping to increase the mobility of your hips. It is also very centring and grounding.

CAUTION: If you find it difficult to cross your legs like this, then leave out this posture.

START by sitting with your left thigh crossing over the right. Bend your knees so that your left foot rests close to your right hip and your right foot is close to your left hip (see Figure 5.9). Both sitting bones should be resting evenly on the ground. If you feel unbalanced, then leave out this posture until your hips become more flexible.

● Place the palms of both hands on your lower back and stroke from the centre outwards with both your hands and feel how this position widens and releases your lower back.

● Now place your hands on your feet or, loosely clasped, rest them on your top knee.

FIG. 5.9
COW POSE

● Find your centre and bring your awareness to your breathing. As you exhale, relax and feel the base of your spine release downwards like a long heavy tail. Feel your hip joints release downwards.

● Feel the way your breathing caresses the curves of your spine. Feel it travelling down towards gravity, towards the roots, when you exhale, starting from the base of your skull and moving down towards the coccyx. Pause and then feel the inhalation rippling from the roots up to the top of your neck.

● Continue for a moment or two longer and then uncross your legs and relax.

● Then cross your legs with the right leg on top, and repeat.

GROUP 2: PELVIC EXERCISES

The following postures (Nos. 9–13) are the basic pregnancy exercises which I recommend you try to practise every day throughout your pregnancy. While they benefit your whole body, they are especially useful in increasing the mobility of your pelvis and enhancing your awareness of the parts of your body which are most involved in giving birth. They will help you to feel at ease and comfortable in natural upright positions for birth and labour, and to be in touch with your instincts. These are the most important postures to practise while you are pregnant.

Your awareness of how these postures benefit you will be enhanced if you first pause to read the section below in order to understand how your pelvis is structured and the way that it functions during childbirth.

THE PELVIS

In addition to its function as the main weightbearing part of your body, your pelvis is also the bony base and outlet of your trunk through which your child must pass to be born. Through exercising in pregnancy and practising the yoga positions, you can work along with nature to increase the flexibility of your pelvic framework in readiness for the birth. It is therefore helpful, before you begin to learn the exercises, to understand how your pelvis is designed to accommodate your baby's passage during labour and birth.

FIG. 5.10
THE FEMALE PELVIS
(a) Front view, *showing sacrum (A), iliac or hip bones (B), coccyx (C), pubic bone (D), ischial bones (E), pelvic cavity (F).*
(b) Back view, *showing sacro-iliac joints (G), sacro-coccygeal joint (H) and symphysis pubis (I).*
(c) Side view, *showing iliac bone (B), sacrum (A), sacro-coccygeal joint (H), hip joint (J) and pubic bone.*

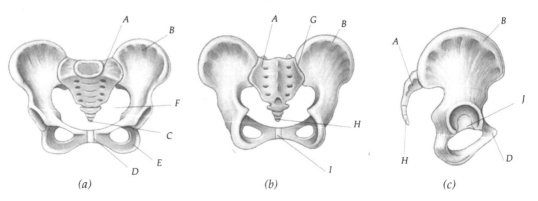

(a)   (b)   (c)

Shaped like a funnel with a curved canal, your pelvis is made up of four bones. The sacrum forms the back wall of the pelvic canal. It is made up of five fused vertebrae to which the coccyx is attached at the base, and is ideally shaped as a triangle to transfer your body weight down to your legs (see p. 76). The sacrum is flanked on either side by the large hip bones, each of which is made of three bones fused together since puberty. These are the ilium (flank or side), ischium (buttock or 'sitting bones') and the pubis in front. The two pubic bones meet in front at the powerful joint which is known as the symphysis pubis, so that the pelvic girdle forms a continuous ring which surrounds the pelvic canal.

THE BABY'S JOURNEY
THROUGH THE PELVIS DURING BIRTH

The rounded entrance to the pelvic canal at the top is called the pelvic inlet, while the opening at the base through which the baby will pass as it is born is called the outlet. In the weeks before labour starts, the baby's head usually engages in the pelvic brim or inlet, so that the top of the head descends below the edge of the rim.

The widest diameter of the pelvic inlet is crosswise from side to side. The widest diameter of the baby's head is from the crown to the forehead (front to back). As the baby's head enters the inlet, its widest diameter aligns with the widest diameter of the pelvic brim. During labour the baby's head descends deep down into the pelvic canal.

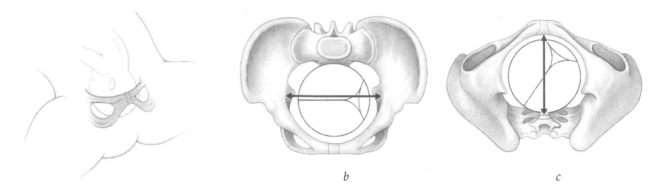

b *c*

However, the widest diameter of the pelvic outlet is from front to back (pubis to coccyx). Therefore, towards the end of labour, the baby's head must rotate so that the widest diameter is aligned with the widest diameter of the outlet for the birth. This spiralling movement of the baby through the pelvis continues with the emergence of the shoulders and the rest of the baby's body. Of course, the baby's journey through the pelvis will be easiest if you are upright in labour and when you give birth, so that gravity can assist the spiral descent of the baby's head (see Upright Labour and Birth Position on p. 178, and Recommended Reading).

EXPLORE YOUR OWN PELVIS LIKE THIS:
- Kneel on the floor with your trunk vertical.
- Place your hands on your hips at the level of your waist and feel your (iliac) hip bones at the sides. Starting at the front corners, press with your thumbs all along the top rim of the iliac bones and feel how they curve around your sides towards the sacrum at the back.
- Now place one hand below your lower belly and feel the top rim of your pubic bone with your fingers. Then lift up one knee and see if you can feel the bottom rim about 1½" further down and leave your hand in position.
- Place the other hand palm down on your lower back with the fingers pointing downwards. Your sacrum is located under your palm while the coccyx lies just under your fingertips. The distance

FIG. 5.11
PELVIC INLET
AND PELVIC
OUTLET
*(a) The baby's head engages in the pelvic brim.
(b) The widest diameter of the baby's head (front to back) engages in the widest diameter of the pelvic brim (side to side).
(c) The baby's head turns inside the pelvic canal so that the widest diameter emerges through the widest diameter of the pelvic outlet which is between the pubic bone and the coccyx (front to back).*

111

between the pubic bone and the coccyx is the widest diameter of the pelvic outlet through which your child will be born. The sacrum under the palm forms the back wall of your pelvis (see p. 110).

● Now remove your hands and remain kneeling, but sit down on your hands. Press your fingers upwards and wiggle your hips a little from side to side so that you can feel the two buttock or sitting bones. Between the two bones is the pubic arch.

● To feel the pubic arch, come back up and, still kneeling, lift your left leg and place the sole of the foot on the floor. Using the fingers of your left hand, find the left sitting bone and then press upwards along the bony rim in front towards the centre. Change legs and repeat on the other side. You have been feeling both sides of the pubic arch. The back of your baby's head will come under this arch as it emerges during birth.

● In the same position, explore the shape of your pelvic outlet from underneath by feeling the coccyx, the tips of the sitting bones, the pubic arch and the base of the pubic joint.

PELVIC MOBILITY

If you look at the diagram on p. 110 you will see where the four pelvic joints are located.

Nature has designed your pelvis so that its joints become increasingly mobile during pregnancy thanks to the softening effects of hormones on the ligaments. These are bands of tough fibrous tissue which hold the bones of your pelvis together at the joints. These ligaments interweave and run in all directions and, with the help of the pelvic muscles, bind the whole pelvis into a single unit.

When they soften they allow greater expansion of the pelvic joints which widens the diameters of the pelvic canal, making more space for your baby. For example, the pubic joint in front is usually held firmly together but during birth it is capable of separating as much as half an inch to widen the pelvic canal. The joints between the sacrum and the iliac or hip bones, known as the sacroiliac joints, are able to make a slight pivotal movement forward and back which allows your sacrum a certain degree of mobility so that it can adjust to the shape of your baby's head as it descends through the pelvic canal. It also makes it possible for the sacrum to tilt backwards so that the diameter of the pelvic outlet from front to back widens as your baby is emerging. This is why it is so important to avoid reclining positions in labour and birth in which your weight rests on your sacrum directly and renders it immobile, thus narrowing the pelvic outlet considerably (see my book *Active Birth*).

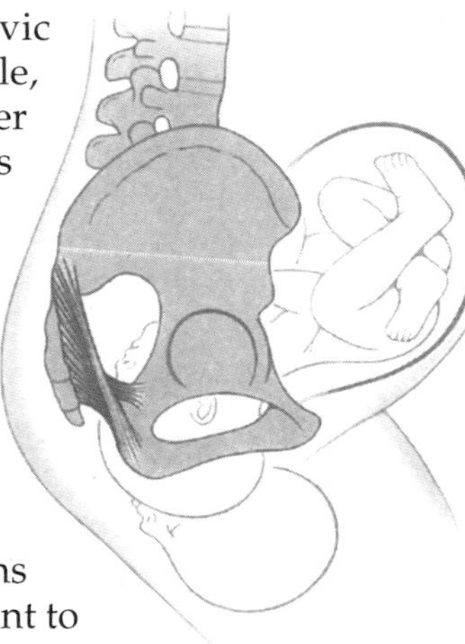

The tiny joint between the coccyx and the sacrum also becomes more mobile, enabling the coccyx to move back out of the way as your baby is being born.

FIG. 5.12
The baby's passage through the pelvic canal

In addition to this increase in pelvic mobility, your baby's skull bones are not yet fused as they are in an adult and they can overlap to allow a certain degree of 'moulding' to adjust to the shape and size of the pelvic canal. The yoga postures in this section enhance this natural increase in pelvic mobility and help to release stiffness or tension in the pelvic joints and the muscles which attach to the pelvis.

WHY THE PELVIC POSTURES ARE SO IMPORTANT IN PREGNANCY

About thirty-six pairs of muscles attach to your pelvis. They include the largest and strongest muscles of your body and control your movements whenever you change your position. They extend up into your trunk and also down into your legs and form important supporting parts of the body wall. Every part of your body, including the head, is connected to the pelvis so that it plays a key role in maintaining the balance and transfer of weight throughout the body.

Deep inside your body, the iliopsoas muscles stem from the spine and then come forward and down inside the abdomen like long straps to attach to the inside surface of the hip bones. As we have already seen on p. 82, they play a key role in maintaining the balanced relationship of the pelvis to the spine and freedom of movement in the hip joints. They also interrelate with the attachments of the diaphragm muscle and play an important part in breathing (see p. 81). The iliopsoas muscles are involved in flexing the trunk when they contract or shorten. For example, when you squat, they bring the spine, pelvis and thighs forward. They also connect your diaphragm with your pelvic floor muscles. The balanced action between the iliopsoas muscles and other deep muscles in the pelvis keeps the pelvis a working unit between the thighs and the spine for weight transfer. This contributes considerably to the stability of the pelvis. If these groups of deep pelvic muscles are not in balance then the pelvis will be out of alignment. As we have seen in Chapter 4, this will result in the ligaments becoming too weak and the joints will be subjected to strain, especially in pregnancy.

Most women underestimate how our Western lifestyle can result in postural imbalances which affect the integrity of the pelvis. This is not always obvious, but can prevent the baby from being correctly positioned for birth or cause damage and injury at the time, so for this reason it is important to take advantage of the exercises in this section to be sure of a strong and well-articulated pelvis. This will increase the likelihood of a physiological birth.

The pelvic ligaments and muscles work together to bind all the parts of the pelvic girdle into a whole and complete the wall of the pelvis so that it is a secure basin of support for the pelvic organs. The yoga postures in this group work on a deep muscular level so that the pelvic muscles come into a harmonious balance to ensure the integrity of the pelvis and its postural relationship to the rest of the body, and also its efficiency as the bony passage through which your baby will be born.

9 TAILOR SITTING

Baddha Konasana – bound angle pose

Tailor sitting is very grounding and centring. It is beneficial to the pelvic area as a whole, including the reproductive organs. It increases mobility of the joints, widening the pelvic diameters, and improves circulation to the whole area. It relaxes the pelvic floor muscles and gives you a sense of how your body can open to give birth. It helps to position your pelvis correctly and improve your posture. Practise daily if possible, for up to ten minutes at a time once it becomes comfortable.

CAUTION: Avoid straining or forcing in this position, by pulling your feet in too close to your body or pushing your knees down towards the ground. Keep it loose and gentle. Relaxation and release of tension will come through gentle breathing, in time, with practice. Never push or bounce the knees.

START in the basic sitting position (see Figure 5.1) with your lower back supported by a wall or a corner if necessary.

● Bend your knees and bring the soles of your feet together at a comfortable distance from your body. Later, when you have relaxed a little, you can draw them in closer. The outside edges of the feet should be touching, with the soles of the feet opening outwards eventually, like the pages of a book (see Figure 5.13a).

● If your thighs are not touching or close to the floor then you can place a soft cushion underneath each knee for support (Fig. 5.13b).

● Focus on your breathing and the way your body contacts the floor.

LEANING BACK

● Now move away from the wall if you are using one. Lean back, supporting your body with your hands, making sure your shoulders are relaxed (see Figure 5.13c).

FIG. 5.13 (a)
TAILOR SITTING

FIG. 5.13 (b)
TAILOR SITTING
With cushions

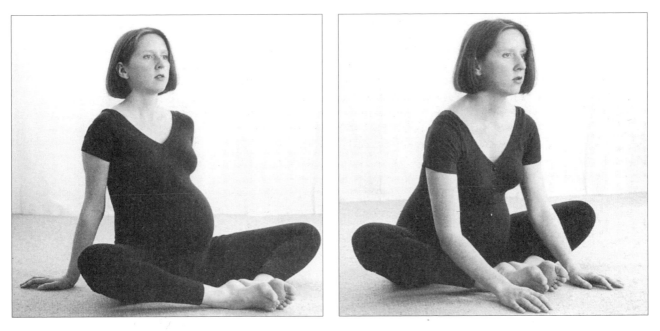

FIG. 5.13 (c)
TAILOR SITTING
Leaning back

FIG. 5.13 (d)
TAILOR SITTING
Leaning forward

● Focus on your breathing and allow the breath to flow through your whole body, imagining the exhalations starting from the base of your skull, travelling down your spine, through your pelvis and hips all the way to your feet. Imagine the inhalations coming through the soles of your feet, around your knees, through your thighs and hips, and then up slowly to fill the whole length of your lungs, from the base to just under the collar bones. Continue in this way in a comfortable rhythm for three or four cycles of the breath, feeling tension in the groin releasing as you breathe.

● Now move back against the wall so that your lower back is supported and, still in tailor sitting, bring your feet towards your body, keeping a feeling of softness in the groin so that the energy can flow freely through your body. Use your hands gently to relax the muscles of your legs, loosening the calf muscles and turning the thigh muscles from the inside to the outside of the thighs.

LEANING FORWARD

● Now lean forward slightly from the hips, touching the ground in front of you gently with your hands (see Figure 5.13d).

● Relax your spine and allow your head to tilt forward a little towards your chest to relax the back of your neck.

● Focus your awareness on your breathing and, as in basic sitting, feel your hips and the base of your spine lengthen downwards as if you are planting the root of the spine into the ground each time you exhale. With each inhalation, keep this grounded feeling and slowly lengthen and uncurl to come up into an upright position, your spine making contact with the wall one vertebra at a time. Take your time, remembering that it is the breath that returns your body to the upright position.

SITTING UPRIGHT

● Relax and spread your shoulders, letting your hands rest on your knees with the palms up (see Figure 5.13a).

● Now close your eyes and feel the pull of gravity underneath you. Notice the way your sitting bones make contact with the floor and release your lower back downwards towards the roots like a long heavy tail. Feel your hip joints dropping on to the ground.

● Bring your awareness to the rhythm of your breathing. Focus on the exhalations and feel the ripple of the breath move from the top of your neck all the way through the curves of the spine to the root, but without pushing the exhalation down. Just let it happen. Imagine the roots going deep into the earth.

When the breath comes in, keep the grounded feeling in the pelvis and the hip joints. Feel the inhalations begin from the roots and ripple from the base upwards, so that your spine releases and lengthens while the roots stay planted. Feel how your chest expands softly to welcome the incoming air and be aware of a gentle lengthening of your trunk each time you inhale. Allow the inhalations to fill the whole length of your lungs from the base to the collar bones.

● Continue breathing comfortably, feeling any tightness in the hips or the groin melting and releasing with the breath. Enjoy a feeling of openness in the pelvis. Relax and release the muscles of the pelvic floor. Be aware of the gentle lengthening of the space your baby occupies between the top rim of your pelvis and the lower rim of your rib cage while releasing and letting go of your shoulders. Continue for up to three minutes. You can continue for up to ten minutes once you feel comfortable and relaxed in the position.

9a TAILOR SITTING BACK-TO-BACK with a PARTNER

This is a very pleasant way to practise Baddha Konasana in a class or when working with a pregnant friend or your partner at home.

FIG. 5.14
TAILOR SITTING
BACK TO BACK
WITH A PARTNER

START by sitting back-to-back with a partner so that your lower backs (sacrum) are touching.

● Then bend at the hips to lean forwards, following the instructions on p. 115 and taking care to keep your sacrum in contact with your partner. Let your breath bring you slowly into an upright position, uncurling gradually so that your back makes contact with your partner's from the base upwards, while the heavy root of the spine releases downwards.

● Continue to sit in this position and breathe, enjoying the support of your partner behind you, for 1–3 minutes.

9b TAILOR SITTING with a PARTNER'S FEET in the BACK

This is a very comfortable way to support the base of the spine in this posture.

START by sitting in Baddha Konasana with your back to your partner. Your partner behind you can then place the soles of both feet firmly against your lower back or, alternatively, with one foot on the base of the spine and the other just above it. Let your partner know which of these options feels most supportive and how much pressure you need. Meanwhile, your partner can lean back on the hands for support (see Figure 5.15), but without tensing the shoulders.

FIG. 5.15
TAILOR SITTING
WITH PARTNER'S
FEET IN BACK

● As you relax into the tailor pose, focus on grounding and releasing your spine with your breathing. The emphasis should be on rooting the spine downwards, facilitated by your partner's support in the base so that your spine can then lengthen and release upwards from this stable base.

● Continue for 1–3 minutes and then change places if you wish to give your partner a turn.

10 SITTING with LEGS WIDE

Sitting on the floor like this with your legs wide apart is both comfortable and beneficial in pregnancy. The pelvis is well grounded and the diameters of the pelvic canal widen, encouraging a feeling of openness. Mobility of the hip joints increases while the muscles of the inner thighs and the backs of the legs lengthen and release. This posture stabilizes and anchors the pelvis and so enhances the release of tension along the spine and in the neck and shoulders.

Regular practice of this position will increase your confidence in being able to open your body to give birth and enhance your awareness of the way your pelvis is widening and loosening to make space for your baby. You can sit like this as often as you like or use this position for your breathing practice. You may also enjoy following this posture with tailor sitting (No. 9) when you practise, alternating from one to the other.

START in the basic sitting position (see Figure 5.1) with your lower back supported by a wall or a corner. This posture can also be done sitting back-to-back with a partner or with your partner's feet supporting the spine (as in No. 9a or 9b).

Spread your legs as wide apart as possible without exceeding your natural limit. It is not important how wide you can open your legs but rather how comfortable you feel. Focus your awareness on your breathing and the way your body contacts the floor.

FIG. 5.16 (a)
SITTING WITH
LEGS WIDE

LEANING BACK
● Move away, if you are using the wall for support, and then lean back on to your hands to release tension in the groin, as you did in tailor sitting (see Figure 5.13c). Support your trunk with your arms without tensing your neck and shoulders.

● Using your imagination, breathe through your whole body as you did in tailor sitting, the exhalations moving from the top of your neck to your feet, and the inhalations from your feet upwards.

LEANING FORWARD

● Lean forward slightly, moving so that your lower back is supported by the wall again if you are using one. Touch the ground lightly with your hands, your weight going down into the ground through your sitting bones and hip joints (see Figure 5.16b).

FIG. 5.16 (b)
SITTING WITH
LEGS WIDE
Leaning forward

● Use your breathing as you did leaning forward in tailor sitting (see p. 115), grounding the root of the spine while exhaling and slowly lengthening and uncurling along the length of your spine while inhaling until you are sitting upright once more.

Then spread out and relax your shoulders and drop your arms by your sides, hands resting lightly on your thighs, palms up.

SITTING UPRIGHT

● Relax in the posture and turn your attention inwards to the rhythmic wave of your breathing (see Figure 5.16a).
● Feel how your lower back and pelvis release downwards with the pull of gravity.
● Massage your thighs so that they feel soft and heavy, turning the big thigh muscles from the inside towards the outside.
● Now gently lengthen your calf muscles and extend your heels without tensing your thighs. Feel the way the backs of your heels rest on the floor. If your feet tend to turn outwards, then allow them to do so for a few seconds and then gently roll the legs so that the knees are facing up towards the ceiling without tensing the muscles.
● Feel your spine lengthen from the base to the top of the neck with the inhalations, like a plant absorbing moisture from the earth, while your hips and heavy pelvis remain grounded.
● Circle your shoulders loosely to release them, and relax the back of your neck by tucking your chin slightly forward.
● As you breathe, be aware of a gentle lengthening of the space occupied by your baby, between the top rim of your pelvis and the lower rim of your rib cage. With the root of the spine and your pelvis firmly grounded in the position, your upper body can blossom upwards like a bouquet of flowers, growing from the ground.
● Continue for 1–3 minutes, your body becoming more grounded from the pelvic rim downwards, while your upper body feels lighter and looser as your spine releases.

10a SIDE BENDS with LEGS WIDE APART

Once you can do No. 10 with ease, you will enjoy these graceful side bends which allow a gentle stretching of the oblique abdominal and side muscles while encouraging release and expansion of the chest and lengthening of the spine.

CAUTION: It is very important to bend to the side moderately and to avoid straining. Do not attempt the full posture until you can do so with ease. Focus instead on exploring your own comfortable limit in a gentle way so that you experience a lovely lengthening feeling all along your side rather than a sense of constriction or strain. A good guideline is to be aware of keeping both sitting bones and hip joints firmly down on the floor. If you feel one buttock bone or hip lifting up, then you know you are beginning to go beyond your limit. Your breathing is also a good guide. If you are breathing effortlessly you are doing well, but if you are struggling to breathe then you are overdoing it . Follow the instructions up to your comfortable limit only, and then focus on your breathing and the way your body is affected by the pull of gravity.

START in the sitting position with legs wide apart (see Figure 16(a)). Spend time allowing your body to settle into the position. Be aware of the way your lower back, hip joints, sitting bones and the

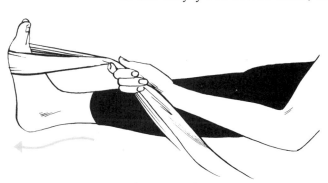

backs of your legs are very well grounded in this position and keep them rooted throughout. Release your lower spine downwards and bring your awareness to your breathing. Breathe comfortably in your normal rhythm, continuing to send deep roots into the ground with the exhalations and be aware of a gentle lengthening of the spine and the upper body with the inhalations. Feel the inbreaths filling the length of your lungs all the way up to the collar bones and the out breaths emptying the lungs completely, releasing the root of the spine downward. Keep breathing gently, without pushing the exhalations or pulling in the inhalations. At the same time, your mind stays in the ground, aware of the pull of gravity at all times.

● As you enjoy the flow of your breathing, bend slightly to the right, extending your right arm towards your right foot until you reach your comfortable limit. You can loop a belt around your right foot (see Figure 5.17)

FIG. 5.17
USING A BELT
If your lower arm does not reach your foot, loop a soft belt around your foot and hold it at a comfortable distance. Keep your elbow towards the front of your knee and bend gently to the side to find your comfortable limit.

FIG. 5.18 (a)
SIDE BEND WITH LEGS WIDE APART
Place one arm behind your back

• Make sure that your left hip and buttock bone remain down on the ground.

• Allow your neck and head to follow the wave of your spine so that the back of your neck feels relaxed.

• Place your left arm comfortably behind your back to help to bring your left shoulder back and to make space in the rib cage, so that it is easy to receive and welcome the breath into your lungs when you inhale (see Figure 5.18a).

• If you can do so without

FIG. 5.18 (b)
Raise the other arm towards the ceiling and lengthen the spine.

FIG. 5.18 (c)
Take your arm over your head without straining.

lifting your left hip or straining, place your right elbow and forearm on the floor inside the right knee and catch the foot using a belt around the foot if necessary (see Figure 5.17). You should feel a gentle stretch along the left hip and side of the trunk.

• If you are able to do so with ease, then you can increase the sideways stretch by lifting your left arm up towards the ceiling, allowing it to extend up loosely from the shoulders as you inhale (see Figure 5.18b). Then, on an exhalation, bend gently to the right, taking your left arm over your head towards your right foot. Go only as far as you can without straining or lifting your left hip off the floor.

• Enjoy the stretch for thirty seconds or so, and then come slowly back to the centre and relax before you repeat on the other side.

10b PARTNER WORK with LEGS WIDE APART

You can work with a partner in this posture in many enjoyable ways. Sitting back-to-back or with a partner's feet in the back (as demonstrated on p. 116-17) can also be done in this position. Or your partner can kneel on the floor facing you and place both hands on your thighs and knees, applying a firm but gentle downward pressure to help you to 'breathe' the backs of the legs towards the floor.

FIG. 5.19 (a)
PARTNER WORK WITH LEGS WIDE APART
Place both hands firmly and gently on your partner's hip bones using a downward pressure.

Alternatively, while you sit with legs wide, your partner might try the following:

• Position yourself comfortably behind her and place both hands around the hip joints, applying a firm but gentle downward pressure to help her to ground the pelvis and release the root of the spine downwards (see Figure 5.19a).

• Complete this part of the exercise by removing your hands slowly and spending some time massaging her shoulders and down her spine.

• Now come around to one side of her, making yourself comfortable with one knee up.

• Take her forehead in one hand so that you support the weight of her head. Encourage her to breathe and relax and let you support the weight of her head (see Figure 5.19b).

• Now massage the nape of her neck, up into the hairline and down the sides of the back of the neck towards the shoulders.

• Then ask her to slowly raise her head, tilting her chin downward slightly at the end, to keep the back of the neck long and relaxed.

• Now sit behind her with both feet placed firmly against her lower back for support, without disturbing the natural balance of her spine. Encourage her to feel grounded in the pelvis as she breathes out, while slowly raising both arms up over her head each time she inhales (see Figure 5.19c).

Do this slowly over several cycles of the breath, raising the arms a little higher with each inhalation, continuing to lengthen the lower back downwards with each exhalation. Keep the arms up for about thirty seconds and then bring them down gently.

FIG. 5.19 (b)
Supporting her forehead with one hand, use the other to massage the muscles at the base of the skull and the back of the neck.

Fig. 5.19 (c)
Place the soles of both feet firmly against your partner's lower back to support the root of the spine. Your partner then slowly raises her arms above her head as her spine lengthens from this stable base.

11 CHILD'S POSE

This posture is one of the most enjoyable and beneficial to practise in pregnancy. It increases mobility of the pelvic joints, gently encouraging the natural widening of the pelvic canal and the diameter of the pelvic outlet, while releasing tension and stiffness in the hip joints and the groin.

The muscles of the lower back and pelvic floor relax, allowing the spine to lengthen while the weight of your baby and uterus hang forward. As the baby grows heavier, this posture is relaxing as it temporarily allows your lower back some respite from supporting the additional weight of the pregnancy. Circulation to the pelvic area is enhanced and your baby may also enjoy the hammock-like support in this position!

CAUTION: If you find it uncomfortable to keep your pelvis down on your heels because of varicose veins in the legs or stiffness in the knees and ankles, then sitting astride a bolster or placing a cushion or two under your buttocks may be helpful (see Figure 5.20).

When going forward, as in Figure 5.21a–d, remember that it is not important how low down you go. Focus instead on feeling

Fig. 5.20
SUPPORTED CHILD'S POSE
Using a bolster and cushions

grounded in the pelvis and the root of the spine, making sure that your back feels loose and free all along its length, rather than straining to go down all the way to the floor.

START by kneeling on a folded blanket or soft surface in the basic kneeling position with your knees as wide apart as possible without straining (Figure 5.21a). Your feet should be turning inwards towards the centre, following the curve of your buttocks.

● Focus on the normal wave and rhythm of your breathing, releasing your lower back downwards with the exhalations so that you feel you are really sitting in your pelvis.

● Feel the inhalations being gently welcomed and received into the whole length of your lungs from the base to the collar bones so that the upper body feels light and free.

● Circle your shoulders loosely and relax your arms.

● Feel the way your head balances on top of your spine and drop your chin down slightly to relax the back of your neck.

● Begin to come forward slowly, moving from the hip joints, lengthening your lower back around the curve of the sacrum towards your heels and without bending your spine. Your pelvis stays down close to your heels throughout this exercise and your spine should always feel loose and free, the forward movement coming from the hip joints. This is more important than going down all the way to the floor.

● Place your palms on the floor, keeping your arms straight and your spine free (Figure 5.21b).

● Focus on lengthening the root of the spine downwards as you exhale and allow the inbreaths to elongate and release your spine from the base to the top of the neck.

● Make sure the back of your neck is lengthened and relaxed by releasing your chin slightly downwards towards your chest.

● Provided you are feeling comfortable in the posture so far, continue moving forward from the hips and come down on to your elbows (see Figure 5.21c). Continue breathing normally,

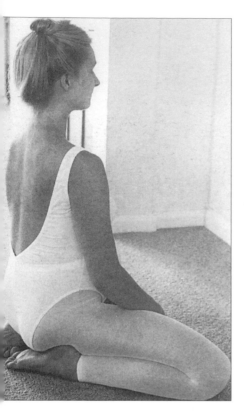

FIG. 5.21 (a)
CHILD'S POSE
Kneel upright and lengthen the base of the spine downwards.

FIG. 5.21 (b)
Come forward from the hips, touch the ground with your hands and release and lengthen your spine

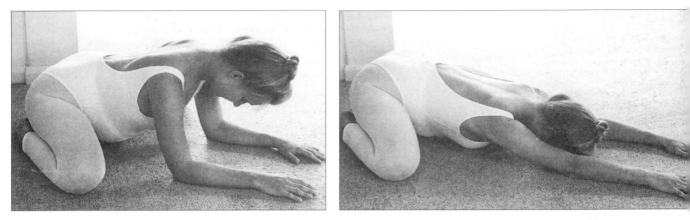

FIG. 5.21 (c)
*Lean further
forward on to your
elbows.*

FIG. 5.21 (d)
*Release your trunk
forward from the
hips with your
forehead resting on
the floor and arms
extended.*

gently lengthening the spine towards the coccyx as you exhale, and then feel the ripple of release which occurs up your spine towards the base of the skull when you inhale. You may find it comfortable to lie forward on to a bolster or long cushion for support, so that you can completely relax in the posture (see Figure 5.20).

● If it feels comfortable, you may be able to relax further forward on to the floor. Stretch your arms out loosely in front of you and place your forehead on the floor (see Figure 5.21d). Make sure there is no sense of strain in your back. Focus on releasing your lower back towards your heels and continue breathing and releasing your spine.

● When you are ready, come up very slowly, lengthening and releasing the root of the spine downwards towards your pubic bone as you do so. Your shoulders should feel light and loose with all your weight settling into the heavy pelvis. Release your lower back down towards your heels.

● Finally, centre your head and feel the way it balances on top of your spine, lengthening and relaxing the back of your neck by tilting your chin slightly downwards. Circle your shoulders loosely a few times to enjoy the feeling of lightness and freedom in the upper body.

11a CHILD'S POSE – PARTNER WORK

NOTE: These instructions are for your partner.

● Kneel or sit comfortably behind her and place your hands gently on her shoulders. Become aware of her breathing rhythm and your own. Tune in to her energy before you begin to do anything.

● Now begin massaging her shoulders, working into any areas that feel tight or tense, and asking her how much pressure feels good. You can work down the arms and also into the back of the neck (see Figure 5.22a).

● End by stroking down the shoulder blades and then massaging down either side of the spine, all the way to the tailbone.

● Kneel comfortably behind her and place your hands on the top rim of her pelvis, with a gentle but firm downward pressure (see Figure 5.22b).

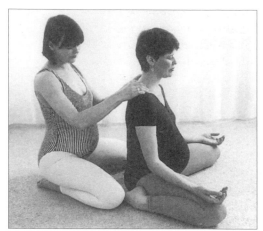

FIG. 5.22 (a)
CHILD'S POSE
WITH A PARTNER
*Massaging the
shoulders*

FIG. 5.22 (b)
*Anchoring the
pelvis*

- Encourage her to breathe and gently release the root of her spine downwards while exhaling so that her pelvis feels well anchored.
- Then, keeping your hands in place, suggest that she slowly raise her arms above her head while inhaling so that she has a sense of lengthening out of the grounded pelvis.
- Ask her to bend forward slowly, moving from the hip joints, until she reaches her comfortable limit.
- Move round to her left side, kneeling with one knee up for your own comfort.
- Place the palm of your right hand over the root of her spine (sacrum) with your fingers facing towards her coccyx. Now lean your weight gently but firmly down and back, asking her to tell you how much pressure to apply (see Figure 5.22c).
- While the right hand anchors the base of her spine, your left hand can massage along its length and into her neck and shoulders. Continue like this for about thirty seconds, encouraging her to breathe deeply and relax.
- Then gently remove your right hand and use both hands to massage more deeply into her shoulders. Continue for about thirty seconds, using your hands to release any stiffness or tension in the neck, shoulders and upper back.

FIG. 5.22 (c)
*Back and shoulder
massage in the
forward position*

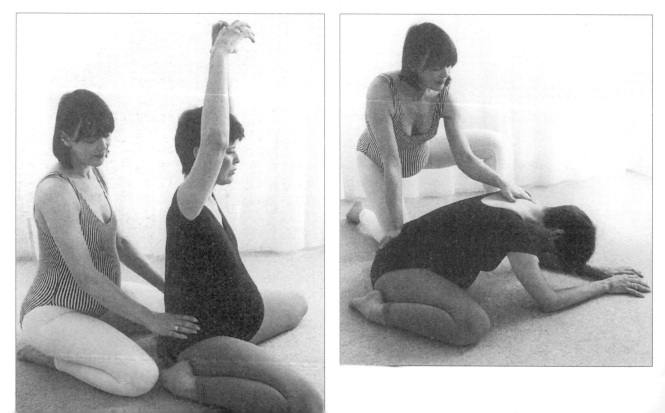

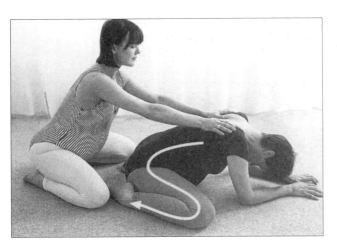

FIG. 5.22 (d)
Clearing the energy – full body strokes

● Finally, kneel behind her and place both palms on her upper back on either side of the spine close to the neck. Now, with a firm, even pressure, using both hands, stroke down her back, around her hips, along her thighs and off her calves and feet in one movement (see Figure 5.22d). Repeat five times.

● Then rub your hands together to make them warm and place the palms of both hands over her lower back for a few seconds, allowing the warmth of your hands to penetrate the muscles.

● Keep your hands in place as she comes up slowly, exerting a gentle but firm downward pressure as she returns to the upright position to remind her to lengthen her lower back downwards around the curve of the sacrum.

12 SQUATTING

Malasana – garland pose
Squatting is the central exercise of your pregnancy yoga practice. A natural position for giving birth, it opens your pelvis to its widest and creates a perfect angle of descent for the baby in relation to gravity (see p. 111). While you are pregnant, squatting regularly helps to increase the mobility of your pelvic and hip joints and to bring your pelvis into the right postural position in relation to your spine (see p. 81). When this happens your uterus is properly supported and the baby is held securely in a good position. In the last few weeks of your pregnancy, squatting will encourage your baby's head to engage in the pelvic brim. Practising squatting will also help you to feel at ease in this position so you can use it comfortably when you are in labour or supported to give birth.

When you squat, the extensor muscles in the back, buttocks and pelvic floor lengthen and relax, while the muscles in front of your body shorten or contract. In this position, your pelvic floor relaxes

FIG. 5.23
SQUATTING

and the blood supply to the whole pelvic area improves. The perineal tissues relax and can stretch evenly when you squat, so regular practice may help to prevent tearing in the final stages of the birth.

You may well find that, at first, it is uncomfortable to squat. If so, you probably have not used this position for many years. In fact, squatting is a perfectly natural sitting and resting position which every toddler uses instinctively before standing and walking. Thanks to the help of the pregnancy hormones, your pelvic ligaments will increase in laxity and, with just a little dedicated practice, squatting will soon become much easier. I have never met a woman who was unable to learn to squat using some form of support, even though many are doubtful when they first begin to try!

Recovering this healthgiving habit will be a true service to your well-being and help to prevent any problems arising with elimination as it also relaxes the bowel and bladder. While you are pregnant it is helpful to place two small plastic stools (of the type used by toddlers) on either side of the toilet and bring your feet up into a position closer to squatting. This will help to prevent constipation. You can also keep a low stool in your living room to use for squatting comfortably when you relax at home, so that squatting becomes a normal part of your life (see p. 129).

The squatting exercises that follow begin with the easiest and end with the full position. Take your time to develop ease in each of them until you are ready for full squatting. It is advisable to practise squatting for five minutes a day throughout your pregnancy in addition to squatting comfortably as a sitting position on a stool whenever you have the opportunity.

CAUTION: If your baby is in the breech position after thirty-four weeks, stop squatting altogether as you do not want to encourage the buttocks to engage. After thirty-six weeks, practise the knee–chest position (see p. 139) several times a day instead (see Appendix – Breech Baby, p. 201).

Avoid full squatting if you have had a cervical stitch (Shirodkar suture) or if you have haemorrhoids or vulval varicosities, severe or painful varicose veins in your legs. However, the squatting exercise (No. 12b), using a stool under your buttocks for support or squatting astride a bolster or large rolled-up cushion, can be practised safely provided it does not cause you any pain or discomfort. Full squatting for a short period of time is not harmful to varicose veins in the legs unless they hurt in this position.

It is useful to prepare for squatting with the following stretch for your calves.

12a CALF STRETCH

This posture lengthens and relaxes the calf muscles and the Achilles tendons, increasing the flexibility of the ankles. It is good preparation for squatting and will also help to alleviate cramps in the calves.

START by standing facing a wall with your right foot close to the wall and your left foot about a yard back

FIG. 5.24
CALF STRETCH

- Bend your right knee.
- Keep your left knee straight, lean forward and, clasping your hands, place your forearms and elbows on the wall.
- Keep the back of your neck and your shoulders relaxed throughout.
- Make sure that both feet are facing towards the wall and are not turning out to the sides.
- Now move your left foot back as far as you can, keeping the heel firmly down on the floor.
- Make sure that your hips are parallel to the wall. Do not allow the right hip to fall forward.
- Breathe your weight back into your left heel and feel it going down on to the floor so that you will feel the stretch in the calf muscles and Achilles tendon. Don't push the heel into the floor, but feel how it is being pulled down by gravity. The front leg should touch the floor lightly with all your weight moving down into the ground through the back heel.
- As the heel drops on to the floor, feel how the back of the knee 'opens' and releases, as if it were yawning.
- Hold for up to thirty seconds and then change legs, bringing the left foot forward and the right foot back. Repeat twice more on each leg and then relax.

12b SQUATTING on a STOOL

- Take a low stool or two or three large books and place them behind you. Use the minimum number of books you need, lowering the height of the pile as you improve until you do not need them.
- Stand with your feet about 18" apart and parallel. Drop your weight into your heels and then, keeping them flat on the floor, bend your knees, lengthen your lower back and lower yourself slowly into a squat with your buttocks resting on the stool or books. Your feet may turn out as you go down, but try to avoid turning them out more than necessary. Your knees should be pointing in the same direction as your feet.

FIG. 5.25
SQUATTING
ON A STOOL

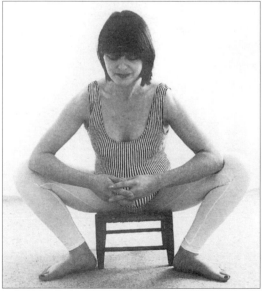

● Pay attention to your feet. Feel the base of the big toe, the heel and the outside edges of the feet making contact with the ground just as if you were standing upright. The inner ankles lift and the toes spread apart, moving outwards from the big toe to the little toe.

● Lean forward from your hip joints, keeping your spine free and the back of your neck relaxed.

● Clasp your hands or bring the palms together in a prayer position and place your elbows inside your legs, using them to help spread your knees out wide. Stay in this position for 1–3 minutes and then come forward on to your hands and knees before coming up, or else come up slowly to avoid straining your knees.

● Repeat twice more, pausing to rest in between.

12c SQUATTING AGAINST a WALL

● Place a pile of three small cushions between your feet and stand with your lower back (sacrum) only just touching the wall and your feet 18" apart and parallel or slightly turned out (not illustrated).

● Keeping your heels on the ground, lengthen your lower back, bend your knees and slide down the wall into a squatting position, keeping your sacrum in touch with the surface. Find the right distance for your feet from the wall so that only your lower back is in contact with it. The rest of your spine should be free and coming forward a little from the hip joints so that you have just a touch of support from the wall at the base of the spine and the cushions under your buttocks.

FIG. 5.26
SQUATTING WITH
SUPPORT UNDER
HEELS

● Spread you toes and let your weight drop into your heels. Feel the inner arches of your feet lifting while the base of the big toe, the heels and the outside edges of the feet go down on to the floor. The toes spread apart, moving outwards from the big toe to the little toe.

● Clasp your hands as in No. 12a or place the palms together in a prayer position.

● Continue for 1–3 minutes and then come forward on to your hands and knees before coming up.

● Repeat twice more, after a little rest.

12d SQUATTING with SUPPORT under the HEELS

● Roll a blanket or a yoga mat and place it under your heels with your feet about 18" apart and as close to parallel as possible.

● Bend your knees and come down into a squat as in Nos. 12a and 12b (see Figure 5.26).

● Make the roll smaller as you improve.

● Continue for 1 3 minutes and repeat. Come up as before.

12e SQUATTING HOLDING on to a SUPPORT

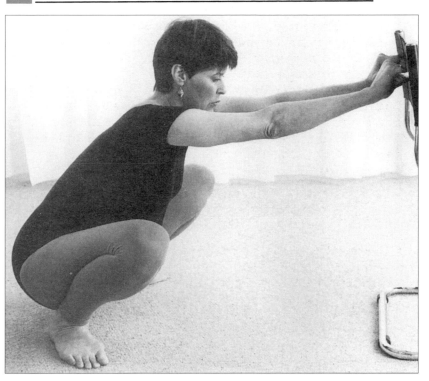

FIG. 5.27
SQUATTING
HOLDING ON TO
A SUPPORT

● Find something secure to hold on to about 2–3 ft high, such as a window ledge, the side of the bath, a radiator or both door handles of a strongly hinged, open door.
● Stand facing your support with your feet 18" apart and slightly turned out if necessary.
● Keeping your heels down on the floor and your elbows straight, lower yourself into a squat (see Figure 5.27).
● Spread your toes, lift the inner ankle bones and spread your knees so that they follow the line of your feet.
● Make sure that the back of your neck is relaxed by dropping your chin down slightly towards your chest, and release and lengthen your lower back downwards.
● Stay in the position, breathing comfortably, for 30–60 seconds. Then exhale, press your heels into the floor and come up slowly and carefully.
● Repeat twice more, with a little rest in between.

12f FULL SQUATTING

● Stand with your feet 18" apart and parallel or slightly turned out. Let your weight drop down into your heels. Breathe for a moment or two and ground yourself by sending your exhalations like roots into the floor through your heels.
● Bend your knees and lengthen your lower back downwards (see Figure 5.28a).

FIG. 5.28 (a)
FULL SQUATTING
Stand with feet wide and bend your knees

FIG. 5.28 (b)
*Lean forward from
the hips and touch
the floor*

FIG. 5.28 (c)
*Squat down
keeping your heels
on the ground,
with hands clasped
and knees spread
wide*

- Bend forward from the hips and place your palms on the floor with your knees still bent (see Figure 5.28b).
- Lower your pelvis down into a squat. Clasp hands and place your elbows inside your knees (Fig. 5.28c).
- Exhale down into the floor through your heels and release your lower back downwards.
- As you inhale, feel the spine lengthen from the tailbone up to the top of your neck, keeping your chin slightly down to relax the muscles in the back of your neck.
- Spread your toes and lift the inner arches of the feet and the inner ankle bones.
- Feel your weight go down from your heels and the outside edges of the feet into the floor.
- Continue for 1–3 minutes, breathing comfortably. Touch the floor with your hands and stand, or come forward onto hands and knees to come up.
- Repeat twice, resting in between.

12g SQUATTING WITH A PARTNER

SQUATTING ONE AT A TIME WITH A PARTNER

● Stand facing a partner and hold each other by the wrists. Place your feet about 18" apart and slightly turned out.

● When your partner is ready, bend your knees and, keeping your heels down on the floor and your elbows straight, lower yourself down into a squat.

● Hold on to your partner for support and stay in the position for 30–60 seconds.

● Focus on your lower back, releasing downwards, your heels going down into the floor and the back of your neck lengthening. Your knees should be pointing in the same direction as your feet.

● Lift the inner arches of the feet and the inner ankle bones, dropping the outside edges and the heels down into the floor.

● Spread your toes and your knees out wide.

● To come up, exhale into your heels and stand up slowly with your partner's help.

● Repeat this two or three times, resting briefly in between.

PARTNER

● Take a good distance from her so that both of you can keep your arms straight without bending the elbows.

Hold her securely by the wrists throughout this exercise.

● Bring your feet a little closer to her, placing one foot in front of the other.

● Lengthen your lower back and tuck your pelvis under when she goes down, so that you are leaning back rather than forward. This way your own back is protected and it is possible for you to support her without straining. Alternatively, you can do this exercise with the supporting partner seated on a chair instead of standing.

FIG. 5.29 (a)
SQUATTING
WITH A PARTNER
Partner squat, one at a time

133

FIG. 5.29(b)
Squatting together

SQUATTING TOGETHER

● Stand facing each other with your feet about 18" apart and slightly turned out.

● Hold each other securely by the wrists and stand far enough away from each other so that your arms remain straight, without bending the elbows, as you both go down. You may need to move a little further back as you go down in order to support each other properly. Your knees should be pointing in the same direction as your feet.

● Hold for 30–60 seconds and then come up by dropping your heels down into the floor and straightening your legs. Keep supporting your partner as you both stand up slowly. Repeat two or three times.

FIG. 5.29(c)
Helping

HELPING

Squat on your own as in 12f or in 12d.

PARTNER

● Stand behind her with your feet under her buttocks and your shins supporting her lower back.

● Bend forward carefully from your hips; don't strain your own back.

● Place your hands on her knees and use your body weight (rather than 'pushing') to allow her to relax down into her heels while spreading her knees apart. Use a firm, consistent pressure but don't be forceful. Check that it feels easier for her to squat with your assistance.

● Hold for about 20 seconds and then suggest that she goes forward on to her hands and knees before coming up.

PELVIC FLOOR MUSCLES

Your pelvic floor is one of the most important parts of your anatomy, especially during pregnancy and birth. Yet because the pelvic floor is not visible, it is easy to overlook the vital role it plays in maintaining your health. While the domeshaped diaphragm muscle (see p. 62) forms the roof of your abdominal cavity, the inner muscles of the pelvis, shaped a little like an inverted dome, form its floor.

The pelvic floor is the term used to describe the layers of muscle which lie within the pelvis, forming its base. These are the muscles that lie right between your legs. They extend deep inside your body from the lower sacrum and coccyx at the back, between your buttock bones and subpubic arch to your pubic bone in front, like a kind of hammock. The deep inner layer is known as the pelvic diaphragm and the outer forms the perineal muscles.

In the midline, where the right and left halves of the pelvic floor

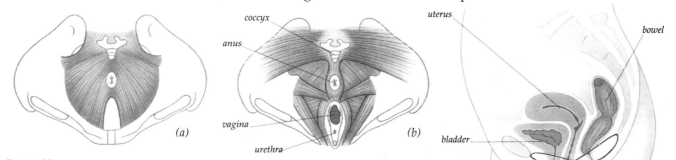

FIG. 5.30
THE MUSCLES OF
THE PELVIC FLOOR
(a) The pelvic floor muscles
(b) The muscles of the perineum
(c) The position of the pelvic floor seen from the side

unite, the pelvic floor is penetrated by three openings, the urethra in front, the vagina in the centre and the anus at the back. The muscle fibres are arranged around these openings and the inner passages they lead to, so that they form circular sphincters which can open or close as needed. They are distributed in a kind of figure-eight pattern with the front loop surrounding the urethral and vaginal sphincter and the other, the anal sphincter, at the back. The two loops and the underlying connecting tissues unite to form the perineal body in the centre so that the whole pelvic floor is continuous.

When one sphincter contracts, the same action occurs simultaneously in the others. The anal sphincter is usually held closed except when you empty your bowels, while the vagina and urethral sphincters are normally in a state of partial contraction. During elimination, when the bladder or bowels empty, or when the baby emerges during childbirth, the sphincters automatically relax to open and then return to the contracted, supportive state.

We can also contract and relax the sphincters of the pelvic floor consciously. Unlike the uterus, the pelvic floor muscles do come under our conscious control and it is possible to release or contract them at will.

Try this: to get a sense of how you can contract and release your pelvic floor muscles, try stopping the flow of urine in midstream. Do it once, but don't make a habit of it!

When you do this, you are voluntarily constricting the urethral sphincter. Alternatively, try inserting one finger into your vagina when you are in the bath and contract your vaginal muscles around your finger. These are also the muscles which can grip the penis when making love. Try doing this with your partner and see if he can feel the tightening movements. You can also contract the strong sphincter of the anal muscles at the back. You will find that, while it is possible to focus on one sphincter at a time, all three will move in unison when the pelvic floor contracts.

The IMPORTANCE of GOOD MUSCLE TONE in the PELVIC FLOOR

In our evolutionary past, when our female ape ancestors went about on all-fours, the pelvic floor was at the back of the body, just under the tail. Its main function was to provide sphincter control of the openings to the bladder, vagina and anus (see p. 76).

However, in the upright position, the pelvic floor muscles need to support the entire contents of the abdomen from underneath and to resist the effect of the downward force of gravity. They need to bear the pressures which occur when we breathe, laugh, cough, sneeze, lift a heavy weight, strain or give birth.

When your pelvic floor is in good tone it is rather like a trampoline slung across the pelvic outlet from front to back, and also attaching to the inside of the sitting bones. It supports the pelvic organs and the abdominal organs above them.

When the pelvic floor is weak, it is like a sagging trampoline with loose springs. Instead of having good rebound and elasticity to counterbalance the weight on top, it drops and consequently all the pelvic organs can descend and sag below the horizontal. Very often, women do not realize that they have a weak pelvic floor but wonder why they feel listless, achy or depressed, or do not have strong feelings or sensations when making love.

While weakness in the pelvic floor may not be obvious at first, eventually it can lead to problems such as urinary incontinence, vulval or anal varicosities (piles) or prolapse of the uterus due to the sagging effect and weakness of the muscle fibres of the sphincters and their surrounding blood vessels. Eventually, if ignored, problems such as these, which can be prevented or healed by exercise in the early stages, may end up needing surgery. It is possible, with pelvic floor exercises, to prevent such problems during your pregnancy.

DEVELOPING POWER in the PELVIC FLOOR

The pelvic floor is the main supporting structure of the uterus. During pregnancy, hormonal softening throughout the body also affects these muscles. This will help during the birth but may weaken the pelvic floor as a supporter. The increase in weight of the uterus in pregnancy places additional stress on the pelvic floor whenever you are upright.

Problems with the pelvic floor are so common that it seems that society just takes them for granted. Since at least half of the female population has some laxity of the pelvic floor, with or without handicaps, doctors tend to think of the firm perineum as the exception.

ELIZABETH NOBLE
Essential Exercises for the Childbearing Year

It is therefore essential to maintain the strength of the pelvic floor with suitable exercises throughout your pregnancy, and to restore and maintain good muscle tone – especially if your pelvic floor was weak at the start of your pregnancy.

Good muscle tone can be successfully restored during pregnancy by dedicated exercise, even if you can hardly move these muscles at first. The yoga postures benefit the pelvic floor indirectly by improving circulation and posture, but specific pelvic floor exercises in addition to these should be practised regularly (see p. 138).

The pelvic floor muscles are internal to the pelvis and need to be exercised separately, and this should receive top priority in pregnancy. Taking the trouble to ensure that your pelvic floor is healthy through exercise will strengthen and thicken the muscle fibres. It will also improve circulation so that blood is pumped efficiently back up to the heart. This will prevent or improve varicosities and reduce the compression caused by the additional weight of pregnancy. It will also help to prevent constipation and increase your awareness of pleasant sensations when making love. This can transform your sex life and increase your orgasmic potential.

Your PELVIC FLOOR during CHILDBIRTH

During labour, your baby's head descends deep into the pelvic canal. Just before the birth it makes contact with the muscles of the pelvic floor and this stimulates the onset of the expulsive reflex in the second stage, and also encourages the baby's head to rotate into the most convenient position for birth (see p. 111). As your baby is being born, the head and body will come through the vaginal sphincter in the centre of your pelvic floor. During labour, the pelvic floor relaxes and softens so that it is capable of the distention and stretching which is needed as the baby's head, shoulders and body emerge during the second stage.

While you are pregnant, practising the pelvic floor exercises will not only enable you to improve muscle tone by contracting, but will also teach you how to consciously relax and release your pelvic floor muscles as you will need to do when your baby is being born. By practising this in pregnancy, you will not need to think about it later as you are giving birth. You will instinctively find it easier to release these muscles when you need to.

The PELVIC FLOOR in UPRIGHT BIRTH POSITIONS

Undue stress on the pelvic floor during the birth can be prevented by adequate exercise in pregnancy and also by choosing active upright positions while giving birth. The pelvic floor muscles belong with the extensors of the trunk which run down the back of your body. The flexors are in front. In the squatting position or its variants (such as kneeling), the flexors in front contract and shorten. The extensors are the opposing team and they relax and lengthen in this position. This means that the pelvic floor muscles are relaxed and lengthening when you use supported squatting positions, which will make it easier for them to open and release for birth (see Squatting on p. 127).

There is also less stress on the perineum in upright birth positions so that it can expand evenly and move up and back out of the way as the baby's head emerges. In the semi-reclining position the perineum cannot stretch easily and the baby's head comes down on to it directly. As it cannot easily move back or stretch in this position, damage or tearing is more likely.

Your PELVIC FLOOR after BIRTH

With good preparation in pregnancy and sensible use of upright positions for birth, the pelvic floor in a healthy, sexually active woman should survive pregnancy and birth without injury. You are bound to feel a little sore and tender at first but the healing and recovery is usually remarkably fast. With consistent exercise of the pelvic floor in pregnancy, a woman's body can tolerate several pregnancies and remain none the worse for wear.

Your body changes rapidly from its pregnant state in the first week or so after birth, so this is the best time to ensure good recovery of the pelvic floor and perineum by continuing to do your pelvic floor exercises. You can begin the day after birth. Do not be surprised if you do not feel very much happening at first – sensation will return as muscle tone is restored.

If you have had stitches or an episiotomy, the pelvic floor exercises are completely safe and beneficial. They will improve circulation and speed up the healing process. The incision is brought closer by the muscular contractions and there is no danger of the wound opening due to pelvic floor exercises.

FIG. 5.31 (a)
PELVIC FLOOR
EXERCISES
*Easy squatting
for pelvic floor
exercises*

PELVIC FLOOR EXERCISES

Pelvic floor exercises should be practised daily during pregnancy. This is even more important than doing them postnatally.

To practise your pelvic floor exercises, squat down on your toes in the easy squatting position (Figure 5.31a) or use any of the supported squatting positions. Your pelvic floor muscles are completely relaxed in this position so if you can tighten them easily, then you know your pelvic floor muscles are in reasonably good tone. If you find it difficult to contract them like this, then you need to practise daily.

Read the cautionary note on p. 128. If any of this applies to you, then use the knee–chest position (Figure 5.31b) instead of squatting to do your pelvic floor exercises and read the advice on p. 216

FIG. 5.31 (b)
*Knee-chest
position for pelvic
floor exercises*

13a CONTRACTING and RELEASING

● Close your eyes and focus your awareness on your pelvic floor.
● See if you can tighten your pelvic floor muscles by drawing them up towards your uterus. Just your pelvic floor muscles should be moving, not your buttocks or abdominal muscles.
● Now breathe out and let them go and feel them release slowly.
● Try doing the same thing – inhaling when you tighten and exhaling when you let go. Repeat four more times.
● Now go one step further. Tighten the pelvic floor muscles when you breathe in. Hold them tight while you exhale and inhale again. Then let them go slowly on an exhalation.

13b The LIFT EXERCISE

Using your imagination, contract your pelvic floor muscles in stages, like a lift going up four floors. Breathe normally on the way up and exhale in stages on the way down.
● Start in the 'basement', breathing normally. Contract to bring the pelvic floor muscles, like a lift, up to the 'ground floor' and pause for an instant. Then contract a little more to bring the lift up to the 'first floor' and pause, and so on until you reach the 'fourth floor'.
● Hold on the 'fourth floor' for a few seconds. Then exhale a little way and let go from the 'fourth' to the 'third floor'. Then exhale a little more and let go from the 'third' to the 'second floor' and pause. Continue like this to the 'ground floor' and pause. Now exhale all the way as you release into the 'basement'. This is how your pelvic floor will release as your baby is being born.

13c QUICKIES

● Tighten and let go in quick succession while breathing normally. Repeat about ten times and then relax. These can be done any time during the day, in any position.

13d VISUALIZATION for BIRTH

This exercise will give you a sense of how you can work with gravity in upright birthing positions and instinctively release your pelvic floor when you give birth.

Do this pelvic floor exercise in the last six weeks of your pregnancy. Stand with your feet about 18" apart and bend your knees, placing your hands on your knees for support (see Figure 5.32). Relax your shoulders, jaw and the back of your neck and allow your head to hang forward comfortably.

● Close your eyes and focus your awareness on your breathing, sending the exhalations into the floor through your feet and heels like roots and receiving and welcoming the inhalations into your lungs slowly as if they are coming to you from the ground. Continue for a few cycles of the breath until you feel securely in contact with the earth.

● Now visualize your baby's head deep inside your pelvic canal, resting just above your pelvic floor, about the size of a small grapefruit.

● Contract your pelvic floor muscles all the way up to the fourth floor.

● Now exhale gradually through your mouth as if you are blowing through a straw, while releasing your pelvic floor muscles slowly.

● As you are doing this, imagine your pelvic floor softening and releasing around your baby's head as it emerges in the second stage. Imagine your uterus contracting and pressing down on your baby's body and your baby's head in turn pressing down on the pelvic floor, helping it to open and release as you exhale.

● Towards the end of the exhalation, feel a slight pressure or bearing down sensation as your pelvic floor releases from 'ground floor' to 'basement'. There is no need to use any force or effort as you do this. It is a gentle bearing down or bulging sensation which is easily felt as your pelvic floor relaxes completely.

● Now try the same exercise again and this time make a low 'ooooooooo' sound as you are exhaling. When you are actually giving birth you are likely to need to make a lot of noise as your baby is being born. This exercise will show you how it is natural to exhale while you make a noise and release your pelvic floor at the same time. This will happen instinctively when you are actually giving birth. Some women find it helpful to consciously focus on releasing the pelvic floor with these exhalations, using them to 'breathe the baby out', while others do so without thinking.

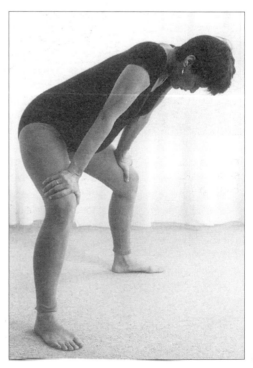

FIG. 5.32
STANDING SQUAT
FOR PELVIC FLOOR
EXERCISES

GROUP 3: KNEELING POSITIONS

14 BASIC KNEELING

Vajrasana – thunderbolt pose

Kneeling with the knees together is a very stable position for breathing and meditation and can be used as a sitting position. It extends the ankle and knee joints and regular practice will improve circulation to the legs. You will need to be on a soft surface such as a carpet or folded blanket for the kneeling positions.

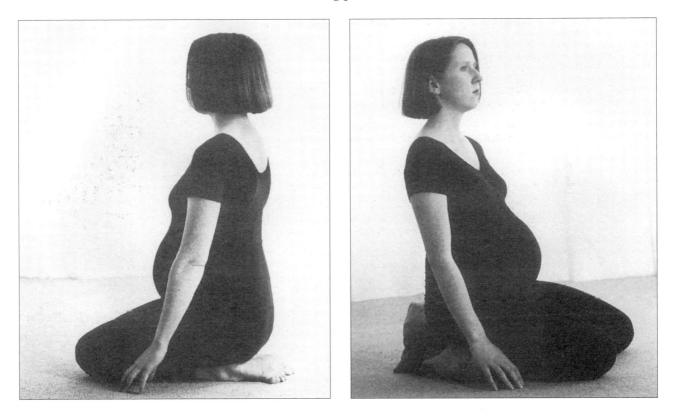

FIG. 5.33 (a)
BASIC KNEELING
Feet together

FIG. 5.33 (b)
BASIC KNEELING
Using a bolster

CAUTION: If you have painful varicose veins or stiff knees or ankles, then use cushions or a bolster to make yourself comfortable or leave out this position (see Appendix – Foot Problems, p. 205).

START by kneeling on the floor with your ankles and thighs together and your pelvis resting on your heels (Figure 5.33a). If your ankles or knees are stiff, this may be too uncomfortable in which case use a cushion underneath your buttocks or a bolster (Figure 5.33b).

● Bring your awareness to your breathing.
● Stroke your hands down your lower back to have a sense of the base of the spine, elongating and releasing the root of the spine downwards along the curve of the sacrum when you exhale, as if you have a long heavy tail pulling down into the floor.

- Focus on the normal rhythm of your breathing, sensing the weight settling into your pelvis as your lower back lengthens with the exhalations and the upper body and chest become lighter as they receive the inhalations.
- Circle the shoulders loosely to release them and lengthen the back of your neck by bringing your chin down slightly towards your chest.
- Continue for 1–3 minutes and then relax and come forward on to your hands and knees.

15 BASIC KNEELING between the FEET

Virasana – hero pose

If your knees and ankles are quite supple you may be able to sit in between the feet. With knees together, the calves fold back and the soles of your feet face the ceiling and follow the curve of your body. Your buttocks should be resting firmly on the ground (Figure 5.34a).

If you are not sitting on the floor then put one or more cushions underneath your buttocks until you can feel your weight drop through your sitting bones towards the floor (Figure 5.34b).

Follow the instructions for kneeling with your feet together.

FIG. 5.34 (a)
BASIC KNEELING
Between the feet

FIG. 5.34 (b)
BASIC KNEELING
Using cushions

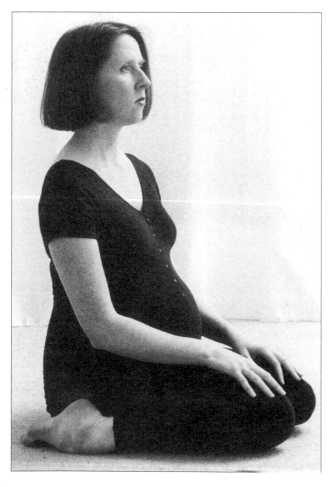

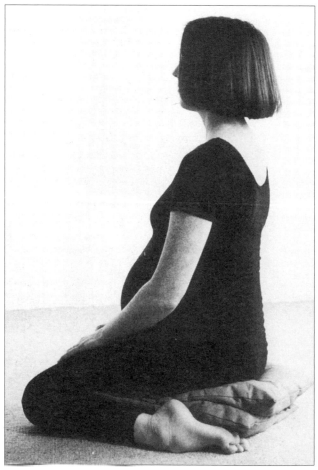

16 THAI GODDESS POSE

This position extends the soles of the feet, making them more lively and receptive to the earth's energy when standing. It also improves suppleness of the toes and develops strength in the arches of the feet. Regular practice will help all the standing postures and improve the general health of your feet.

CAUTION: If your toes are stiff this exercise will hurt at first, but after a few weeks the pain will begin to lessen as your toes become more supple and circulation to your feet improves. To ease pain in the toes, hold the posture only very briefly at first, leaning forward to rest when you need to.

● From the basic kneeling position with feet together, tuck under your toes and then sit back on your heels.

● Drop your weight down into your pelvis, releasing the root of the spine downwards towards your heels. Feel the soles of your feet stretch and 'open'.

● Bring your palms together into the prayer position in front of your breastbone and lengthen the back of your neck. Continue for about thirty seconds and then rest in the all-fours position.

● Repeat two or three times.

● Wriggle the toes afterwards to relax them.

FIG. 5.35
THAI GODDESS
POSE

17 KNEELING TWIST

CAUTION: Make sure when you do this twist that your spine remains vertical while it turns. Avoid leaning back or to the side, and any forceful movement (see caution on p. 102).

START in the basic kneeling position or comfortable variation (see p. 141), with thighs and ankles together.

● Bring your awareness to your breathing and lengthen the base of your spine downwards. Relax and loosen your right arm from the shoulder.

● Now turn gently to the right, keeping a sense of the lower back moving down as the spine turns. Feel the vertebrae turning gently from the base of the spine, slowly up to the neck.

● Bring your left arm across your body and gently hold on to the outside of your right thigh to give you more leverage without straining (see Figure 5.36a and 36b).

● Look round softly over your right shoulder, keeping your neck free and your eyes and jaw relaxed. Relax both shoulders downwards and allow the right shoulder to release down and back so the rib cage can expand comfortably as you breathe. Keep your right arm loose and relaxed.

● Breathe softly and hold for about thirty seconds.

● Come back to the centre slowly, lengthen your lower back, and then repeat on the other side.

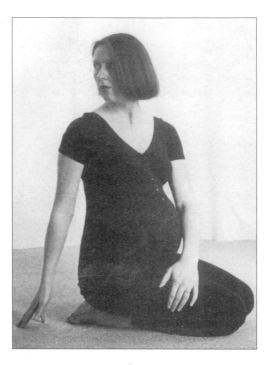

FIG. 5.36 (a)
KNEELING TWIST
Back view

GROUP 4:
NECK and SHOULDER RELEASES

FIG. 5.36 (b)
KNEELING TWIST
Front view

NECK EXERCISES

Start in the basic kneeling position (No. 14) or sit comfortably on the floor with legs crossed or in half lotus (No. 4). Feel the way your body contacts the ground and bring your awareness to your breathing. Lengthen your lower back and release your shoulders.

18a NECK RELEASE

Let your head hang forward, relaxing the nape of your neck, your shoulders, face and eyes (Figures 5.37a and 5.37b).

● Breathing comfortably, rotate your head slowly like a big, heavy ball. Allow its own weight to carry it round over your shoulder (Figure 5.37c) and then continue rolling your head back (Figure 5.37d). Feel the back of your skull roll past your spine to your other shoulder and forward so that your chin sweeps past your collar bone, in a loose circle (Figure 5.37e).

● Continue circling slowly three or four times, feeling your neck become soft and loose as the neck muscles relax.

● Now come back to the centre and repeat in the other direction.

You can vary this exercise by pausing to feel the stretch for a few seconds at each stage.

FIG. 5.37 (a)
NECK
RELEASE
*Starting position
for head roll*

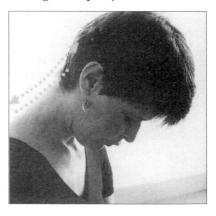

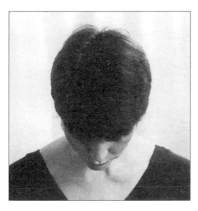

FIG. 5.37 (b)
Releasing the back of the neck

FIG. 5.37 (c)
Roll gently to one side

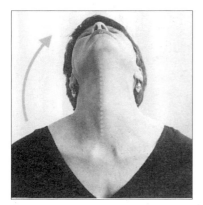

FIG. 5.37 (d)
Softly roll your head back

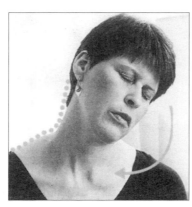

FIG. 5.37 (e)
*Roll gently forward down
the other side*

BACK OF THE NECK

- Now relax your jaw and bring your head forward slowly.
- Clasp your hands and place them on the back of your head so that your chin comes forward towards your chest.
- Drop your elbows towards the floor, relaxing your arms. (Don't 'pull' on the neck, just allow the weight of your arms to gently help the lengthening.)
- Elongate the lower part of your spine downwards and breathe deeply, allowing your neck and shoulders and upper back to release.
- Sense the exhalations travelling all the way down your spine to the tailbone, and the inhalations as if they were coming up from the root of the spine to the nape of the neck.
- Continue for a few seconds.
- Slowly lift your head and lower your arms to your sides.

SIDES OF THE NECK

- Lengthen your lower back and relax your shoulders with your head centred.
- Release your head slowly towards your left shoulder, relaxing both shoulders downwards.
- Raise your left arm and place the palm on the right side of your head so that you feel the stretch all along the right side of your neck from your ear to your shoulder. (Don't 'pull' on the neck – just allow the weight of your left arm to assist the lengthening gently.)
- Breathe and hold for a few seconds, and then come back to the centre and repeat on the other side.

FRONT OF THE NECK

- Release your head backwards and feel the front of your neck lengthen.
- Open your mouth wide, releasing tension in your jaw (yawning will help!).
- Continue for a few seconds. Then close your mouth, bringing your teeth together to lengthen and stretch the front of your neck. Hold for a few seconds.

TURN TO THE SIDE

- With your trunk facing forwards, turn your head and neck and look round over your left shoulder. Hold for a few seconds.
- Come back to the centre and repeat on the other side.

19 SHOULDER RELEASES

The shoulder girdle is made up of the two collar bones, which attach to the breastbone in front, and the shoulder blades towards the back. Together, they form a kind of bony yoke which hangs over the top of your rib cage. It is not directly attached to the spine at all and is suspended from the head by the strong neck muscles you have been releasing in the previous exercise.

Your shoulder girdle supports your arms which are connected to it by the round ball and socket joint in the shoulders. This joint is capable of a wide range of movements like the hip joint. Muscles which attach to the entire trunk all converge in the shoulder joint rather like the spokes of a wheel.

Stiffness in the shoulders is very common. Our modern, mechanized lifestyle does not give us much opportunity to use the full range of movement that our arms and shoulders are designed for. Emotional tension and stress often result in tightness and tension in the shoulders. Most of us have one shoulder stiffer than the other, depending on how we use our bodies. So, for many reasons, postures which specifically release the shoulders are very important since imbalance or tightness in the shoulder girdle will affect and disturb the whole body.

In pregnancy and during breastfeeding, the weight of the enlarged breasts in front of the body tends to pull down on the front of the shoulder girdle. Some exercises which counterbalance this tendency should be included in your practice. You will be spending many hours carrying your child throughout the first three years of life. This too will take its toll on the shoulders so that shoulder exercises are very important if the body is to stay structurally balanced.

All the standing positions help to release tension in the shoulders (Group 5), especially dog pose (No. 25). The exercises below are all basic shoulder releasing positions. It is helpful to do them before you begin Group 4 but they can also be practised separately.

The shoulder postures can be done in the basic standing, kneeling or sitting positions, but since it is wise to avoid standing for too long in pregnancy, begin in the basic kneeling position. If you find this uncomfortable, then sit in half lotus (see p. 104) or simply cross-legged on a small cushion, or with legs wide.

The shoulder releases help to make more space for your breathing, so make the most of the opportunity to be aware of the inhalations filling the three parts of the lungs (see Breathing exercise on p. 71), and the exhalations releasing the lower back downwards in all these exercises. Since you probably have a good sense of this by now, the instructions below simply say 'breathe deeply'.

19a COW POSE, ARMS ONLY

Gomulkhasana

CAUTION: Avoid forcing or struggling to do these positions. Focus instead on the moderate positions, going only to your comfortable limit and breathe. By breathing, the tension will release and the shoulders will loosen by themselves with practice.

START by exhaling and lengthening the base of your spine downwards. Lengthen the back of your neck by bringing your chin down slightly. Breathing comfortably, roll your shoulders backwards a few times to release them.

With your lower back lengthening downwards around the curve of the sacrum, and your pelvis well grounded, hold a belt in your right hand. Stretch your right arm up, then bend the elbow and drop the belt down your back, bringing your right hand down the back of your neck as far as possible.

● Now reach behind your back with your left hand and catch the belt. Hold it as high up as you can manage without straining (see Figure 5.38a). Keep your neck free and in the centre. If your fingers touch, then you do not need the belt. Follow the instructions above but link your fingers or clasp your hands behind your back (see Figure 5.38b).

● Stay in the position for about a minute, lengthening both your lower back and the back of your neck as you breathe deeply, with your right elbow pointing to the ceiling and the left elbow pointing towards the floor.

FIG. 5.38 (a)
COW POSE, ARMS ONLY
Using a belt

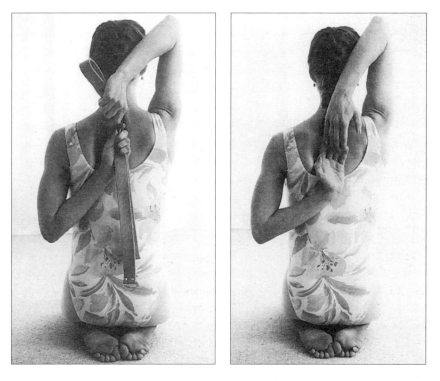

FIG. 5.38 (b)
COW POSE, ARMS ONLY
With clasped hands

● Be aware of the gentle lengthening of the space between the top rim of your pelvis (the hip bones) and the lower rim of your rib cage as you breathe, making more space for your baby.

● Then release your arms, bringing them down to your sides. Find the centre and repeat on the other side.

19b PRAYER POSITION behind the BACK

Roll your shoulders backwards a few times to release them and then bring both arms behind your back, placing the wrists, palms, thumbs and fingertips together (see Figure 5.39).

● Bring your hands higher up the centre of your back and place them between the shoulder blades. If you find this difficult at first, then keep your hands lower down at the back of the waist.

● Breathe normally and lengthen your lower back downwards, keeping your neck loose and free. Feel the upper spine releasing underneath your hands.

● Relax your shoulders downwards and allow the chest to widen as you breathe.

● Hold for up to a minute and then relax your arms by your sides.

19c CROSSED ARMS

*Garudasana –
eagle pose,
arms only*

This posture releases the thoracic spine between the shoulder blades.

● Cross your arms at the elbows, bringing your left arm over your right. Now wrap your forearms around each other, bringing the palms together with your fingers pointing to the ceiling (see Figure 5.40).

If this is difficult at first, start by hugging your arms across your chest to release the shoulders and then cross the forearms.

● Lengthen your lower back downwards and, while you do so, raise your elbows slightly until you feel the space between the shoulder blades widen.

● Breathe deeply and continue for up to a minute, feeling the entire spine lengthen from the base through the upper back to the top of the neck.

● Uncross your arms and then repeat on the other side.

FIG. 5.39
PRAYER POSITION
BEHIND THE BACK

FIG. 5.40
CROSSED ARMS
*Widening the
upper back*

F IG . 5.41 (a)
WRISTS AND HANDS
Reversing the palms

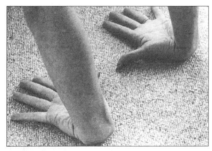

F IG . 5.41 (b)
Wrist stretch, fingers forward,
palms down

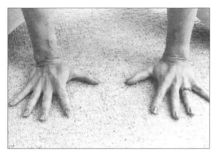

F IG . 5.41 (c)
Wrist stretch on the back of hands

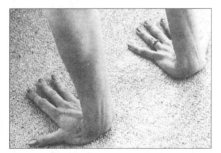

F IG . 5.41 (d)
Wrist stretch, fingers back, palms down

20 | WRISTS and HANDS

These exercises help to improve flexibility of the wrists and fingers, and to ease any discomfort from oedema.

FIGURE 5.41 (a) Clasp your hands and interlock the fingers. Reverse the palms outwards and extend your arms so that you feel the stretch in the fingers.

- Hold for fifteen seconds and then release.
- Now clasp your hands and interlock the fingers in the 'non-habitual' way so that the other forefinger is on top. Reverse the palms, hold for about fifteen seconds, and then release.

FIGURE 5.41 (b) Start in the basic kneeling position with knees wide and place your palms on the floor about 12" apart and parallel. Spread your fingers out wide like starfish and feel how your palms contact the floor.

- Lean forward over your hands until you feel the stretch in the wrists and palms.
- Hold for about fifteen seconds, breathing palms, wrists and fingers down on to the floor, then release.
- Repeat twice more.

FIGURE 5.41 (c) Now turn your hands under and place the backs of the hands on the floor with the fingers pointing towards you. This time lean back until you feel the stretch in the back of the wrists.

- Hold for about fifteen seconds, breathing your wrists down into the floor and then release.
- Repeat twice more.

FIGURE 5.41 (d) With the fingers still facing inwards, reverse the hands, placing the palms on the floor. Lean back until you feel the stretch in the wrists and palms.

- Hold for about fifteen seconds and then release.
- Repeat twice more.

FIGURE 5.41 (e) Bend your left hand forward from the wrist. Using your right hand, place your fingers above the left wrist and your thumb under the left thumb.

- Press the left thumb up towards the forearm, to touch if possible.
- Hold for about ten seconds and then release and move the wrist up and down a few times.
- Repeat on your right hand.
- When you have completed these exercises, clench both hands into a fist and then unclench, stretching the fingers several times. Finish by shaking both hands loosely from the wrists.

F IG . 5.41 (e)
Thumbs up

GROUP 5: STANDING POSTURES

The standing positions are wonderful to do when you are pregnant because they bring your whole body into harmony with the earth, giving you a sense of postural balance in action.

In these positions the feet are all important. Starting with your awareness centred in your wide, spread-out feet, you feel the 'intelligence' of the ground which we call gravity, pulling you downwards into the earth like the roots of a tree. When your feet are well positioned and become grounded, the large muscles of your legs can relax. Then, somehow, a ripple of muscular release occurs from the ground upwards through the muscle systems of the whole body, right up to the neck.

When your muscles relax, the weight of your bones which they support can sink downwards as your body rediscovers its alignment with gravity. As the root of your spine, your pelvis and legs are drawn down, you will begin to feel a deeper sense of both physical and emotional grounding. Then, from above the pelvis, tension and tightness gradually begin to release so that a feeling of freedom and space develops in the upper spine, chest, shoulders and neck. As the weight of all your body parts come into balance along the vertical axis of the spine, misalignments disappear and your posture becomes naturally more elegant.

You will rediscover how to walk and how to stand with grace and without effort. Minor aches and pains will slowly disappear.

The earth is there to nourish you unconditionally like a mother is there for her baby. It is not surprising that she is called Mother Earth in so many cultures. Developing this awareness of your body in the upright position, and its direct relationship to the earth, allows you to benefit from the bountiful energy she offers you at all times.

If you practise just a few of the simplest standing positions regularly you will soon notice a sense of increased vitality, energy and confidence. You will also discover the power to calm and ground yourself. This can be useful at any time, even in the midst of the most tumultuous contractions in labour. You will also know how to 'stand your ground' and increase the power of your presence. Before you start these postures, turn back to p. 82 and reread the information about feet.

CAUTION: In pregnancy, it is generally best to choose one or two of the standing postures to practise in any one session rather than working through them all at once. Take your time to really discover each posture and vary your practice according to your needs.

There are some women who find that they quickly feel faint when standing still for any length of time in pregnancy. This is usually the result of circulation changes and is not usually a cause for concern. If this happens to you, then it is best to leave out the standing positions altogether until after the birth, or else to do them for only a very short time and sit or lie down to rest before you feel faint (see low blood pressure, fainting, etc. on p. 207).

21 BASIC STANDING

Tadasana – mountain pose

In this position you are like a mountain, completely still and stable, rooted into the earth by your feet with your upper body and head free and light, reaching upwards to the sky without effort. Tadasana, when done correctly, brings a physical and emotional balance to the body which is gentle and quiet and yet strong and alert. In pregnancy it is invaluable as a reminder of the way to carry your baby correctly when standing and walking during your daily activities.

START in the basic standing position you learnt in Chapter 4 (see p. 84). Here is a checklist of important points to remember:

● You feet should be placed about 12" apart and parallel. Turn the heels out slightly so that the outside edges of the feet are in line.

● Drop the base of your big toe down into the ground and then spread all your toes out so your feet become wide, and then relax the base of the toes on the ground.

● Lift the inner ankle bones and the inner arches of the feet, bringing the outsides edges down on to the floor.

● Allow your weight to drop down into the floor through your heels. Feel the little toes extend and lengthen as the feet find their balance, keeping the base of the big toes down.

● Your knees should be straight but not tightly locked, so that the creases at the back of the knees open.

● Release and lengthen your lower back downwards so that your pelvis tucks under gently, supporting your baby from underneath.

● Circle the shoulders backwards a few times and then release them downwards so that your arms hang loose and heavy by your sides.

● Lengthen and relax the back of your neck, tilting your chin down slightly towards your chest. Feel how your head balances in the centre on top of the vertebrae. Relax your jaw, the muscles of your face and your eyes.

● Centre all your awareness in your feet. Feel the vitality of the earth beneath you and your invisible 'roots' just under the ground.

Now you are standing in Tadasana. Relax into the posture for a minute or so, surrendering your body weight to the active pull of gravity through your feet and legs. Let all the muscles of your legs become soft. Breathe comfortably and normally so that you feel your bones sinking on to the floor as your weight settles.

● Keep your natural breathing rhythm flowing and then, without pushing or pulling the breath, imagine the exhalations going down into the ground like the roots of a tree.

● Relax at the end of each exhalation and allow the inhalations to come slowly, as if the air were coming up from the roots into your lungs, filling them from the base upwards.

● Feel gravity working, pulling your body downwards from the waist, drawing the root of the spine down as you exhale.

● Feel the ripple of release coming up through your whole body from the ground as you inhale, all the way up to your neck.

● Continue for a few more cycles of the breath and then relax.

FIG. 5.42 (a)
BASIC STANDING
Tadasana – Basic standing

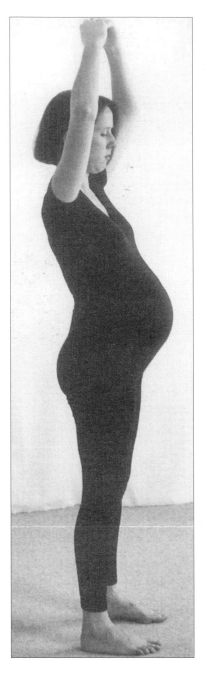

21a TADASANA LIFTING the ARMS

START in Tadasana and relax into the position, breathing comfortably, your awareness centred in your feet throughout.

● Without disturbing the roots or the rest of your body, slowly raise your arms in front of your face with the elbows coming in towards each other (see Figure 5.42b).

● Raise your arms over your head very slowly as you inhale, keeping your neck and shoulders loose, your lower back releasing downwards and your awareness in your feet.

● Now drop your arms loosely by your sides as you exhale, making the sound HA! Repeat three or four times, releasing your weight into your heels, letting go in your shoulders, each time you drop your arms.

21b TADASANA SLIDING DOWN the WALL

This is really a skiing exercise which is very effective as a strengthener of the large thigh muscles. It is useful in pregnancy because developing some strength in the thighs can be helpful if you squat to give birth. This exercise also helps you to better understand what it means to lengthen the root of your spine, and helps to prevent the development of excess flab in the thighs.

Relaxing your neck and shoulders, jaw and arms while only your thigh muscles are working is good practice for staying relaxed while your uterus is contracting in labour.

START in Tadasana, with the back of your heels about 18" away from the wall. Bend your knees and, keeping your feet where they are, bring your back up against the wall. Check that your feet are parallel and toes spread out wide.

● Feel the way your back contacts the wall and notice which parts of your spine are touching.

● Now bend your knees a little and slowly release the root of your spine downwards until the back of your waist makes contact with the wall. Eventually there should be no gap between your lower spine and the wall surface.

● At the same time as releasing the root of your spine, bend your

FIG. 5.42 (c)
TADASANA
SLIDING DOWN A
WALL

FIG. 5.42 (b)
TADASANA
LIFTING THE ARMS

knees and slide slowly down the wall until you are 'sitting' on an imaginary chair. You will feel your thigh muscles working.

● Allow your jaw, back of your neck, shoulders and arms to relax.

● Hold the position for a few moments, breathing normally and then slowly come up.

● Repeat twice more.

21c STANDING TWIST

This position has similar benefits to the twisting positions you have already learned and begins to introduce you to the twisting variations which are possible in the standing postures. It is helpful for freeing and releasing the upper spine.

START in Tadasana with your feet 12" apart and parallel, facing towards a stool or chair. Relax for a few moments, centring your awareness and your weight in your feet, following the instructions for grounding the feet on p. 151.

● Lift your left leg up on to the stool, keeping the foot facing forward.

● With your weight going down your right leg into the floor, release and lengthen your lower back downwards.

● Keep your right heel, the outside of the right foot and the base of your big toe firmly down on the floor, lifting the inner ankle bone and the inner arch of the foot.

● Spread the toes of both feet.

● Be aware of the crease at the back of the right knee opening out as if it were yawning.

● Letting the movement begin with the awareness of your lower back lengthening and your weight dropping down into the floor through your right heel, turn your trunk very slightly to the left. Have a sense of the movement continuing upwards from the base of your spine and ending with your head, turning gently to look over your left shoulder.

● Breathe comfortably in your normal rhythm and allow this rotation to happen slowly and gently without losing the awareness of your weight releasing downwards with the pull of gravity, through the root of the spine and the right heel on to the floor.

● Feel your left shoulder and arm releasing back and down as your upper spine gently turns.

● Be aware of the inhalations being received into the whole length of your lungs, from the base to the collar bones, so your chest becomes more relaxed and open.

● If it is comfortable, you can hold the outside of your left thigh with your right hand (see Figure 5.42d).

● Continue breathing and releasing in the position for up to thirty seconds and then come slowly back to the centre.

● Change legs and repeat, turning in the other direction.

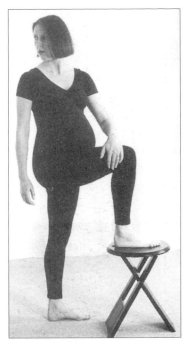

FIG. 5.42 (d)
STANDING TWIST

22 TREE POSE

Vrksasana

This posture is all about stability, balance and becoming grounded. Like a tree, your roots go down deep into the earth, while your branches extend up towards the sky. Gravity draws your weight down through the base of your spine, your hips and the standing leg, deep into the roots. This allows the rest of the spine to lengthen upwards towards the light and releases the shoulders.

START by standing in Tadasana facing a wall, an arm's length away from it so you can touch the surface lightly with both hands for balance. Your feet should be 12" apart and parallel. Become aware of your breathing and centre and ground yourself for a few breaths before you move, taking care that your feet, knees, hips, lower back, shoulders, neck and head are positioned correctly. Focus your awareness on the roots and the contact your feet are making with the floor.

FIG. 5.43 (a)
TREE POSE
*With one
knee bent*

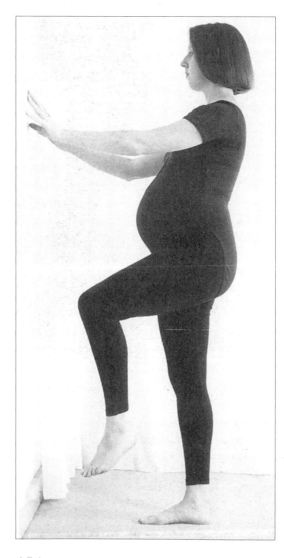

● Now bring your weight on to your right leg, taking care to keep the right hip in towards the centre. Keep the foot very 'intelligent'. Spread the toes. Press the base of the big toe down. Lift the inner arch and ankle bone and release the outside edge of the foot and the heel down.

● Touching the wall with both hands lightly, slowly lift your left foot off the ground, focusing your awareness on your weight dropping down through the right leg and heel into the floor along the plumbline of gravity. Make sure the inner arch of your left foot is lifting, the outside edge going down, and use your toes to balance.

● Bend your left knee and raise it up slowly in front of you (see Figure 5.43a). Concentrate on the right foot only.

● Continue breathing normally. Release the base of your spine downwards, grounding the right heel, sending roots deep into the earth like a tree with your exhalations. Let your weight drop through the heel into the floor.

● Feel the breath being received gently into your lungs when you inhale, allowing your spine to lengthen and grow effortlessly from the roots, all the way up to the top of your neck.

● If you can without straining, place the left foot on the inside of the right thigh with the heel as high as possible. Extend the heel to help it stay in place (see Figure 5.43b). Keep touching the wall lightly to keep your balance.

● Centre your hips so that they are parallel to the wall and make sure that the left hip is drawn in towards the centre and the lower back lengthens.

● Make sure your shoulders are relaxed and let your head find its balance, lengthening the back of your neck by dropping your chin slightly forward.

● Hold the position for a few breaths and then slowly lower your arms and place your right foot back where it was originally on the ground.

● Feel the difference between both legs, and repeat on the other side.

23 STANDING FORWARD BEND

Uttanasana

The standing forward bends are a progression from Tadasana in which the feet and legs remain grounded as the pelvis rotates forward from the hip joints, allowing the upper body to extend and lengthen, freeing and releasing the spine. The forward movement lengthens and relaxes the muscles at the back of your legs as well as your pelvic floor muscles, reducing stiffness in the hamstring muscles in particular.

This results in improved blood circulation and energy flow through the legs so that you receive more energy from the ground and your vitality increases. The overall effect is energizing, preventing unnecessary fatigue caused by blocked energy in the legs and spine. With practice, this posture will also help to improve the alignment of your pelvis and, thus, your postural balance.

CAUTION: When bending forward be sure that the movement originates in your hip joints so that your spine hangs free without straining. Explore your comfortable limit without bending further forward than you can manage. It is an excellent idea, especially in late pregnancy, to place your hands on a table top, window sill, the back of a steady chair, or a stool for support to allow your spine to extend and lengthen without strain (see Figure 5.44a). It is more important to lengthen your spine than to touch the floor.

FIG. 5.43 (b)
TREE POSE
With one foot on thigh

155

In pregnancy it is best not to hold the position for longer than about 30–60 seconds. Rather, come up slowly, rest for a few minutes and repeat a couple of times. Always pay very careful attention to the way that you come up.

A few women find that the circulation changes in a forward bending position cause feelings of dizziness. This may be caused by very low blood pressure or a tendency to feel faint when standing (see p. 39). If this happens to you, then leave out these positions. Women with severe haemorrhoids or vulval varicosities should also avoid this exercise, or else use a window ledge or table for support.

FIG. 5.44 (a)
STANDING
FORWARD BEND
Holding on to a
support

START facing a window ledge or table in the basic standing position (p. 151) with your feet parallel, about 12" apart. You can place them slightly wider to make space for the baby in late pregnancy if it is more comfortable. Clasp your hands loosely behind your back holding the wrist of one hand with the other.

● Ground yourself through your heels and release and lengthen your lower back downwards. Meditate for a few seconds on the way your feet contact the ground and allow the muscles of your legs to relax so that your weight sinks downwards with the help of gravity through your heels.

● With your awareness still focused on the pull of gravity through your heels, allow your upper body to release forward very slowly on an exhalation, moving from your hip joints until your trunk is parallel to the floor.

● Now gently extend your arms out in front of you and place your palms on the ledge so that your arms, neck and spine can extend comfortably in one straight line, parallel to the floor. Your hips should be above your feet so that your legs are vertical (see Figure 5.44a).

● The creases at the back of the knees open like a yawn and the muscles just under your sitting bones lengthen and relax, making more space right at the top of your thighs. You should feel the stretch in the muscles at the back of your legs.

● Focus on your natural breathing rhythm, allowing your spine to lengthen and release as you breathe, keeping your awareness of the roots going down into the ground through your feet.

● Your lower back feels long, curving down towards your heels. Then the rest of the spine extends from this stable base so that the upper back feels loose and the neck lengthens in line with the rest of your spine. Your shoulders remain loose and relaxed.

● Continue in the position for up to a minute and then release your arms. Clasp them behind your back and return very slowly to Tadasana by bending your knees, releasing your weight down into your heels, tucking under your tailbone to lengthen your lower back as you come up. Bring your shoulders and your head up last, and then unclasp your hands and circle your shoulders backwards a few times to release them.

● Most people need support as in figure 5.44a. It is crucial for the spine to be free and to avoid straining the lower back. However, if your body is very supple you may prefer to bend forward fully (see Figure 5.44b).

● Be aware of your weight going down towards gravity through your heels, and stay grounded in the heels throughout.

● Lengthen your lower back down and back, having a sense of the hip joints being directly above your heels. You may need to lean forward a little to do this, and then breathe your heels back down on to the floor.

● Allow your arms to hang down loosely towards or on to the floor, and let go of your head, releasing your neck and shoulders.

FIG. 5.44 (b)
STANDING
FORWARD BEND
Full position

● Focus on the normal rhythm of your breathing.

● As you inhale, feel your spine lengthen from the base to the top of the neck. As you exhale, breathe down from the lower back into the heels.

● Feel the back of the knees open and the little space between the top of the thighs and the buttocks lengthen.

● If your hands touch the ground easily, then you may like to place your palms flat on the floor in this posture.

● Hold for up to a minute and then come up on an exhalation by curling up slowly, lengthening your lower back and feeling your weight settling into your heels as you return to the basic standing position.

24 WIDE STANDING FORWARD BEND

Prasarita Padottanasana

You will need to do this posture on a firm, non-slippery surface such as a wooden floor, or else use a non-slip yoga mat. As in the previous exercise, use a window ledge or a table for support unless you can touch the floor easily without straining your back.

START in the basic standing position with your feet 3–5 feet apart, to suit your own comfort. Make sure that your feet are parallel by turning out the heels. Press the base of your big toe down, spread the toes out wide and lift the inner arches of the feet. Feel the outer edges of the feet going down into the floor from the outside of the knee through the outside of the ankle bone, as if down the outside seam of a pair of trousers (see Figure 5.45a).

● Allow the creases at the back of your knees to open like a yawn.

● Lengthen your lower back downwards around the curve of the sacrum and then release your shoulders and elongate your neck by releasing your chin slightly downward towards your chest.

● Focus on the normal rhythm of your breathing and ground yourself through your heels. Now release your upper body forward slowly, moving from the hip joints, and place your palms on top of a table, window ledge or a stool of suitable height to allow your arms and upper body to be in one straight line so that your spine can lengthen.

● Make sure that your hips are in line with your feet.

● Breathe and feel your weight going down into the floor through the outside of your heels.

● Release your lower spine towards your heels and feel your spine lengthen all the way up to the top of your neck as you breathe. Keep your neck and shoulders relaxed.

● You will feel the stretch in the backs of your legs. Sense the heels going down, the backs of the knees opening and the little space between the top of the thighs and the buttock bones lengthening.

● Continue for up to 30–60 seconds, breathing normally, and then come up slowly. Bring your feet closer together and then come up on an exhalation. Bend your knees, tuck under your tailbone, lengthen your lower back and drop your weight down into the floor through your heels.

● If you do not need support, release your upper body forward and let your arms hang down loosely, placing your palms lightly on the floor if it is comfortable. Follow the instructions above, letting go of your head, lengthening and releasing the back of your neck. Exhale into the feet, bend your knees and lengthen your lower back downwards as you come up slowly (see Figure 5.45b).

● If you can touch the floor with ease, place your palms on the floor in line with your feet, but do not strain (Figure 5.45c). Feel the pull of gravity under your feet and wrists. Come up as before.

FIG. 5.45
WIDE STANDING
FORWARD BEND
(a) Standing with feet parallel and legs wide

(b) Come forward from the hips and touch the floor

(c) Place the palms of the hands on the ground between the feet

25 DOG POSE

Svanasana

This stretch reminds us of the lovely stretching movements dogs and cats make to release their spines when they wake up after sleeping. It releases the neck and shoulders and also lengthens and relaxes the muscles at the back of your legs.

CAUTION: Most people have a lot of stiffness at the backs of the legs which will become painfully apparent when you first try this posture. However, with practice you will soon loosen up and begin to enjoy it. If you feel lightheaded or dizzy when doing this in pregnancy, then leave it out. It is essential to practise the dog pose on a hard, non-slip surface such as a wooden floor or a yoga mat. In pregnancy, do this for short periods only, repeating two or three times if you wish after a little rest on your hands and knees.

FIG. 5.46 (a)
DOG POSE
Prepare on all-fours

START on all-fours with your palms face down on the floor under your shoulders and your knees under your hips. Tuck your toes under to stretch the soles of your feet. Spread your fingers out wide like starfish. Breathe your wrists and palms down into the floor when you exhale and release your neck and shoulders, feeling the upper back widen between the shoulder blades. This is the resting position.

● Come up on to your toes and then, pushing the floor away from you with your hands, turn out your heels slightly and bring them down to the floor if possible. (With practice your heels will eventually rest on the ground.)

● Release your neck and shoulders and bring your weight back and down towards your tailbone, then bypass the pelvis and go down into your heels. At first this posture may feel a bit top-heavy but remember you are aiming for lightness and release in the shoulders and upper body with the weight going back into the ground through your heels, rather than falling forward on to your hands.

FIG. 5.46 (b)
DOG POSE

● It is important to open the creases at the back of your legs and keep your legs straight.

● Come back into the resting position (Figure 5.46a) and wait for half a minute or so before trying again.

● Now come up into the posture once more and, this time, begin to get the feeling of looseness in neck and shoulders and weight going down into the heels.

● Open the backs of your knees and elongate your calves and Achilles tendons down as you exhale. Hold for up to thirty seconds and then return to the resting position.

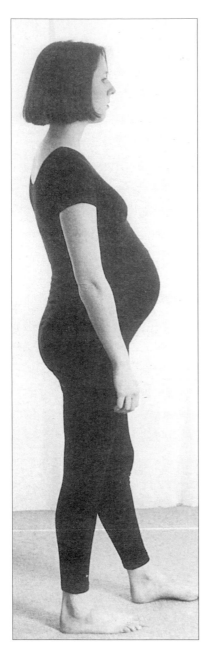

FIG. 5.47 (a)
TRIANGLE POSE
Take a small step forward with one leg

● Repeat one more time.

If Svanasana (dog pose) is easy for you, you may enjoy going into it from Uttanasana (the standing forward bend) and Prasarita Padottanasana (wide standing forward bend) (Nos. 23 and 24). You do this by walking your hands forward while keeping your heels on the ground.

26a TRIANGLE POSE

Trikonasana

Probably one of the most misunderstood yoga postures, Trikonasana is rarely taught correctly. The essence of this posture is that it is a progression from Tadasana which involves taking a small step forward while remaining as stable as a mountain in the base. Then your pelvis rotates forward from the hips and your spine extends sideways. The triangle formed by your legs remains stable with your weight centred firmly in the back heel. The back leg stays straight and the back heel is planted, rooted, into the floor throughout. This allows your shoulders to relax and your arms to extend freely.

The pregnant women I teach love this posture, saying it makes them feel graceful and powerful, and frees the upper body of tension.

CAUTION: Since most of us carry a lot of tension in the shoulders it is important to progress very slowly with this one. It is not important to bend all the way down. Rather, allow your spine to extend freely and keep your shoulders and arms relaxed. As soon as you feel them tensing up, you know you are bending too far.

START in Tadasana (No. 21) and relax and breathe, feeling your connection with the ground.

● Keep your right foot where it is and take a small step forward with your left, as you would do if you were about to walk.

FIG. 5.47 (b)
Slowly raise both arms to shoulder height

FIG. 5.47 (c)
Raise the opposite arm up over your head

FIG. 5.47 (d)
Turn your head to look towards the back hand as your arm extends to shoulder height behind you

FIG. 5.47 (e)
Relax your shoulders, arms outstretched

- With your lower back long and releasing downwards, let your weight fall down your right leg and heel into the ground. Both feet continue to point forwards.
- Keep the creases behind both knees open and the legs straight, but do not lock your knees.
- Focus on the natural rhythm of your breathing and very, very slowly raise both arms up in front of you until they reach shoulder height. Feel as if it is your breathing rather than muscular movement that is enabling your arms to come up.
- Keep your left arm where it is and, almost in slow motion, breathe your right arm up over your head and then behind you until it is level with the right at shoulder height.
- Follow this graceful movement with your head to look back at your right hand.
- Turn both palms up and focus on the natural rhythm of your breathing.
- Your weight continues to fall through your right hip, leg and heel down into the floor.
- Breathe in your natural rhythm and feel the exhalations creating roots through your left foot down into the ground. Feel the inhalations coming effortlessly in to fill your lungs so that your chest feels free and open, and your arms open outwards as if you were about to embrace someone, or fly.

On an exhalation, with your right heel still firmly grounded, bend slightly to the left from your left hip joint. Let your spine lengthen as you breathe, keeping your head in line with the whole spine and looking up gently towards your left hand.

- Bend only as far as you can without tensing your shoulders, even if it is only an inch or two.
- Continue breathing in the position for a few more breaths and then slowly, on an exhale, return to the upright position, lengthening your lower back and keeping your weight going down through the right leg and heel.
- Relax your arms, return to Tadasana, and repeat on the other side.

FIG. 5.47 (f)
Bend to the side slightly, lengthening your spine

FIG. 5.48 (a)
BENT KNEE TRIANGLE POSE

FIG. 5.48 (b)
BENT KNEE TRIANGLE POSE
Extending slightly to the side

26b BENT KNEE TRIANGLE POSE

Parsvakonasana

This posture is very similar to Trikonasana (triangle pose) but the front leg bends slightly.

Your weight is still centred in the back leg and heel, and this is the important thing to focus on throughout. You will find it easier to bend to the side without tensing your shoulders than in Trikonasana, but remember to stay grounded through the back heel.

START in Tadasana basic standing (No. 21).
- Take a natural step forward with your left leg while keeping your weight on your right leg, with the heel well grounded.
- Slightly bend your left knee, keeping the right leg straight.
- Now continue as you did in Trikonasana (triangle pose).
- Breathe both arms up to shoulder height, then breathe the right arm slowly up, over your head and down behind you until it is level with the left arm at shoulder height.
- Open your arms, palms up, and breathe quietly.
- With your weight in the left leg and heel, bend slightly sideways to the right while looking up at your left hand. Go only as far as feels comfortable, keeping your shoulders and neck relaxed. The main emphasis is on lengthening the spine – the sideways movement coming as the spine releases.
- Continue in the position for a few more breaths and slowly come up, dropping your weight back into your left heel.
- Return to Tadasana and repeat on the other side.

27 TRIANGLE FORWARD BEND

Parsvottanasana

Unless you have been practising yoga for a long time you will need a chair for this posture (see Figure 5.49a).

START in Tadasana basic standing with your feet about 12" apart and parallel, and focus on your breathing and your connection with gravity.

- Place your hands behind your back in the prayer position (see Figure 5.49b). The wrists, palms and thumbs should be touching with the fingers pointing upwards towards your neck. Place your hands between your shoulder blades, if you can do so without straining.
- Now relax your shoulders and allow them to open outwards and back, as well as

FIG. 5.49 (a)
TRIANGLE
FORWARD BEND
With support

FIG. 5.49 (b)
*Take a small step forward
with one leg*

releasing downwards. Bring your elbows back and towards each other. This widens the front of the chest and makes plenty of space for your breathing. (If this hand position is difficult, clasp your hands loosely behind your back instead, holding one wrist in the other hand.)

● Lengthen your lower back by releasing it downwards and lengthen your neck by dropping your chin down slightly towards your chest.

● Take one small step forward with your left leg as if you were about to walk, but keep your weight centred in your right leg.

● Keep your weight firmly in the right heel throughout when you practise this posture.

● Make sure that both hips and feet are facing forward.

● Now, very slowly, with your weight in your right heel, exhale and bend forward slightly from the hips, keeping your spine free. At first the forward movement should only be a few inches.

● Your left foot rests softly on the floor throughout but remains sensitive to the ground to prevent your left hip moving.

● Go only as far forward as you can manage without bending your spine or tensing your back. When you find your comfortable limit, stay in the position for 30–60 seconds, focusing on your natural breathing rhythm.

● Ground the right heel with each exhalation and feel your spine lengthen with each inhalation. Relax the back of your neck by tucking your chin down slightly.

● If your hands are in the prayer position, you will be able to feel your upper back lengthening as you breathe.

● If the forward movement is easy for you, you can place your palms on the back of a chair in front of you to really lengthen your spine. Remember to keep your weight centred in your left heel.

● If this movement comes easily for you, then you can continue to bend forward slowly from the hips, keeping your spine free (see Figure 5.49d and e).

FIG. 5.49 (e)
*Release forward
completely from
the hips,
lengthening your
spine as you
breathe*

FIG. 5.49 (c) (ABOVE)
*Bend forward slightly
from the hips*
FIG. 5.49 (d) (RIGHT)
Bend further forward

GROUP 6: ADVANCED POSTURES

This section is only for those who have learned yoga before pregnancy and are used to practising these postures regularly. If you have never tried them before, pregnancy is the wrong time to begin. Rather allow them to inspire you to take your practice further after your baby is born.

Inverted postures give you energy and help you to feel balanced. If you are in the habit of doing some inverted postures and it feels like a galling limitation to give them up, there is no reason why you should not continue during your pregnancy, provided you are enjoying them and doing them correctly. The way you feel is the best guide as to how long to continue. In my experience, most women begin to feel uncomfortable in the shoulder balance around the seventh month. I have known women who have continued with supported headstands and full arm balance right up to the end of pregnancy without any ill effects, but most mothers begin to feel the baby's priority is to go downwards and may leave out these postures during the heaviest weeks before the birth.

If you love doing back bends you may want to continue doing them in pregnancy. It is perfectly safe to do so provided you are doing them correctly and it feels completely comfortable. Most women stop doing them in the last three months and wait to begin again for at least three months after the birth until the lower back has regained its strength.

28 SHOULDERSTAND

Sarvangasana

This position is a wonderful release for the neck, spine and shoulders. Once you are comfortable in it, shoulderstand is deeply relaxing and calming, having a very quietening effect on the mind. It is said to have a beneficial influence on the endocrine glands and to enhance hormone secretion.

CAUTION: Beginners should not attempt this position in pregnancy, and neither should anyone with neck or back problems. This is only for those who practised it regularly before pregnancy and wish to continue. When it begins to feel uncomfortable or top-heavy then it is time to stop until after the birth. Even for those who are very experienced, it is best to do this posture from midpregnancy onwards with the support of a wall since your body and breasts are heavier than usual.

Attention to detail so that your body is lying straight and properly

FIG. 5.50 (a)
SHOULDERSTAND
Preparing for shoulderstand

aligned is very important in shoulderstand. Never turn your head to the side while in this position.

It can be misleading to think of your weight resting on your shoulders in this posture. In fact, the weight flows from your elbows into the floor, and the shoulder blades move towards each other, allowing your shoulders to relax and protecting the small vertebrae of the neck.

START by lying down on the floor at right angles to the wall with a folded blanket under your back up to your shoulders. Your head should be resting in the centre on the floor and your buttocks close to the wall. Place your arms by your sides with the palms down (see Figure 5.50a).

● Bend your knees and put the soles of your feet flat on the wall a few inches apart.

● Relax in this position and breathe. With the exhalations, lengthen your lower back and bring the back of your waist down on to the floor.

● Elongate the back of your neck by bringing your chin down towards your chest.

● Relax your shoulders and walk your fingers towards your feet so that your shoulders move down away from your ears.

● Keep your arms tucked in close to your sides.

● Breathe and allow your spine to release before you begin.

● Breathe your shoulders, upper arms and elbows down on to the floor.

● On an exhalation, lengthen your lower back, press the soles of your feet into the wall and slowly lift your pelvis so that your weight comes up on to your shoulders, upper arms and elbows. Make sure your elbows do not splay out to the sides to ensure that you are well supported.

It helps to focus on keeping the elbows grounded. When the elbows are resting correctly down on the ground, the shoulders can release.

● Support your back with your hands, placing them at the back of the ribs as low down towards your head as you can manage.

● Slowly straighten your legs on the wall.

● Feel the back of the head, neck, shoulders and upper arms and elbows contact the floor, and breathe your elbows away and down when you exhale.

● Hold the posture for 30–60 seconds and then very slowly lower yourself to the ground, one vertebra at a time from the neck downwards, until your whole spine rests on the floor.

● Bend your knees for a few seconds to release your lower back and then roll over slowly on to one side before coming up.

FIG. 5.50 (b)
Half-shoulderstand

FIG. 5.50 (c)
Supported shoulderstand using a wall

FIG. 5.51 (a)
HEADSTAND
*Full headstand
against a wall*

29 HEADSTAND

Sirsasana

This is a very strong and invigorating pose. It can be done in pregnancy if you are used to doing it regularly and know how to do it correctly.

It is essential to do this posture in the right way, with attention to detail to avoid strain from the additional weight of your body in pregnancy. It is also very important to recognize when to stop practising the headstand if you begin to feel uncomfortable in any way. Unless you are very confident, headstand should be done against a wall or with a supporting partner in pregnancy.

Place a folded blanket on the floor before you begin. It is helpful to do headstand facing a floorlength mirror to check that your body is symmetrical.

The name of this posture is misleading as it is not, in fact, your head which carries your body weight. Your weight rests mainly on your wrists, forearms and elbows in this position, with your head balancing lightly, neck and shoulders releasing.

START by kneeling on the floor on your hands and knees facing your partner or the wall (see Figure 5.51b).

● Link your fingers together so that the thumbs cross, the wrists go down on the floor, the palms face down and the little fingers rest on the ground (see Figure 5.51c).

● Take plenty of time to prepare for headstand. Your forearms rest on the ground with the elbows positioned shoulders' width apart. Before you think of going up, breathe your wrists, forearms and elbows down on to the ground. This is the base which will support your weight when you go up so focus throughout on grounding this stable base with your exhalations.

FIG. 5.51 (b)
*Preparing for
headstand on
all fours*

FIG. 5.51 (c)
*Detail of head,
arm and hand
positions*

- Relax your shoulders and place the top of your head in the centre of the triangle made by your forearms.
- Now straighten your legs with your toes tucked under and bring your weight down into your elbows. Walk in with your toes so that your hips are above your head and your spine is straight while your partner supports your hips (see Figure 5.51d). Make sure that your shoulders stay relaxed and don't tighten.
- Now slowly take your feet off the floor with knees bent, your partner still supporting your hips. Lengthen your spine all along its length from the head to the tailbone, keeping your neck long by tucking your chin in slightly towards your chest (see Figure 5.51e). Breathe down into the floor, grounding the base between your wrists and your elbows. Keep your shoulders relaxed.
- Now exhale and slowly straighten your legs so that your whole body is vertical. Breathe and find your balance by concentration on grounding the elbows. Your partner can stay close and help to gently check that your body forms a vertical line from your head to your heels. If the balance is correct then the position feels effortless and the shoulders relax (see Figure 5.51f).
- To come down, your partner should stand behind you and support your hips as before. Then bend your knees and slowly return to the straight leg position, placing your feet on the floor.
- Then relax on to all-fours, and come up.

FIG. 5.51 (e)
*Bend your knees
and lengthen
your spine*

FIG. 5.51 (d)
*Coming up, your
partner supports
your hips*

PARTNER:
- Stand with your feet steady behind her, and breathe and centre yourself.
- As she straightens her legs, hold her hips firmly but lightly so that she is supported but can find the balance herself, with your assistance.
- Check that her head is centred, her shoulders relaxed and her neck and lower back are lengthening so that her spine extends vertically.
- Support her feet lightly when she is up, letting her know you are still there, and then support her hips again as she comes down.

30 FULL ARM BALANCE

This posture should be done against a wall or with a supporting partner in pregnancy. It is very invigorating and gives a feeling of lightness which is most welcome in pregnancy.

CAUTION: Beginners should not attempt this in pregnancy. However, for the regular practitioner, full arm balance can be done throughout pregnancy. I found it very relieving when carrying my son Theo who was 11 lb at birth! You can continue until close to the birth provided it feels comfortable.

FIG. 5.51 (f)
*Full headstand
with partner
support*

START in the standing position facing your supporting partner. Now bend forward from your hips and place your palms on the floor about 12" apart and parallel, on either side of your partner's front foot. Ground your wrists and hands, rooting them down into the floor with your exhalations. Your partner should hold your hips firmly but lightly.

● When you are ready, come up gently, one leg at a time, into the hand balance, placing your legs together and gently supported by your partner as you find your balance (see Figure 5.52b).

● Lengthen your lower back and relax the back of your neck, breathing down and pushing into the floor through your wrists. Release your neck and let your head hang freely, chin towards your chest.

● Find the balance and hold for up to thirty seconds, breathing comfortably.

● To come down with your partner supporting you, lower your legs slowly from the hips one at a time, and come back on to your feet in the standing position.

PARTNER:

● Stand with one foot in front of the other so that you feel completely stable.

● Breathe so that you centre and ground yourself.

● Place your hands on either side of her hips and support her as she comes up, helping to lift the hips upwards gently while allowing her to find the balance herself.

● Remind her to relax her neck and lengthen her lower back.

● Guide her to keep her body and legs centred, and then support her securely as she comes down.

FIG. 5.52 (a)
FULL ARM
BALANCE
Against a wall

FIG. 5.52 (b)
FULL ARM
BALANCE
With a partner

31a BACK BENDS

Urdhva Dhanurasana – upwards bow pose

This posture can be done in pregnancy up until around the end of the seventh month, but only if you practised it regularly before pregnancy with ease and it feels comfortable.

It should certainly not be attempted by the beginner until six months after childbirth, and then only with the help of a teacher.

When this position is done correctly the whole body opens and releases freely like a ripple growing from the ground through the firmly rooted feet and hands. The spine extends along its length from the base, and the neck, shoulders and chest release.

In back bend your body is like a bridge. The hands and feet are the support for the structure so it is important that they rest firmly on the ground and do not move or the bridge will collapse.

CAUTION: Avoid trying to do this one on your own unless you are experienced. Take plenty of time to relax in the starting position, only going up when the urge to do so comes from the ground and is irresistible. Avoid pushing yourself up forcefully, and focus instead on the instructions below – taking the time to follow them accurately.

It is helpful to have a partner hold your feet firmly in position as you go up. Stop practising back bends as soon as you feel uncomfortable when you do them.

31b HALF BACK BEND

Start by lying on your back with your knees bent and your feet parallel, with your heels close to your hips. Place your arms close to your sides with the palms of the hands facing downwards (see Figure 5.53a). Tuck your chin towards your chest to lengthen the back of your neck.

FIG. 5.53 (a)
HALF-BACKBEND
Preparing for half-backbend

● Relax and breathe for a while, feeling your lower back lengthen and the back of your waist releasing on to the floor. Feel your heels planting firmly on to the ground.

● On an exhalation, lengthen your lower back and, at the same time, press your heels down and allow your pelvis to lift gently so that your spine comes off the ground slowly, all the way up to your shoulders (see Figure 5.53b).

● Hold for a few seconds breathing normally and then come down slowly on an exhalation, releasing your spine down on to the floor, one vertebra at a time, from the shoulders to the tailbone. Relax then repeat two or three times more.

FIG. 5.53 (b)
HALF-BACKBEND

31c FULL BACK BEND

START by fastening a soft belt at hips' width and place this around your thighs just above the knees to help keep your legs in position (see Figure 5.54a). Lie on your back with your knees bent and your

feet parallel, with the heels close to your hips. Pay attention to the way your feet are positioned, as in basic standing. Devote plenty of time to the preparation.

● Lengthen your lower back downwards, tucking under your pelvis, so that the back of your waist releases into the floor.

● Bend your elbows and place your hands on the floor, palms down, just under your shoulders (see Figure 5.54a).

FIG. 5.54 (a)
BACKBEND
Preparing for backbend

● Stay like this for several minutes, breathing into your lower abdomen and feeling the back of your waist and lower back lengthening downwards, and your heels and wrists sinking into the floor. Take your time until you feel that your feet are really well grounded and the pull of gravity reaches your hips.

● Then exhale and, starting from your heels going down, allow yourself to come up in one smooth movement which ripples up from the ground. Your heels and wrists go down into the floor and your spine bends freely along its length without tightening in the lower back. It is essential that your hands and feet do not move (see Figure 5.54b).

● Tuck your chin towards your chest to lengthen the back of your neck.

● Hold the pose for just a few seconds and then slowly come down again to rest your spine on the floor.

● Bend your knees up to release your lower back before rolling on to your side to come up slowly.

FIG. 5.54 (b)
BACKBEND

GROUP 7: RELAXATION

At the end of your yoga practice you need to lie down and relax for at least ten minutes. Normally this position is done lying flat on the back. However, during pregnancy it is best to lie on your side. Use plenty of cushions so that your body is well supported with your whole spine, including your neck, in a straight line. Place a cushion under your head and then stretch out your bottom leg and bend the top one. Place another cushion under the top knee. It may be helpful to read these suggestions into a tape recorder so that you can listen and relax.

Relaxation involves allowing your body and mind to become completely still and peaceful. The way to do this is to focus on your breathing rhythm and also on the way that gravity totally supports your body so that you can let go of your muscles.

If thoughts arise or sounds from the environment distract you, acknowledge them and then try to release your awareness from them by focusing again on your breathing. This will become easier with practice. Relaxation is not like sleeping in that your body is totally relaxed but your mind is both silent and alert, and focused only on your breathing.

When you are completely comfortable, bring your awareness to the rhythm of your breathing. As you exhale, relax and release each part of your body in turn, feeling a warm glow travelling through you as your muscles release. Start with the toes and feet, and then work your way slowly through the legs, pelvis, spine, shoulders, arms, hands, fingers, neck, throat, jaw, face and eyes. Always wait for the inhalations to come in quietly of their own accord, and focus on releasing with the exhalations. Finally, notice the movement of your breath in your chest and in your belly.

You might like to end by bringing your awareness to the presence of your baby. Spend the last few minutes resting and relaxing with your baby and then take your time to open your eyes. Stretch out and come up slowly. Follow the relaxation with a refreshing drink before you continue your day.

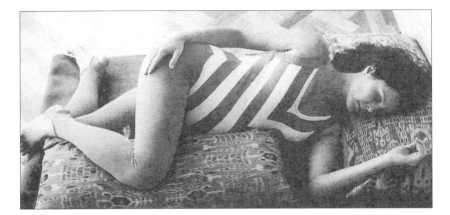

FIG. 5.55
RELAXATION

APPROACHING
LABOUR

Towards the end of your pregnancy you will begin to anticipate the birth and want to prepare yourself for labour. It is important that this preparation includes all the information you need to understand what is about to happen. However, it is vital that you also prepare with your body.

This chapter should be used in the last two or three months of your pregnancy and contains suggestions about how you might want to move and position your body and use your breathing to help you through the intensity and power of the experience in the most practical way. It will be helpful to practise these movements regularly in late pregnancy so that they become comfortable and familiar body habits. Then you will find that you move instinctively when you are actually in labour, without having to remember any specific positions or information. The knowledge will be 'embodied' and your instincts will guide you. If your labour is uncomplicated, this will increase the chances of your having a physiological birth without the need for any intervention. However, if you do need some help, something of value that you have learnt from your yoga will probably be there to help you at the time. Whatever happens on the day, yoga will enable you to approach the experience from a position of inner power.

Further information and guidance about active birth, water birth and obstetric interventions can be obtained from my other books listed on p. 218. In the pages which follow you will be discovering in practice how the yoga you have learnt in pregnancy can be used in labour and when you are actually giving birth. Essentially you will be learning with your body rather than your mind, and once again a little practice prior to the event will make all the difference.

Whatever happens on the day, yoga will enable you to approach the experience from a position of inner power.

CREATING a SETTING for LABOUR

Whether you are intending to give birth in your own home or in a birth centre or hospital, you will probably spend some hours around the house in early labour. Being in a familiar, intimate environment will enhance your body's secretion of hormones which stimulate contractions and help to establish the rhythm and progress of your labour.

You will need to let go of your thinking and allow yourself to be instinctive and spontaneous. This means that you will need to be able to surrender to the sensations you are feeling in your body. Your yoga practice throughout pregnancy has been wonderful preparation for this.

The ability to let your body take over while your mind is quiet is very similar to what happens during lovemaking, when one's inner feelings and physical sensations predominate while the mental processes subside. In fact, when creating the right setting for your birth, the analogy of lovemaking is useful since exactly the same hormones – oxytocin and endorphins – will be produced by your body when you are in labour as those you secrete when you make love. They are even called the 'love hormones'. The environment most conducive to labour is similar to an intimate setting suitable for lovemaking.

When practising for labour it is a good idea to create the same sort of setting and atmosphere that you will want to be in on the day. The hormone oxytocin which stimulates your uterus to contract and the endorphins which give natural pain relief are produced more readily by your body when you are relaxed, in intimate surroundings. An atmosphere which is conducive to labour and is 'hormone enhancing' will need to be quiet and calm with a feeling of privacy.

Low lighting or semi-darkness, perhaps even candle light, will enhance relaxation. It is a good idea to have a fragrant massage oil which is suitable for use in pregnancy to hand. Some quiet, meditative music may be enjoyable, or perhaps the sounds of nature or the ocean. Make sure that the room is warm and has a few useful props such as a low stool or a pile of books for squatting on, a simple upright chair, a beanbag and a selection of large cushions.

Wear something soft and comforting which you can take off easily if you feel like being naked or getting into the bath or shower. If you are planning to use a water pool during labour, try to have at least one practice session in the pool prior to the birth so you can experiment and try out a variety of positions and ways to use the pool. It is generally best to reserve the birth pool for strong labour when you are going beyond 4 or 5 cm dilation or feel the need of some additional help with the pain. If progress is good in the pool then you may want to remain there. If, however, your contractions weaken in the water, it is wise to get out and use the help of gravity to get things going again. Alternatively, if you are not progressing well 'on land', getting into a pool of warm water may dramatically intensify the contractions and also offer some relief from the pain.

Being in water is a wonderful way to enhance deep relaxation and helps many women to let go more easily during contractions. Since the possibility of using a birth pool is becoming more widely available, the birth positions I am suggesting include information about how they can be used in a birth pool (see Resources).

Always start your practice session with 10–15 minutes of breathing and meditation. Tune in to the presence of your baby so that you are conscious of your baby being there with you throughout.

When you begin to try the positions, take your time and let go of your inhibitions, allowing yourself to make any movements which come easily, such as rolling your hips, rocking backwards and forwards or swaying. Think of your labour as being a kind of personal birth dance – one in which you will move in complete freedom, following your inner feelings at the time. Allow yourself to express the way you feel with your body and also with your breathing and the sounds you make. You may breathe quietly and slowly, focusing on the exhalations, or make deep chanting sounds. You may want to sing or to moan and groan. Towards the end, as the intensity of your labour increases, you are bound to need to be much more noisy and, finally, as you are giving birth, you may want to roar like a lioness, or scream and shout out freely as your baby is being born, or alternatively to breathe your baby out quietly. The free expression of sound is a great help in releasing and letting go of pain. It is important not to try to contain your feelings or the pain, but to be fully uninhibited about letting them out.

Giving birth is passionate, powerful and deeply sexual. It involves many intense sensations both painful and pleasurable. It is a time to let go to your instincts, to let your body take over and to be completely free.

CONNECTING to the EARTH

Giving birth involves many intense sensations both painful and pleasurable. It is a time to let go to your instincts, to let your body take over and to be completely free.

When you are in labour you will understand the relevance of having meditated so deeply during your yoga practice on your roots, your connection with the earth. Whether you give birth at home or in hospital, as soon as you close your eyes and focus your awareness inwards, Mother Earth will be there to support, nourish and sustain you. Just as she is when you practise the postures, gravity is a great friend and helper during labour and birth. Tuning in to this fundamental force during your contractions will help you to feel centred and grounded. There will be a constant exchange between your body and the ground, where the earth absorbs the pain and gives back new, fresh, energy.

The power and efficiency of your contractions will be increased, easing your baby's passage down the birth canal, if you know instinctively how to position your body and move in harmony with gravity. You will be more comfortable and cope better with the intensity of the sensations you experience as your uterus contracts. The pain at the peak of the contractions, when the wave or rush of energy opening your body is strongest, will be easier to bear and less overwhelming when you are upright and mobile, in touch with your roots. The pages which follow go through the stages of labour in sequence, with some practical suggestions for your practice sessions.

SHARING the EXPERIENCE – the Partner's role

If you are planning to share the experience of labour and birth with a partner, include him or her in some of your practice sessions, experimenting with ways to be helpful at the time. Always start the session with ten minutes or so of quiet breathing practice together, so that you can tune into a deeper, more meditative state of mind before you begin, and also acknowledge the presence of your baby (see Simple Breathing, p.69).

When working with a partner it is as important to be able to be silent and quiet together without doing anything in particular, as it is to do practical things. At times you may want to be alone, or to have your partner there in the room but not actually doing anything or watching you. It is very important that your partner's presence helps you, rather than distracts or inhibits your progress.

It is difficult to predict the way that you will want your partner to help you at the time. You may simply want to know that he or she is in another room nearby, ready to be called when you are in need. On the other hand, you may want intensive help from your partner, to be held or massaged through every contraction. Or you may want the midwife to do all or some of this during labour.

Some women prefer their partner not to be present, and partners themselves are also bound to have their own preferences and ideas about the ways they would like to share the experience. The current fashion is for partners to be present and sometimes they may feel somewhat pressurized into performing in a certain way or indeed to be there when, in reality, they would prefer not to be so intimately involved. If these underlying feelings remain hidden, the result could be counterproductive, creating a feeling of anxiety or conflict in the birthing room.

It is vital to be truthful and honest about these issues and to allow for the most appropriate solution to unfold at the time. This is impossible to anticipate in advance, so it is a good idea to learn how you might share the experience and to practise positions and massage together, whilst always keeping an open mind as to whether or not this will be useful on the day. Having said that, many couples experience great pleasure in sharing the intimacy of labour and the birth of their child. For some, this sharing is a highlight of parenting together and is an important beginning to family life in the future. Many fathers have told me this was one of the most profound experiences of their life and that witnessing their child being born resulted in a special sense of closeness in later years. Many women also find the help and support of their partner invaluable.

Good communication in pregnancy will lead to the right way to share the birth experience. It is a good idea to sit down together from time to time, facing and preferably touching each other. Allow each other five or ten minutes to express any feelings about the birth or any other issues which are relevant at the time. Make sure that each of you has space to speak uninterrupted while the other listens. It is always helpful to begin by expressing some appreciations – things you enjoy or like about being together in general, or specifically at the time, or perhaps from the last practice session. If you wish to complain about anything, then follow it with a recommendation. For example: 'Yesterday I found your touch too deep, too firm when you were massaging my back. Could you try to do it more softly and lightly today?' This will aid your ease of communication in labour.

Ending the session with your hopes, dreams and visions is a way to let your partner know more about the way you are anticipating the future. Developing these skills will also be very useful after the birth.

Being together in labour is very much a matter of sensitive communication and appropriate practical help where it is needed, so beginning with good communication in pregnancy is vital. The practical suggestions which follow can then be used as and when they are needed.

Good communication in pregnancy will lead to the right way to share the birth experience.

PRE-LABOUR

Sometimes labour starts without any warning but most women experience a gradual build-up to the real thing.

Early labour usually begins very slowly and some women experience runs of contractions which may last several hours at a time in the days leading up to established labour. You may be very aware of this happening or you may not feel it at all.

During this time your cervix will be thinning and softening as your uterus prepares for labour, but no real dilation will be happening yet. This is important work which must happen before your uterus can open, but you may yet have a long time to go before your baby is born so it is not necessary to start using labour positions until you absolutely have to. Rest or sleep as much as possible when the contractions subside, and fall into rhythm with what is happening in your body. If these pre-labour contractions are keeping you awake at night, try kneeling over a beanbag or a pile of large cushions on your bed so that you can doze between them with your body well supported.

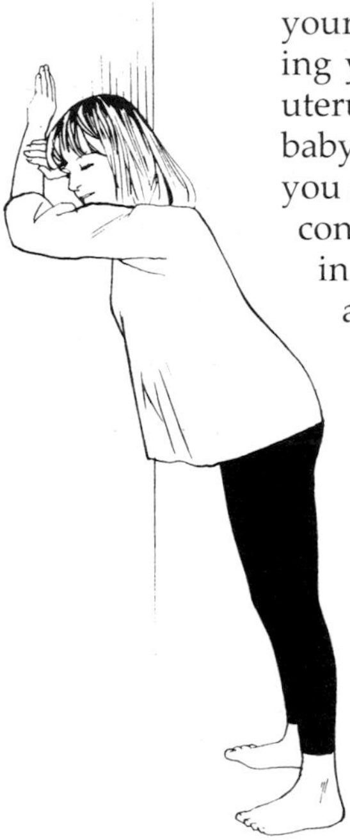

PRACTISING FOR BIRTH – the first stage

When labour begins in earnest, the contractions will become increasingly strong. It is best to do nothing special for as long as possible, but eventually you will find that you need to focus on your breathing and to find comfortable upright positions in which you can move freely during contractions and rest supported between them.

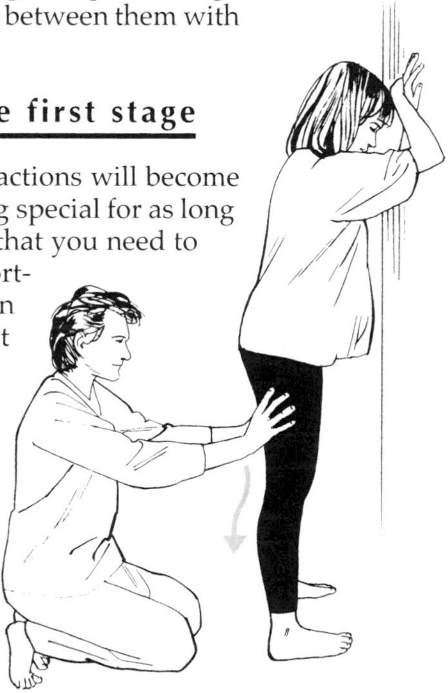

Try each of the following positions as if you were breathing through a few practice contractions. Imagine the contraction beginning, then relax your whole body and centre your awareness on your breathing. Most women prefer to breathe out through the mouth and in through the nose during strong contractions in labour. Focus on long slow exhalations, pausing to let the inbreath come in calmly and slowly before you exhale again. There will be about four or five cycles of the breath per contraction. Contractions in early labour last about thirty seconds, with resting intervals of anything between half an hour and five minutes between each one. By the end of the first stage the contractions last from a minute to a minute and a half, with intervals of about the same duration in between.

It may help you to remember your 'roots' and direct the exhalations down to the ground, receiving energy from the earth without effort each time you slowly inhale (see p. 73). This will enable you to feel grounded and to avoid becoming too exhausted. You can

FIG. 6.1
Stand with your feet comfortably apart and heels well grounded, leaning forward on to a wall. Bend your knees slightly and roll your hips, or move freely to release the pain during contractions. Focus on releasing and discharging tension and pain into the ground with the exhalations, inhaling slowly in between.

FIG. 6.2
Your partner can massage gently down the back of the legs and inside of the thighs towards the ground during contractions.

also try the sound breathing on p. 72 while practising the positions to get used to releasing sounds spontaneously when you are in strong labour. At the same time, move your body intuitively, rolling or rocking or moving in any way you want to, as this will help to dissipate the pain. Once you are familiar with the positions, try moving from one to another, from standing to squatting, squatting to kneeling, swaying your hips, and enjoying the sensuality of your body. Allow yourself to be uninhibited and to discover your own intuitive movements.

Being aware of the intelligence of the earth, the pull of gravity beneath you as you do this will ensure that you feel grounded and centred at the same time. Resting between contractions is vitally important. Labour can go on a very long time and if you are overly active without plenty of rest and relaxation between contractions you may waste your energy. So practise the working positions as well as the resting positions, making sure that you relax deeply and let go of all tension when you are resting. At this time it is important that your partner rests too, avoiding talking to you or massaging you so that you can make the most of the breaks between contractions to replenish your energy.

FIG. 6.4
Some women like to be held while standing. Relax completely in your partner's arms, moving and breathing together – sharing the contraction.

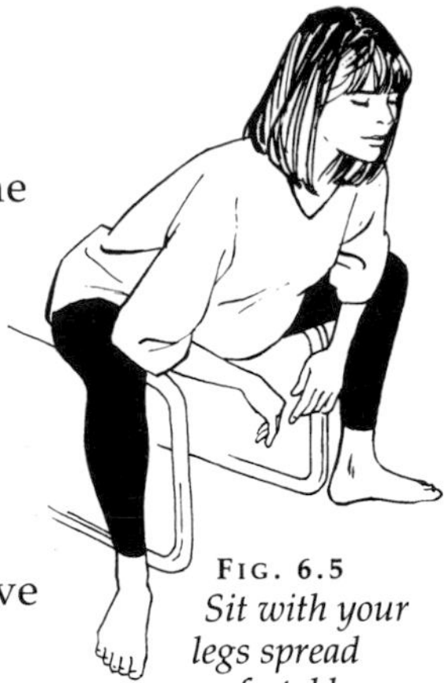

FIG. 6.5
Sit with your legs spread comfortably apart and your feet resting flat on the floor. Lean forward from the hips on to your thighs or on to a support. Rocking backwards and forwards may be helpful during contractions.

STANDING and WALKING

You may enjoy standing or walking about slowly during the first stage of labour, leaning forward during the contractions. Between them you will need to rest by sitting on a chair, kneeling forward on to cushions or a beanbag, or squatting on a stool. These vertical positions stimulate the contractions and make them more efficient and less painful. Gravity helps the weight of the baby's head and body to press down on the dilating cervix, encouraging it to open. You may enjoy being held by your partner or midwife or you may prefer to be alone, with your helpers nearby in case you need them.

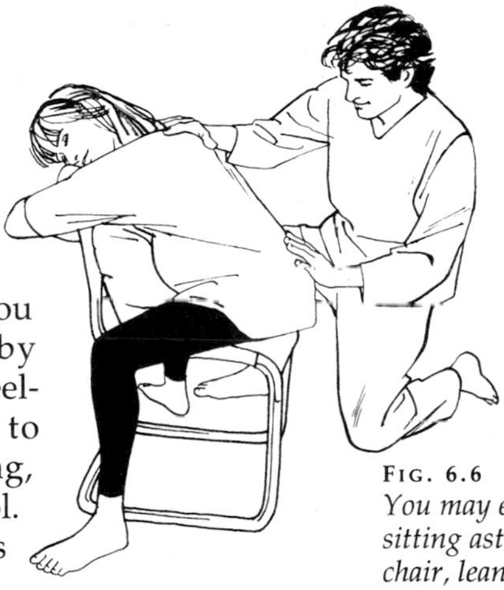

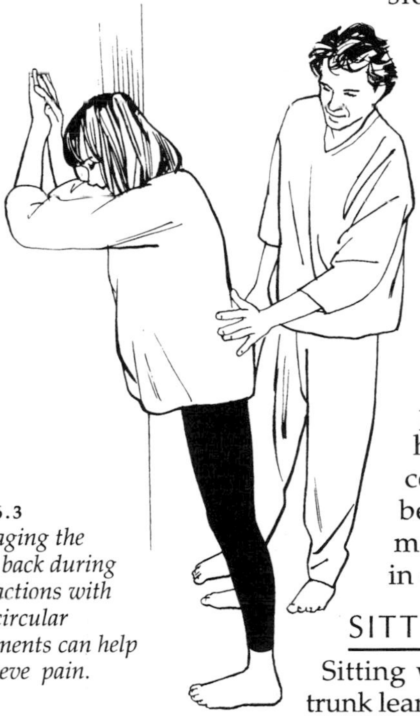

FIG. 6.3
Massaging the lower back during contractions with slow circular movements can help to relieve pain.

SITTING

Sitting with your knees spread wide apart and your trunk leaning forward may be very comfortable in labour. You could sit on a chair or bed, and many women find sitting on the toilet very comfortable.

FIG. 6.6
You may enjoy sitting astride the chair, leaning over the back on to a soft cushion. This is a useful position for a partner to massage your back. The masseur can use a comfortable half-kneeling position to prevent strain and fatigue. It's usually best to massage during the contraction and rest in between.

FIG. 6.7
Sitting on a chair and leaning forward on to soft pillows on a bed or other support is comfortable during contractions and can be used as a resting position in between.

FIG. 6.8
Sitting in a birth pool, or in the bath, in warm water which is as deep as possible, will enhance relaxation in strong labour. The buoyancy of the water supports your weight so that it may be easier to move and change positions. It is usually best to enter the pool when labour is very well established, at about 4 or 5cms dilation.

FIG. 6.9
Squatting in labour will widen the pelvic diameters and bring the baby's head down on to the dilating cervix. This usually intensifies and strengthens the contractions. Use a low stool for support to avoid getting tired, and rest in between contractions, and stand up slowly when you feel the contraction coming on.

FIG. 6.10
Leaning forward on to a soft but firm support and placing firm cushions or a rolled mat under the heels may be comfortable while squatting.

FIG. 6.11
Squatting against your partner's body can be comforting during or between contractions. Your partner should sit towards the front of the seat of the chair so that your back is not touching the rim.

FIG. 6.12
Squatting in warm water is easier than on land. You can hold onto the firm rim of the pool and swing or rock your pelvis rhythmically during contractions to release and relax your pelvic muscles. Between contractions, lean forward on to the rim of the pool and relax deeply.

SQUATTING

Squatting in labour widens your pelvis and brings the baby down on to the dilating cervix, helping to position the head correctly. Because of the increased pressure from the baby's head on the cervix in this position, squatting intensifies the contractions, making them stronger and more efficient.

Squatting positions should be well supported to avoid making you tired and can be used between or during contractions. This can be done by squatting on a stool or using a partner for support. If contractions feel too intense while squatting, try squatting between them and standing up when the contractions come on.

KNEELING

Most women find the kneeling positions most comfortable when the contractions are very strong. They help to reduce pain and help you to feel more grounded during very intense contractions. They also increase your sense of privacy and help you to focus your awareness inwards. As you may be in these positions for a long time, it is important to kneel on a soft surface to protect your knees. You will need a large beanbag as well as a pile of cushions so that you can rest between contractions with your whole body supported. If you feel like kneeling during early labour, make sure you vary the position from time to time, by standing or lifting one knee up, or stretching your legs out one at a time behind you.

The kneeling positions are especially helpful if the baby is lying in a posterior position with his or her spine facing yours. This can extend labour and there may be more pain in the lower back caused by the back of the baby's head pressing against the sacral nerves. Kneeling forward or standing and leaning forward while circling your hips will encourage the baby to rotate into the more usual anterior position and help to relieve backache.

It is important to understand that the more vertical kneeling positions are the most gravity effective. So if you have quite a long way to go, make sure you kneel quite vertically with a high pile of cushions to lean on. Kneeling with the body more horizontal tends to slow things down a little, and may be more helpful if contractions are close together and rather fierce and overwhelming. It is useful to remember that the lower you go, the slower. The 'slow down' position is the least gravity effective and is very helpful in any situation when you need to slow down – for example, if you feel an overwhelming urge to push before you are ready to. In most cases, it is best to go along with your body and push whenever you feel like it but if the pushing is causing the cervix to swell rather than dilate this 'slow down' position will reduce the pressure by taking the baby's head back and away from the cervix. It is also a good position for a very fast birth when the baby is expelled in just a few contractions, as it will help to slow things down as much as possible so that the baby emerges less forcefully, allowing the vaginal tissues more time to expand and release.

FIG. 6.13
By kneeling upright with your trunk more or less vertical, you will make the most of the help of gravity to enhance dilation. Slow circling of the hips or rocking the pelvis helps to dissipate the pain.

181

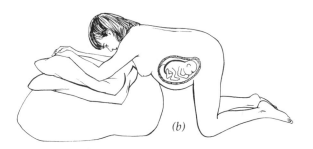

FIG. 6.14
Kneeling over a beanbag or a pile of cushions helps you to feel grounded and slows down very fast or intense contractions by bringing the baby's head off the cervix. Figure 6.14a shows the baby's head in the most common, occipito-anterior position, facing towards the mother's spine. Figure 6.14b shows a baby lying in the occipito-posterior position, facing away from the mother's spine towards her belly. This position will help to ease backpain and encourage the baby to rotate into the anterior position.

FIG. 6.15
When kneeling for a long time, make sure you have something soft under your knees. Stretching your legs like this between contractions helps to release stiffness in the knees and muscles of the legs.

(b)

FIG. 6.17
This half-kneeling, half-squatting position allows you to rock forward and back. Many women enjoy asymmetrical positions, and find this a comfortable variation to use from time to time when kneeling.

FIG. 6.16
The Child's Pose (see p.123) can be used in labour. Modify it using comfortable cushions, or try rocking forward (as in (a)) and back (as in (b)) during contractions. Try inhaling as you come forwards, and exhaling as your pelvis moves towards your feet going back. Be aware of the ground beneath you, and breathe the pain away with the outbreaths.

(a)

FIG. 6.18
The 'Knee Chest' position brings the baby's head down away from the cervix. This will help reduce the intensity of contractions in very fast labour, if there is a swelling of the cervical rim or if there is an 'anterior lip'.

FIG. 6.19
Kneeling in a water pool, or in the bath leaning forward, is a very relaxing position for strong labour. Kneeling positions help you to turn your attention inwards and to concentrate on the contractions. This is enhanced in water, where the pool encourages a feeling of privacy.

LYING DOWN

Despite all the advantages of being upright and active, some women need to have a 'couch potato' birth in order to really let go.

It is best to avoid lying down on your back in labour (see p. 193). If you feel like lying down, lie on your side with your upper body well propped up with cushions. Then it will be quite easy to come up on to your hands and knees if you want to during contractions.

Relaxing and floating in a birth pool or bath may be appealing if you do not feel like being very active or are too tired to support your body weight in an upright position.

FIG. 6.20
Lying on the side, well propped up with cushions.

FIG. 6.21
Floating in water is a wonderful way to relax during and between contractions.

FIG. 6.22

MASSAGE STROKES FOR LABOUR

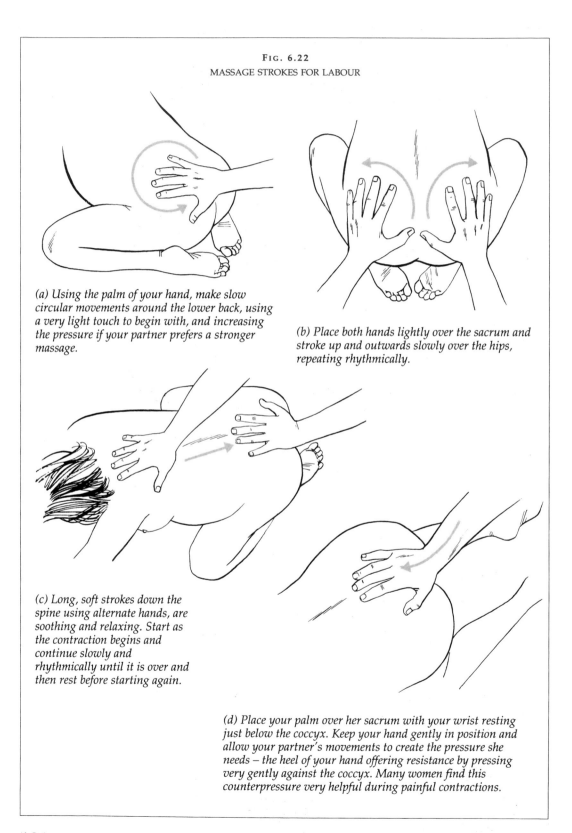

(a) Using the palm of your hand, make slow circular movements around the lower back, using a very light touch to begin with, and increasing the pressure if your partner prefers a stronger massage.

(b) Place both hands lightly over the sacrum and stroke up and outwards slowly over the hips, repeating rhythmically.

(c) Long, soft strokes down the spine using alternate hands, are soothing and relaxing. Start as the contraction begins and continue slowly and rhythmically until it is over and then rest before starting again.

(d) Place your palm over her sacrum with your wrist resting just below the coccyx. Keep your hand gently in position and allow your partner's movements to create the pressure she needs – the heel of your hand offering resistance by pressing very gently against the coccyx. Many women find this counterpressure very helpful during painful contractions.

PRACTISING for BIRTH – the second stage

During the second stage your baby's head will descend deep down into the birth canal, then turn under the pubic bone and finally the crown of your baby's head will appear through your vagina just prior to the birth. During the birth the baby's head will emerge first, followed by the shoulders, one at a time, and then the rest of the baby's body will be born.

It is helpful to understand that the second stage has three phases. In a fast birth they follow in such quick succession that they are not usually noticeable, but when the second stage goes more slowly, these phases are more obvious. The first phase involves the descent of the baby's head deep into the pelvis; the second is turning around the curve of the pubic bone up to crowning, and the third is the emergence of the baby's head and body. Bearing this in mind , the positions for the practice sessions which follow have been arranged in two sections. The bearing down second stage positions should be used until the baby's head is crowning, and the birth positions for the actual birth of the baby.

It is easiest to be on the floor or in a birth pool for the second stage so that you can move freely, but many positions can also be used on a bed if necessary. The positions suggested below are variations of basic squatting which is the physiological position for birth, since gravity helps the baby to descend at the best possible angle while the pelvic canal is open to its widest capacity.

Once your cervix is fully dilated you will begin to feel an urge to push as the expulsive reflex of the second stage gets underway. These contractions will press your baby downwards through the pelvic canal in readiness for the birth. It is impossible to practise pushing since it is an involuntary reflex which will occur spontaneously at the time, but it is helpful to practise the positions which will be most effective and practical. Doing this is important, especially since most of us have been conditioned to expect to give birth lying on the back.

POSITIONS for BEARING DOWN

During the first phase of the second stage you will be pushing your baby down into the pelvis and around the pubic arch. There is no need to use the actual birthing position yet, until the baby's head 'crowns' (when the top of the baby's head begins to show through your

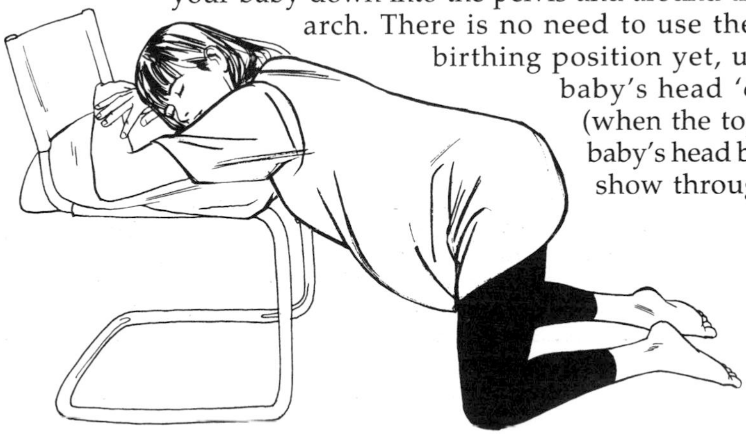

FIG. 6.23
Kneel forward on to the chair to rest between contractions. When the urge to bear down or push arises, kneel upright and hold on to the chair, pushing down towards the ground.

FIG. 6.24
Kneeling on your hands and knees is a useful bearing down position, but is less 'gravity effective' than kneeling upright. Therefore it is most suitable for a fast, efficient second stage of labour where the baby's head is descending well. During contractions, push down into the floor through your hands and knees while relaxing and releasing your pelvic floor muscles.

vagina). Very simple upright positions can be used for pushing until you are ready for the actual birth and you can use any of the same positions you used during labour.

Bearing down positions are usually very simple. You will feel the need to hold on to something when the contractions come on. Pushing is instinctive and there is no need to hold your breath when you push. In fact, releasing your breath and releasing sounds freely without inhibition while you are pushing will help you to let go. It helps enormously to be aware of gravity and to focus on pushing down into the ground, allowing your pelvic floor muscles to relax and release as you push.

FIG. 6.25
Kneeling to bear down in a birth pool, you can spread your knees wide apart and hold on to the firm rim of the pool.

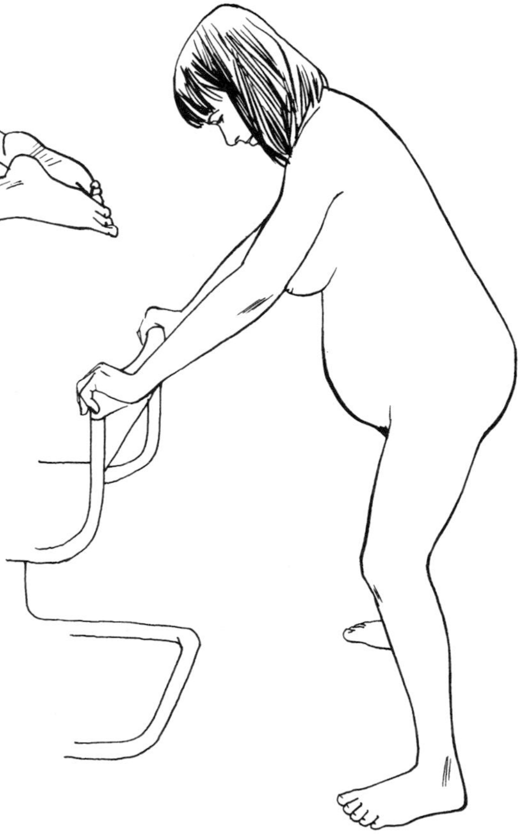

FIG. 6.26
When standing to push, the power of the expulsive contractions is assisted by gravity. Stand with your feet a comfortable distance apart and bend your knees. Lean forward on to the back of a chair or another firm support and push down towards the ground.

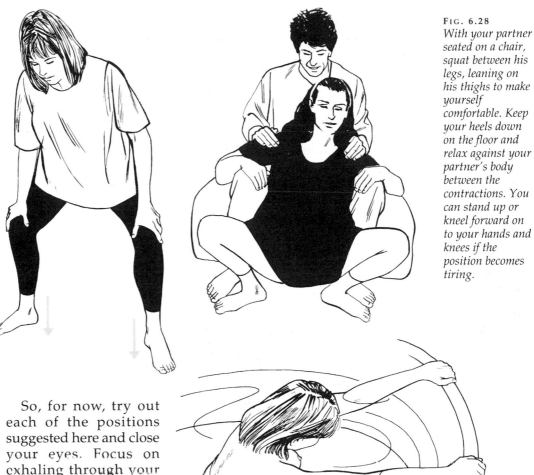

FIG. 6.27
Bear down in the standing squat position by bending your knees and holding on to your thighs and then pushing down towards the floor.

FIG. 6.28
With your partner seated on a chair, squat between his legs, leaning on his thighs to make yourself comfortable. Keep your heels down on the floor and relax against your partner's body between the contractions. You can stand up or kneel forward on to your hands and knees if the position becomes tiring.

So, for now, try out each of the positions suggested here and close your eyes. Focus on exhaling through your mouth and send the breath down into the floor while relaxing all the inner muscles of your pelvis.

HELPING the BABY DESCEND

Sometimes it takes a long time for the baby's head to descend to the base of the pelvis. If progress is slow, the hanging standing squat in Figure 6.30 may help the baby to descend as it is the most gravity-effective position. Your partner should get into position first so that the support is secure. Your baby can also be born in this position with the midwife receiving the baby from behind.

CAUTION: Partners who have back problems should avoid this position and use those shown in Figures 6.28 and 6.37 instead.

The upright support combined with the feeling of hanging helps the baby to drop downwards.

FIG. 6.29
You can squat in a birth pool to bear down by placing your feet flat on the bottom of the pool and holding on to the firm rim. Push down into the floor as if you were on dry land.

187

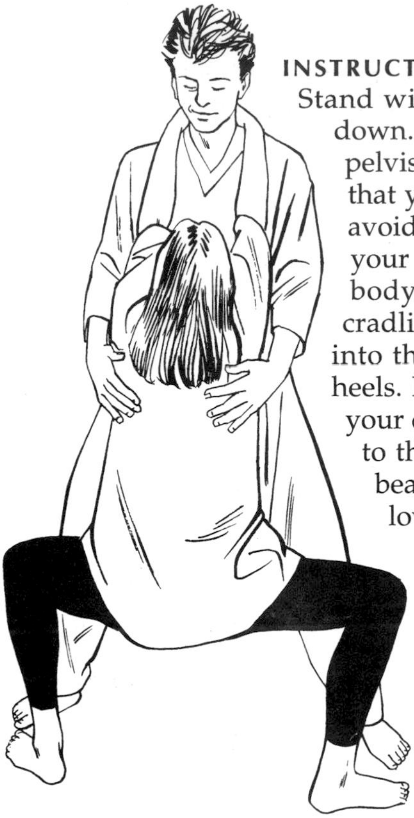

INSTRUCTIONS FOR PARTNER

Stand with feet about 12–18" apart, keeping the heels down. Bend your knees and lean back, tucking your pelvis under and forward. This is very important so that you support her weight against your pelvis and avoid straining your back. The strength comes from your thighs and buttocks. Your shoulders and upper body can then stay relaxed with your arms softly cradling her body. Exhale down through your heels into the floor to stabilize yourself and ground your heels. Keep the back of your neck relaxed by tucking your chin down towards your chest. If you have time to think of it, it is a good idea to have a chair or a beanbag behind you in case she squats down very low during the contractions.

INSTRUCTIONS FOR MOTHER

Place your feet apart, wider than your partner's, keeping your heels down on the floor. Clasp your hands around your partner's shoulders and slide down his body slowly so that you both keep your balance. Go very slowly when you first practise, taking your time to let your weight go fully. Relax against his body and hang, drop your pelvis and allow it to be heavy, with your feet flat on the floor. Your feet still carry some of your weight but you should feel as if you are really hanging. Use this position during the contractions, coming up to rest in between. With practice, this way of supporting will become much easier to do, as you get a feel for the dynamics and become more relaxed and balanced.

FIG. 6.30
HANGING SQUAT
WITH A PARTNER

BIRTHING POSITIONS

It is impossible to predict which position you will use to give birth. It is wise to try them all out many times so that you can spontaneously use the most appropriate position when the time comes.

When you practise these positions, try visualizing your baby's journey through the birth canal. Imagine the baby's head emerging as the tissues of the vagina soften and release while you focus on exhaling, relaxing and releasing, breathing your baby out.

In general, the 'hold your breath and push' approach to the second stage should be avoided. Spontaneous pushing in harmony with the inner sensations you feel while exhaling or releasing sound is likely to be far more effective in helping you to relax and release the muscles of the birth canal as your baby is born. Some women naturally hold their breath for short periods while pushing, but prolonged breath holding is unwise as it reduces the oxygen supply to the baby. Many

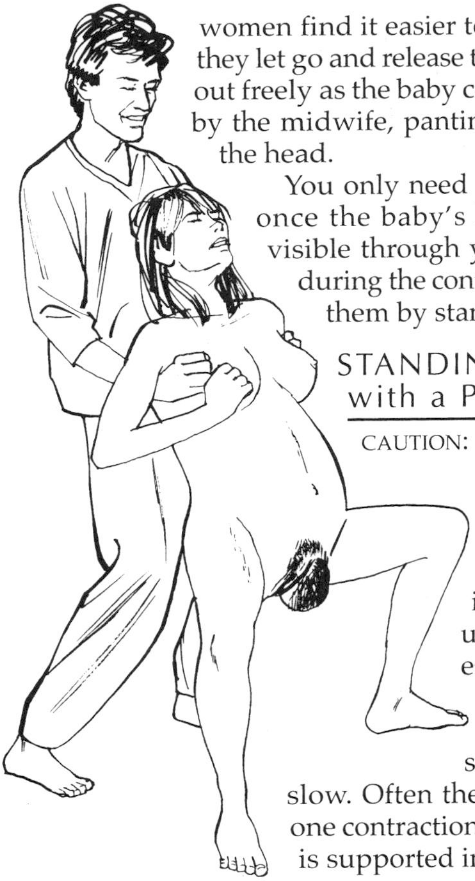

FIG. 6.31
STANDING SQUAT
WITH A PARTNER

women find it easier to be in touch with their power if they let go and release the primal cries of birth and shout out freely as the baby comes. Others prefer to be guided by the midwife, panting to slow down the delivery of the head.

You only need to get into the birthing position once the baby's head crowns and begins to be visible through your vagina. Adopt the position during the contractions only and rest in between them by standing, kneeling or squatting.

STANDING SQUAT with a PARTNER

CAUTION: This position is not for partners with back problems, they should concentrate on 6.28 and 6.39 instead. This is the most gravity effective birthing position and can be used for any birth, but is especially useful if the baby is breech, posterior or the second stage is slow. Often the baby is born in one contraction when the mother is supported in a standing squat.

FIG. 6.32(b)
HAND POSITION
LINKING THE
FINGERS
The partner puts his arms under the mother's arms and offers her his hands with the palms facing up. The mother can then place her hands on top, palms down, linking her fingers with his. The partner should concentrate on keeping arms and hands as relaxed as possible, lowering them to a comfortable height to avoid excessive strain under the mother's arms.

INSTRUCTIONS FOR PARTNER
Place a chair or a beanbag behind you in case she squats down very low. Stand, preferably barefoot, with your feet wide apart. Bend your knees and lean back to support her against your pelvis. Keep your thighs and buttocks firm and relax your arms and shoulders as much as possible. Breathe down into the floor through your heels. If you are able to at the time, it may help to lean against a wall or sit on the edge of a bed. Choose one of the following hand positions shown above, making sure to reduce the pressure under the arms as much as possible by relaxing your own arms and shoulders as she sinks down.

FIG. 6.32(a)
HAND POSITION
HOLDING THE
THUMBS
The mother makes a fist with her thumbs up. The partner then places his arms under her arms and holds her thumbs with his hands.

INSTRUCTIONS FOR MOTHER
Stand with your back to your partner and choose your preferred hand position. Place your feet comfortably wide apart. Bend your knees and lean back against your partner, sliding slowly down his body, keeping your heels down until you find the balance together. Then, when the position feels secure, release your weight and your pelvis down and hang, letting your neck and head relax back against your partner. Come up and rest between contractions.

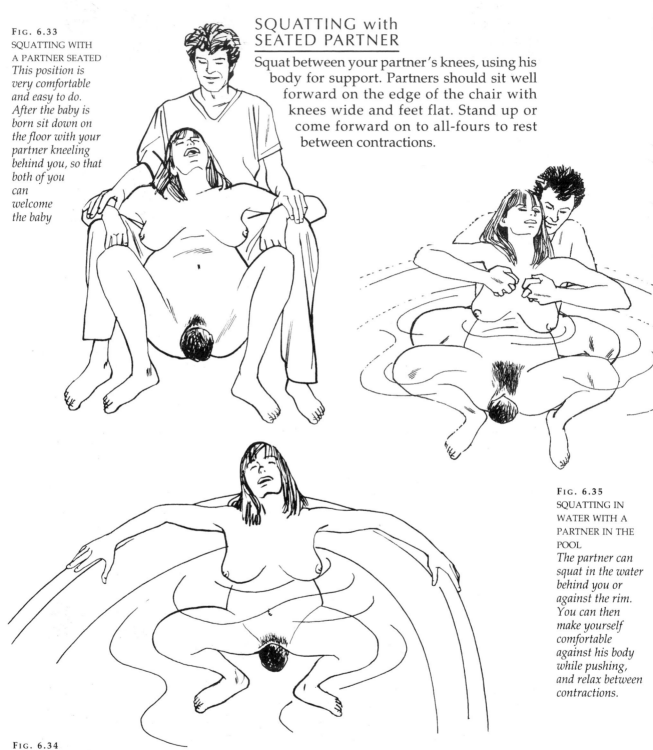

FIG. 6.33
SQUATTING WITH
A PARTNER SEATED
*This position is
very comfortable
and easy to do.
After the baby is
born sit down on
the floor with your
partner kneeling
behind you, so that
both of you
can
welcome
the baby*

SQUATTING with SEATED PARTNER

Squat between your partner's knees, using his body for support. Partners should sit well forward on the edge of the chair with knees wide and feet flat. Stand up or come forward on to all-fours to rest between contractions.

FIG. 6.35
SQUATTING IN
WATER WITH A
PARTNER IN THE
POOL
*The partner can
squat in the water
behind you or
against the rim.
You can then
make yourself
comfortable
against his body
while pushing,
and relax between
contractions.*

FIG. 6.34
SQUATTING IN A WATER POOL
It is easier to squat in water than on land while giving birth, and you can do so by leaving back against the side of the pool holding on to the rim. The buoyancy of the water supports your bodyweight and your baby's body as he or she is born.

FIG. 6.36
SQUATTING IN WATER WITH A PARTNER OUTSIDE THE POOL
Squatting with a partner supporting you from outside the pool is comfortable and easy to do. Your partner kneels beside the pool and places his arms underneath yours so that you can lean back and hold his hands.

FIG. 6.37
STANDING UPRIGHT WITH TWO HELPERS
This method of supporting often happens spontaneously. The mother's weight is supported against both helpers' thighs. Use this position when gravity is needed to help your baby to be born.

SQUATTING on the FLOOR with TWO HELPERS

This method of supporting often happens spontaneously. The mother's weight is supported against both helpers' thighs.

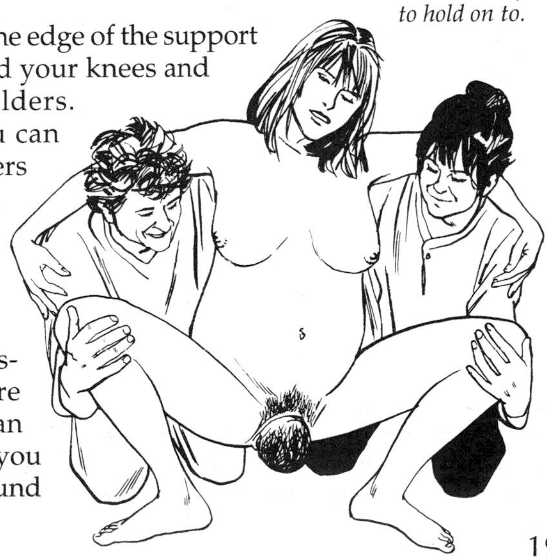

FIG. 6.38
SQUATTING ON THE FLOOR WITH TWO HELPERS
Many women enjoy giving birth in this supportive squat and find it very comforting to have two helpers to hold on to.

INSTRUCTIONS FOR HELPERS
Kneel on either side of her with your inside knees touching. Lean forward with one hand behind her back and the other under her knee nearest to you, if she finds it helpful.

INSTRUCTIONS FOR MOTHER
Squat down, resting your buttocks on the edge of the support formed by your helpers' knees. Spread your knees and place your arms around their shoulders. Keep your feet flat on the floor. You can stand up using your helpers' shoulders for support as you get up, or kneel forward on all-fours to rest between contractions. You can also bring your arms down easily to touch your baby's head as he or she is being born.

   This position can be used on a hospital delivery bed if your helpers are of similar height. In this case they can stand on either side of the bed while you squat on the bed with your arms around their shoulders.

191

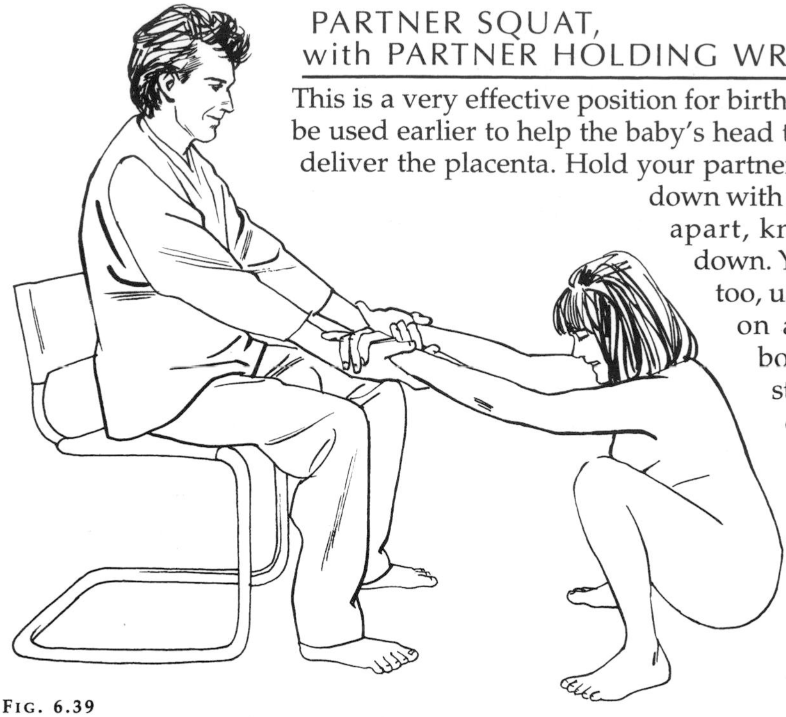

PARTNER SQUAT, with PARTNER HOLDING WRISTS

This is a very effective position for birth itself, which can also be used earlier to help the baby's head to descend, or later to deliver the placenta. Hold your partner by the wrists. Squat down with your feet comfortably apart, knees wide and heels down. Your partner can squat too, using a low stool, or sit on a chair. You should both have your elbows straight so you can pull on your partner and release your weight down through your heels into the floor.

FIG. 6.39
PARTNER SQUAT, WITH PARTNER HOLDING THE WRISTS
This position is gravity effective and enhances the baby's progress through the birth canal.

KNEELING

This is a very popular and instinctive birthing position and is most useful when the second stage is progressing well. If the baby crowns rapidly it will ease pressure on the perineum and slow down contractions. However, if progress is slow, change to a more gravity effective, upright position if you can. Once born, the baby can be placed on a soft towel between your legs so that you can sit upright to welcome him or her.

FIG. 6.41
KNEELING TO GIVE BIRTH UNDER WATER
The baby emerges behind you and is gently 'caught' by the midwife under the water, turned, and then passed under your leg. You can put your hands down and help to bring the baby slowly up to the surface to greet each other for the first time.

FIG. 6.40
KNEELING TO GIVE BIRTH

LYING on the SIDE

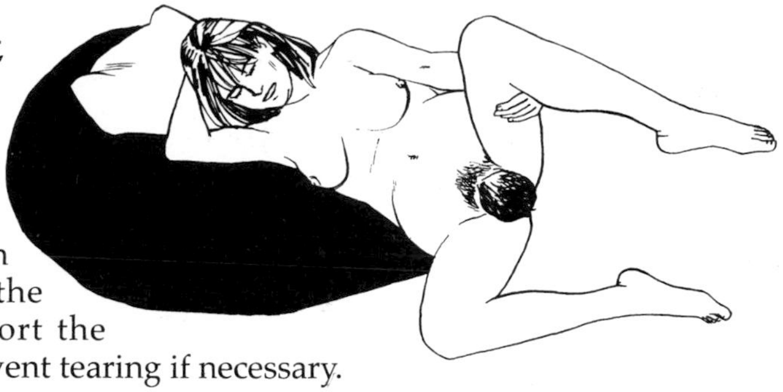

Known as the 'left lateral'
position this is favoured
by mothers and mid-
wives when the baby is
emerging very fast. It
will help to slow down
contractions and give the
midwife time to support the
perineal tissues and prevent tearing if necessary.

POSITIONS TO AVOID

Generally, try to avoid lying on your back as this position does not
allow the sacrum to be mobile and works against gravity. However,
if you have a very ample pelvis and the second stage is progressing
easily, being in a gravity effective position is not so crucial.

Unless you find them very comfortable it is best to avoid chairs,
stools or birthing beds which place you in a semi-upright squat
position in which your weight is resting on your coccyx and your feet
are on platforms or supports. While this looks like squatting it is, in
fact, more like reclining since your weight rests on your coccyx, limiting the mobility of the sacrum. It may be difficult to change positions
if you feel uncomfortable or need to move. In any true squat the
sacrum and coccyx are free and your weight goes down into your
heels or knees. This allows maximum
opening of the birth canal for your baby
and makes the most of the help of gravity.
People usually provide the best support
for giving birth, but these special birth
stools or beds are certainly preferable to
lying on your back!

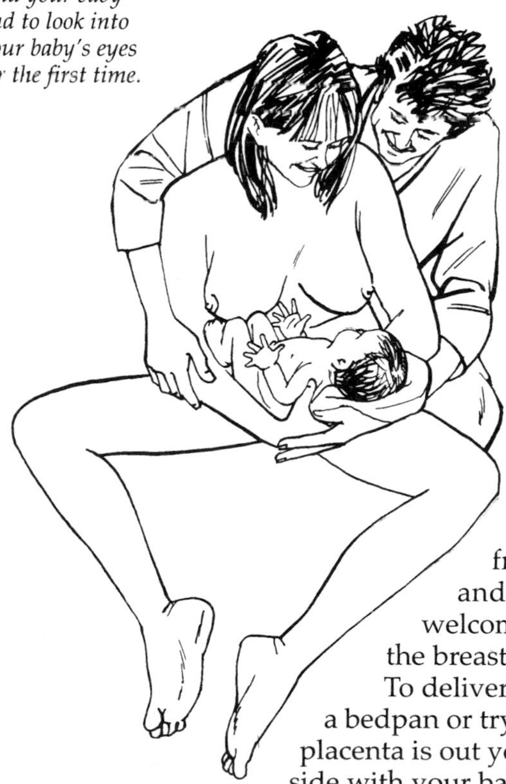

AFTER THE BIRTH –
the third stage

When you first welcome your baby and
the first contact takes place, try to stay
an upright sitting position without
leaning or lying back.

This position helps the placenta to
separate efficiently and fluids to drain
from the uterus. It is also easiest to position
and hold your baby comfortably while you
welcome your baby and introduce him or her to
the breast.

To deliver the placenta you can stand up, squat over
a bedpan or try the partner squat (see Fig. 6.39). Once the
placenta is out you will want to relax and lie down on your
side with your baby nestling beside you under your arm.

FIG. 6.43
SITTING UPRIGHT
WITH YOUR BABY
AFTER THE BIRTH
*This position helps
the placenta to
separate efficiently
and fluids to drain
from the uterus. It
is also easiest to
hold your baby
and to look into
your baby's eyes
for the first time.*

FIG. 6.42
LYING ON YOUR
SIDE TO GIVE BIRTH
*This position does
not make the best
use of gravity but
if the second stage
is progressing
rapidly some
mothers feel most
comfortable lying
on the side to give
birth. You can
support the top leg
yourself with one
arm, or with the
assistance of a
helper.*

APPENDIX

AN A-Z OF YOGA FOR
SELF-HELP

P ractising yoga is a way of life which teaches you to love and respect your body. By gently working on relieving stress and relaxing, by invigorating every cell in your body with healthy breathing, you are constantly encouraging your body to heal itself.

Regular practice of a few yoga positions helps you to maintain your natural equilibrium and is thus essentially an ideal form of preventive health care.

The ability to heal yourself is present throughout your life and is usually even more active in pregnancy. The natural tendency is towards an increase in health and vitality at this time.

However, the additional work your body has to do to support and nourish your baby during your pregnancy can result in discomfort or strain. If your life is stressful or you are anxious, this can undermine your health and sense of well-being. An underlying imbalance, whether physical or emotional, which you may not have been aware of before pregnancy, may surface during these months. Muscular stiffness, restricted mobility of the joints or mild postural distortions are likely to become more apparent now, when aches and pains can arise due to the impact of pregnancy on your system.

Regaining suppleness and flexibility and correcting postural imbalances is slow work, which usually takes years of dedicated exercise. However, the softening effect of the pregnancy hormones does enhance this process, and progress can be faster than usual and very encouraging.

Yoga can also be very helpful when you are out of sorts or ill. By concentrating on the appropriate postures you can enhance your body's natural healing powers. On the other hand, sometimes it is best to stop your yoga practice for a while to allow a healing process to take place undisturbed.

Neglecting a problem which is causing you discomfort can have an insidious and draining effect, causing you unnecessary misery – despite the fact that it is considered to be a 'minor discomfort' one puts up with in pregnancy. In fact, most of these need not be taken for granted as simply 'part of being pregnant', and can be eased or cured by sensible exercise.

The first thing to do if you have a problem is to seek medical advice and an accurate diagnosis. Possibly, then you can also consult an alternative practitioner (see Useful Addresses).

You can then turn to the appropriate section in this chapter to find guidance as to which yoga positions or exercises might enhance your body's innate healing powers and whether any of them should be avoided.

It is important, before you start to use the postures for therapeutic reasons, to discuss your self-help programme with your midwife or doctor who can help you to observe and check your progress and ensure that there is no possible risk or danger to yourself or your baby

FIG. A1
ABDOMINAL
RECTI MUSCLES
(a) Normal

(b) Separated

ABDOMINAL MUSCLES – SEPARATED

The recti muscles are the longitudinal muscles of your abdominal wall, which run vertically from your pelvis to your ribs on either side of the umbilicus. Occasionally these recti muscles can separate due to the stretching of the abdominal wall which happens in pregnancy.

The most common cause is poor posture (see Back Pain), where the exaggerated arch and shortening of the lower back results in the pelvis tipping forward so that the uterus is thrown forward on to the abdominal muscles, which then must do more by way of support than they were intended to. When the lower back is encouraged to lengthen, then the pelvis supports the baby from underneath and the abdominal muscles are less strained. So constant awareness of gently lengthening the lower back is vital if you discover that you have this condition.

Other causes may be a very large baby, a lot of amniotic fluid, multiple birth, obesity or strenuous pushing when emptying the bowels. Separation may be noticed in late pregnancy by lying for a few minutes on your back with your knees bent and slowly lifting your head as if to pull yourself up. This will make the recti muscles tighten. If there is any separation in pregnancy a pencil-shaped bulge will appear down the centre line of the belly. (This should not be confused with the dark line, or 'linea nigra', which often appears down the centre of the abdomen in pregnancy.) After the birth you will be able to feel a gap with your fingers.

Immediately after childbirth these muscles are always slightly separated and this generally rights itself as your body strengthens and recovers. This is not a dangerous condition, even when the gap is quite large, and, although the muscles are unlikely to rejoin completely, it can be healed by doing exercises which strengthen the recti muscles. Most of this work can be done postnatally but the exercise below is recommended in pregnancy if your doctor confirms that the recti muscles are separating.

CAUTION: If you feel uncomfortable or faint lying on your back, especially in late pregnancy, avoid the exercise below and wait until your pregnancy is over to work on strengthening these muscles. Concentrate on lengthening your lower back instead. It is best to avoid side bends, back bends and twists if you have separated recti muscles.

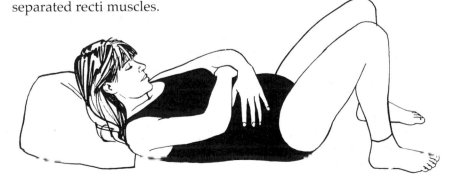

FIG. A2
*Exercise for
separated recti
muscles in
pregnancy*

Lie on your back in the basic reclining position. Cross your hands over your belly to support the abdominal muscles and keep them together.

- Breathe in, breathe out slowly, while raising your head forward towards your chest, until the point just before the bulge appears. Keep your shoulders on the floor.
- Return slowly to starting position.
- Repeat up to five times, twice daily, to keep good muscle tone and avoid further separation.
- Then relax, roll over on to your side and come up slowly.

ADDICTION

If you have an addiction to smoking, alcohol, drugs or overeating, it is vital that you seek supportive professional help in pregnancy. You need medical help and counselling in order to help yourself to change any compulsive patterns and it is not easy to do this on your own. So do discuss the problem with your midwife as your addiction is likely to affect your baby's healthy development if it is ignored.

Yoga can be a great helper when overcoming an addiction and daily practice is recommended. All the postures are useful, especially the standing positions, and the breathing exercises in Chapter 3.

ALLERGIES

Regular practice of the full programme of postures and breathing exercises may improve general relaxation and help allergies. Lots of rest and relaxation is important. Avoid any position which causes discomfort to conditions such as eczema which sometimes worsen in pregnancy. Consulting a homoeopath and a nutritionist is helpful if allergies persist or worsen.

AMNIOCENTESIS

If you are having an amniocentesis you will find the relaxation and simple breathing very useful before, during and after the test is carried out.

It is advisable to rest in bed immediately after an amniocentesis and to avoid all postures for one week. This is because of the slightly increased risk of miscarriage. While yoga is unlikely to encourage a miscarriage it is better to err on the side of caution.

During this time you will benefit from practising the breathing exercises in Chapter 3 and the relaxation on p. 171. After one week you can return to your normal yoga practice, which will help to reduce tension and anxiety until you get the results of the test.

ANXIETY – *see Emotional problems*

ASTHMA

Yoga practice can be very calming and helpful if you suffer from asthma but avoid any postures which make you feel uncomfortable or breathless.

The standing postures in Group 5 are good to do regularly. The breathing exercises in Chapter 3 and the postures which release the neck and shoulders (Nos. 18 and 19) are especially helpful.

BACKACHE – *see Pain*

BLEEDING

Although a small amount of bleeding is usually nothing to worry about, bleeding can sometimes signal a problem or possible miscarriage. If you notice any bleeding in pregnancy then stop practising yoga altogether and visit your doctor or midwife. Slight spotting or bleeding is common in some women in pregnancy and you can continue with your practice provided your doctor says it is safe.

Avoid full squatting (No. 12) until the tendency to bleed completely stops.

The breathing exercises in Chapter 3 and relaxation on p. 171 can be practised daily even if there is bleeding and will not be harmful.

BLOOD CIRCULATION (POOR)

Regular yoga practice combined with massage, walking and swimming will help to improve circulation.

All the yoga postures are beneficial and it is wise to vary your practice throughout the week to include some from each group.

Circulation to and from the legs will be improved by the foot exercises in Chapter 4, as well as No. 12a calf stretch, Nos. 14 and 15 kneeling positions, No. 16 Thai goddess pose, No. 22 tree pose and No. 25 dog pose.

Avoid standing for long periods or crossing your legs when sitting (see Low Blood Pressure and Fainting).

BRACHIAL PLEXUS SYNDROME

Pain, pins and needles or numbness in the hand, forearm or arm are caused by pressure on the nerves which supply the arm. The cause is usually strain or tension in the neck and shoulders. Follow the same exercise suggestions as for carpal tunnel syndrome.

Osteopathic treatment is recommended.

BREATHLESSNESS

This is common in late pregnancy after exertion and is usually no cause for concern. If, however, you are breathless while at rest or after minimal exercise, check with your doctor in case the cause is anaemia or dietary deficiency. Poor fitness will result in breathlessness and you will need to work on improving this gradually through gentle exercise. Gentle yoga and swimming are ideal ways to begin to increase your level of fitness.

It is normal to feel slightly breathless if you are carrying twins or a very large baby. When you lie on your back this diminishes the blood flow to your heart and can cause breathlessness. Avoid lying on your back if this is the case (see Supine Hypotension).

BREECH BABY

Babies usually settle into position for the birth in the last four weeks or so of pregnancy, but some do not do so until a few days or even hours before labour starts. This is more common with second or subsequent babies. The majority of babies lying breech in late pregnancy do turn head down in their own time, but some will remain in breech position for the birth. After about thirty-five weeks of pregnancy many babies lying breech will respond to some gentle encouragement to turn, as detailed below.

Use position one shown in Figure A3 for up to ten minutes at a time, several times a day. It will encourage your baby to turn and prevent the buttocks from engaging in the pelvic brim. While in the position, gently massage your belly with your hands in the direction in which your midwife thinks the baby is likely to turn most easily. This may take time.

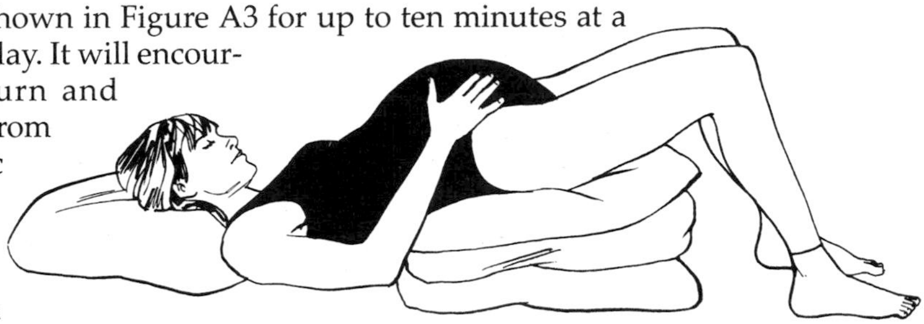

Begin at thirty-five weeks and continue daily until labour starts. After the baby has turned, discontinue this exercise and squat to encourage the head to engage. Acupuncture and homoeopathy can be used to good effect in conjunction with this exercise. The knee–chest position (Figure 6.18, p. 183) is another good exercise to do regularly throughout the day and has a similar effect. Walking for an hour a day will also help the baby's head – which is the heaviest part of the body – to descend down towards gravity.

Emotional conflict, turmoil or anxiety about the birth can be a contributing factor to breech position.

If the baby remains breech for the birth, it may be possible for the baby to be born vaginally if labour progresses well. It is sensible to use the most gravity-effective positions such as these shown in Figures 6.30 and 6.31 (see pp. 188–9) in the second stage, if your birth attendants will support you. Approximately fifty percent of breech births, or more, can take place actively but it is wise also to prepare yourself to accept obstetric assistance if necessary. Some obstetricians have a policy of assisting all breech births, while others may be open to attempting an active vaginal birth.

CAUTION: If your baby is breech at thirty-five weeks, avoid squatting until the baby turns as this may encourage the breech to engage. By all means start squatting if the head moves down.

FIG. A3
POSITION FOR TURNING A BREECH BABY
Make a pile of two or three large cushions. Sit in the centre of the pile with your feet flat on the floor and your knees bent. Then slowly lower yourself down, resting your head on a pillow so that your hips are higher than your head. Massage your belly gently for up to ten minutes several times a day.

CARPAL TUNNEL SYNDROME

Carpal tunnel syndrome is common in pregnancy. You may experience pins and needles, tingling, burning, swelling or pain in one or both hands. Often the condition is worse at night.

The increase in your body's fluids during pregnancy, as well as the general softening of your body tissues, makes it more difficult for fluids to return from the extremities. Carpal tunnel syndrome is caused by pressure on the nerves of the wrist from oedema or swelling. The exercises in Group 4, Nos. 18, 19 and 20, are the ones to concentrate on. Ice packs can be applied and, in extreme cases, a wrist splint from a physiotherapist should be used at night. Osteopathic treatment is recommended and the following massage may be helpful. Helper: Use both thumbs to massage your partner's wrists in the direction of the arrows. To massage yourself: Stroke down in the direction of one arrow at a time.

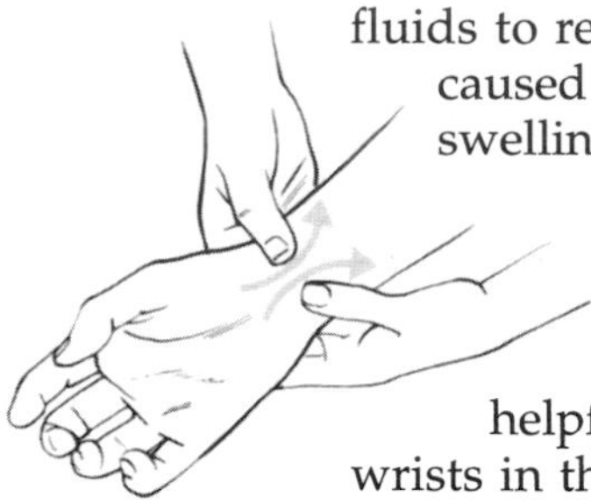

FIG. A4
MASSAGE FOR
CARPAL TUNNEL
SYNDROME

CERVICAL STITCH

Known as a Shirodkar suture, this helps to hold together a loose cervix. If you have a cervical stitch inserted, avoid full squatting. All other postures are safe to do provided your doctor is informed.

CONCEPTION DIFFICULTIES

Daily practice of yoga will improve your overall health and relaxation, enhancing your chances of conception. The pelvic exercises in Group 2 can be practised daily to promote optimal health of the reproductive organs. Acupuncture and homoeopathy may also be helpful.

CONSTIPATION

If you suffer from constipation it is important to exercise regularly. Walking, swimming and yoga will all help. The squatting position is invaluable as it relaxes the pelvic organs, including the bowel. You can squat when you defaecate to help release your pelvic floor and bowel. Respond immediately when you feel the urge to defaecate and then take plenty of time, breathing and relaxing without straining.

Make sure that your diet is not causing constipation. You need plenty of fibre from whole grains, fruit and vegetables and plenty of fluids. Eating some stewed or pureed prunes, figs or apricots before you go to bed at night will help to soften your stools. Synthetic iron supplements or emotional tension may be causes of constipation.

COUGHS, COLDS AND CHEST INFECTIONS

If you get an infection of the upper respiratory tract in pregnancy it can be very difficult to clear. This is because hormonal changes often cause the linings of the nasal passages and sinuses to swell.

Take care not to strain the abdominal or back muscles when you cough by leaning slightly forward. Homoeopathic remedies and steam inhalations may be helpful, as will using a humidifier in the room at night. If the infection is severe and very stubborn, antibiotics may be necessary. Avoid yoga and breathing exercises when you have a fever or feel stiff and achy, and concentrate on relaxation. In the recuperative phase, gentle yoga may be very helpful in restoring your energy.

The alternate nostril breathing may help to clear the nasal passages at the tail end of a cold (see Chapter 3).

CRAMP

Muscle cramps in the legs and feet are very common in pregnancy and often occur as sudden spasms in the calves which can even arise while you are asleep. Some of the kneeling postures will cause cramp in the feet when you first begin to do them if your ankles are stiff. This will stop with practice.

When cramp occurs, the first thing to do is to stretch the muscles by hooking your foot up towards you while extending the heel and massaging the calf muscles vigorously until the cramp passes. The foot exercises in Chapter 4 and the calf stretch (No. 12a) will help to prevent cramps and should be practised a few times during the day as well as last thing at night. Dog pose (No. 25) is also a useful posture to practise. To improve the general condition of your feet, try alternating Thai goddess pose (No. 16) with basic kneeling (No. 14) and do this daily for a while.

CYSTITIS

You need medical advice for cystitis and alternative therapies such as homoeopathy and aromatherapy can be very helpful.

Yoga is very useful as the profound relaxation helps to reduce tension and promote healing for this condition. Daily practice of the postures you find most relaxing is recommended.

DEPRESSION – *see Emotional problems*

DIABETES

Yoga is beneficial and can be practised regularly if you are diabetic.

DISC PROBLEMS

Great care has to be taken not to strain your back when you practise yoga, especially if you have disc problems. Any extreme forward, back or side bending or twists should be avoided.

Before you do any yoga at all, consult an osteopath who is used to treating pregnant mothers and get some personal guidance as to which postures are best for you. Then keep your practice very simple and gentle, concentrating on breathing. The postures in this book are very carefully designed to protect your spine and are safe to do provided you avoid the more advanced movements and do not overextend yourself. Personal tuition with a specialized pregnancy exercise teacher is recommended. (See also Pain – backache.)

EATING DISORDERS

If you suffer from anorexia or bulimia it is very important to talk to your midwife or doctor about this and to seek professional help from a specialized counsellor.

Yoga can be very helpful in overcoming these difficulties, but is not enough without a proper course of treatment or therapy.

Eating disorders can endanger both your own and your baby's health if ignored. Your nutrition needs to be carefully monitored to avoid problems arising and it is recommended to contact a breast-feeding counsellor while you are pregnant (see Useful Addresses, p. 220). This will help to prevent your own eating problem affecting the way you feed your baby and will be supportive for you both.

ECTOPIC PREGNANCY

A previous ectopic pregnancy can be quite a shocking experience, leaving you anxious and unconfident about conceiving again. Regular practice of yoga is one of the best ways to overcome these feelings and promote your general health. Focusing on the pelvic postures in Group 2 will help to ensure optimal health of the reproductive organs. Alternative therapies or counselling may be helpful.

EMOTIONAL PROBLEMS

Yoga can be a great aid if you are anxious or depressed. No matter how low you are feeling, try to discipline yourself to set aside one hour a day to practise, and work through each of the postures throughout the week, starting each session with breathing and ending with relaxation. Read Chapter 2 and the information on p. 64-6 about releasing feelings.

If you are still feeling very troubled after a few weeks of regular practice and anxiety, worry or fears persist, do seek help from a therapist, counsellor or your midwife or doctor. Try to nourish yourself by eating well and spend some time each day walking out of doors. It is important to seek help for your own sake, as well as your baby's, if you feel continually listless, weepy or despondent. Make sure you are not anaemic if you are feeling low, as this can be a cause of depression and listlessness in pregnancy.

EXHAUSTION – *see Tiredness*
FAINTING – *see Low blood pressure*
FATIGUE – *see Tiredness*

FIBROIDS

These can cause acute abdominal pains during pregnancy as the uterine tissues stretch. It is quite safe to practise yoga provided your doctor agrees, but be sure to avoid any postures which increase or cause pain and concentrate on those which seem to help.

Lots of gentle breathing and relaxation in the quieter postures is what you will want to focus on. Gentle swimming may be a very good way to exercise, rather than walking for long distances if the fibroids are causing you discomfort.

FITNESS

Pregnancy, birth and motherhood require a lot of energy and fitness is important. Yoga practice should be combined with walking and swimming to raise your fitness level.

Doing gentle yoga exercises in the shallow end of the pool and slow swimming are the easiest ways to approach exercise if you are very unfit, and then start to practise on land as well when your energy improves, beginning with breathing and sitting positions, progressing slowly to the standing positions (see Weight).

FOOT PROBLEMS

Most of us have problems with our feet, which go unnoticed as we cram them into shoes which cramp the toes or have high heels. Really healthy feet are supple and springy with wide, spread-out toes that adjust constantly to help us find our balance. However, feet are relatively easy to improve with sensible exercise. The simple foot exercises and advice in Chapter 4 are useful, as is regular foot massage. Self-massage of the feet is easiest to do while in the Tailor sitting position (see Figure 5.13a, p114). Massage the arches and soles of the feet as well as the toes, but avoid strong pressure around the ankles.

Postures which especially help the feet are Nos. 14, 15 and 16. Do these often, alternating them from one to the other. If your feet are very stiff use a bolster and cushions as suggested, and place a rolled blanket under your feet if it is helpful.

Work on the toe exercises on p. 83 to encourage your toes to spread.

FIG. A5
USING A ROLLED BLANKET UNDER THE FEET WHEN KNEELING

HAEMORRHOIDS – see Varicosities
HEADACHES – see Pain

HEARTBURN

This is often an inevitable part of pregnancy caused by hormonal softening of the valve between the stomach and the oesophagus.

Try all the postures to see if any in particular help to relieve discomfort. Many women find the shoulder exercises helpful. Eat small meals more frequently rather than large ones, and eliminate foods which seem to make the heartburn worse. Homoeopathy is helpful for extreme heartburn.

HERNIA

If you have an inguinal hernia you need to avoid any posture which causes a feeling of pressure, bulging or pulling in the area. Provided your doctor agrees, you can practise most of the yoga postures very gently.

Standing for long periods, side bending or twisting should be avoided. You need to use your own judgement to be aware of the slightest feeling of strain which indicates that you should avoid a particular movement.

HIGH BLOOD PRESSURE (HYPERTENSION)

The non-strenuous nature of yoga makes it an ideal form of exercise for people with a slightly raised blood pressure as it has been scientifically shown to lower blood pressure.

When you practise your yoga, avoid forward bends (Nos. 23 and 24) and do plenty of slow breathing and relaxing in each posture. Leave out any postures which you find uncomfortable.

Gentle swimming is a good way to exercise if you have a tendency to high blood pressure as it tends to lower blood pressure and does give you effective exercise without strain.

If you have been told to rest in bed, concentrate on the breathing exercises and general relaxation. If your doctor agrees you can also do some gentle sitting positions for half an hour or so, returning to bed to relax afterwards.

The foot exercises on p. 83 will help to keep your circulation moving and you can sit up on the edge of the bed to do some gentle head, neck and shoulder exercises (Nos. 18 and 19) to relieve stiffness. Spinal massage will be very helpful too. Make sure your doctor agrees, but this sort of gentle exercise can help you to feel human if you have to stay in bed for a while and should not raise your blood pressure.

INCONTINENCE

This is caused by softening of the pelvic floor muscles due to the pregnancy hormones, or by weakness in the pelvic floor. The pelvic floor exercises on p. 138 are the ones to concentrate on. Try also exercising your pelvic floor as much as you can during your normal daily activities. Brace your pelvic floor by contracting it before coughing, sneezing, laughing or blowing your nose, or in any situation which may stimulate leakage.

If there is no improvement after the birth, it is advisable to visit an obstetric physiotherapist.

INSOMNIA

Insomnia is common in pregnancy, especially towards the end. The first thing to explore is whether any worry or fear is keeping you awake. Make sure you get some exercise in the day, including walking and swimming two or three times a week if possible. Before going to bed at night have a warm bath, adding a few drops of essential oil of camomile, and then do one hour of gentle yoga ending with a long relaxation in bed, focusing on your breathing. This will all probably help you to fall asleep, but even if you cannot sleep, the deep relaxation will be a reasonable substitute. Do ask your partner to massage you last thing at night with a camomile-based soothing massage oil. This is a good way to induce sleep.

A warm milky drink before bed may also be helpful, and using plenty of pillows to make yourself comfortable is a good idea. If insomnia is severe you need to discuss the problem with your midwife or doctor and counselling may be needed.

IVF PREGNANCY

After in vitro fertilization, it is best to err on the side of caution and wait until the pregnancy is securely established before you start doing yoga. You will need to be guided by your doctor as to when you can begin. Usually, after the fourth month, you can regard the pregnancy as perfectly normal. Up until then, you can benefit very much from the breathing exercises on p. 67 and the relaxation on p. 171.

LOW BLOOD PRESSURE AND FAINTING

Feeling faint and dizzy can be caused by posture in pregnancy, especially from changing position suddenly, standing for long periods or lying on your back. If you feel faint, sit down quickly but carefully to avoid falling and put your head down or else lie on your side until you recover. Pumping your foot, leg and buttock muscles by contracting and releasing them when you stand helps to improve circulation and make sure you lie on your side in bed or when resting.

Yoga practice will help the problem in the long term but follow the signals your body gives you very carefully. If you begin to feel queasy in any posture, sit down and rest. Pace yourself so that you learn to anticipate the point at which you need to stop. Sometimes being overenthusiastic about breathing can cause faintness while you practise. Remember that you should never push or pull the breath, or try to alter its normal rhythm (see p. 70).

Avoid the standing postures for any length of time and leave them out altogether if you feel faint in them from the start. While there is no danger to you or your baby from postural low blood pressure, make sure you discuss the problem with your doctor. Rescue Remedy, one of the Bach Flower Remedies, is useful, so keep some on you if you feel faint often. Make sure that you are not anaemic as this can be a cause of faintness in pregnancy.

MISCARRIAGE

If you have any bleeding at all, stop exercising until you have investigated the cause with your doctor (see Bleeding). If you have had one or more miscarriages previously, or are threatening to miscarry in this pregnancy, then all exercises should be avoided until after the sixteenth week. Breathing and relaxation are most useful until then.

The yoga postures are not strenuous and are unlikely to be the cause of a miscarriage but, as a precaution, it is wisest to begin to practise after your pregnancy is well established.

MULTIPLE SCLEROSIS

Gentle yoga is an ideal form of exercise for this condition as you need to move without getting tired or straining.

Practise just a few postures each day, giving yourself plenty of time for breathing and relaxation at the end. Practise a little regularly and modify the postures so that you never try to strain beyond your comfortable limit. Personal tuition with a qualified pregnancy yoga teacher will be helpful, but make sure that the method being taught is gentle and non-strenuous, compatible with the approach in this book.

NAUSEA AND VOMITING

These are common symptoms of early pregnancy and should begin to clear by the end of the third month. Occasionally they persist throughout pregnancy. From an exercise point of view, gentle breathing, meditation and yoga are usually very helpful and a good walk in the open air every day is recommended. Avoid overbreathing when you practise yoga as this may make you feel nauseous (see p. 70).

If some postures make nausea worse, leave them out. For severe nausea, homoeopathy can be very helpful. Persistent vomiting needs medical attention.

OBESITY – *see Weight*

OEDEMA

The general increase in body fluid and muscular laxity caused by hormones sometimes causes some water retention in the feet, legs and fingers. This is normal in pregnancy and may worsen in the weeks prior to the birth. It is more common with twin pregnancy, excessive weight gain, in hot weather or after prolonged standing. On its own, oedema is not usually a cause for concern but should be checked because, in the presence of other symptoms, it may indicate a possible problem.

Oedema is uncomfortable so avoid any movements which make it feel worse, and try to put your feet up and rest whenever you can. Yoga will be beneficial, but leave out any posture which feels uncomfortable. Homoeopathy is helpful. Oedema usually goes soon after the birth.

ORGASM – *see Sexuality*

OSTEOPATHY

Osteopathy is a system of treatment with the hands which works on the musculo-skeletal system, assisting the body's own healing process. The work is carried out on the body's framework and helps the postural changes to occur without stress. It ensures that the spine is functioning normally and relieves aches and pains associated with the stresses and strains of pregnancy by using gentle relaxation and soft tissue stretching. Both acute and chronic problems such as back pain, sciatica, brachial plexus syndrome and disc problems can be helped with osteopathy so I have made frequent recommendations in this book to osteopathic treatment. Check that the osteopath you consult is registered and has the letters MRO or MCO after their name. It is wise to enquire whether they are experienced in working with pregnant women or new mothers.

Problems associated with a previous pregnancy or birth can be helped, as can the return to normal postnatally. If you are suffering pain, consultation with an osteopath can be very reassuring as you will understand what is causing the pain and know better how to go about helping to relieve it and prevent it getting worse. This is an ideal form of alternative therapy for someone who is practising yoga in pregnancy and complements the work of the postures.

A cranial osteopath uses an extremely gentle yet powerful technique working on a very deep, subtle level with the circulation of cerebrospinal fluid in the spine. This can be a very suitable form of treatment in pregnancy. Some osteopaths practise regular osteopathy and cranial osteopathy, depending on which is more appropriate to the problem.

OSTEOPOROSIS

This kind of gentle yoga is ideal for osteoporosis as the emphasis on gentle lengthening and releasing of the spine is exactly what is needed. Results can be very positive in pregnancy but careful personal tuition is recommended. Avoid extreme twists or side bends, or anything that does not feel comfortable.

PAIN

HEADACHES AND NECK PAIN

Headaches which arise in pregnancy are usually caused by strain on the neck. This may be stemming from tension in the shoulders, postural imbalance or emotional stress. If you are prone to headaches, try to avoid becoming overtired or stressed. Pay careful attention to your posture and make sure that you are not habitually contracting and shortening the back of your neck. Keep it lengthened by releasing your chin slightly down towards your chest and relaxing the muscles at the base of the skull.

As first aid, have a warm bath combined with a relaxing massage and then lie down in a darkened room. The breathing exercises in Chapter 3 and neck and shoulder exercises (Nos. 18 and 19) are most useful for the prevention and treatment of headaches. If they persist or occur frequently, osteopathy or cranial osteopathy is recommended. Headaches with visual disturbances should be taken seriously and reported to your doctor.

BACK PAIN

Back pain is common in pregnancy and is a warning that your posture is unbalanced or your body is not getting enough rest or is being abused by your daily habits or lifestyle.

Postural changes as the weight of the baby increases are inevitable and a woman with well-balanced posture prior to pregnancy will be able to adapt to these changes without getting back pain. However, well-balanced posture is fairly rare and most pregnant women vary between two postural types:

Kypholordotic posture   Here the normal curves of the spine are exaggerated so that the pelvis tilts forward rather than backwards as the weight of the baby increases and is thrown towards the front of the body. This results in strain on the abdominal muscles and lower ribs as well as compression in the lumbar spine and excessive weight on the pubic joint in front. This can cause lower back pain as well as strain higher up on the dorsal spine and in the neck and shoulders.

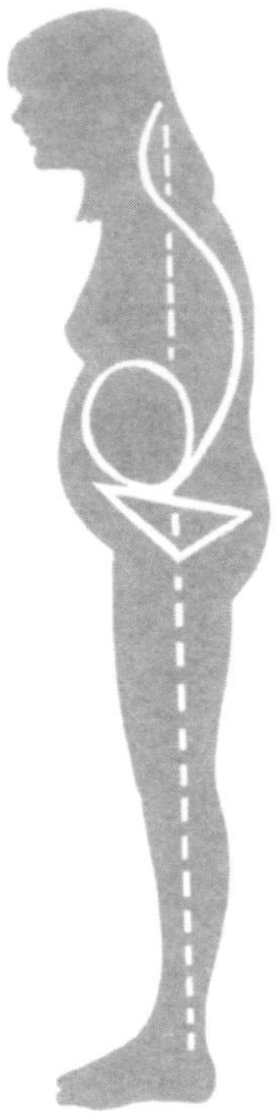

Swaybacked posture Here the curves of the spine are reduced rather than exaggerated so that there is one extended curve which looks like a slouch. In this case the pelvis tilts back too much and the baby is carried towards the back. In late pregnancy the pressure on the lumbar spine from the heavy uterus can be enormous and the result may be chronic back pain.

Treatment of back pain needs to be comprehensive. When pain arises in the back during pregnancy it is an indication of the body's failure to adapt to the normal postural changes of pregnancy. Osteopathic treatment is highly recommended and will complement the yoga postures and general postural awareness you will cultivate using this book.

Back pain may be very much helped in this way and often eradicated. All the postures in this book will be helpful in the long run, but use your own responses to decide which are most helpful, avoiding anything which causes you an increase in pain or feels like a strain. Work very gently and slowly, always applying the principle that 'less is more', and read the cautions carefully.

The child's pose (No. 11) is usually a great relief to those suffering from back pain as it takes the weight of the baby off your spine for a while and releases all the spinal muscles. Avoid going too far forward and lean forward on to a large cushion, chair seat or beanbag if it helps you to relax your spine.

The neck and shoulder exercises (Nos. 18 and 19) and standing positions will help to release the upper body and complement the postures which work specifically on the pelvis (Group 2). Standing positions rebalance posture and release the shoulders, but avoid bending forward more than an inch or two. The back arch on page 168 should be avoided if you have backache, even if you were doing it before you became pregnant, and any movement which involves extending the spine backwards should be avoided in pregnancy and after the birth until your back strengthens. You will need good tuition from a yoga teacher as well as osteopathic help to ensure that your posture has returned to normal and is not still disrupted by the strain of feeding, carrying and lifting your child. Back pain cannot be seen in isolation and involves your whole body and lifestyle. Your daily postural habits and occupation may be contributing to the tension so you will need to pay special attention to Chapter 4.

Swimming can be very relieving if you have backache, allowing you to improve your overall muscle tone and joint mobility in a gravity-free medium. You can try doing some of the yoga positions (Group 2) under water in the shallow end of the pool.

SACROILIAC PAIN and SCIATICA

This is usually experienced as a shooting pain on one side of the lower back that may extend down the leg. It is very common in pregnancy, particularly when lying on the back. Shooting pains down the leg are called sciatica.

FIG. A7
SWAY-BACKED
POSTURE

FIG. A6
KYPHOLORDOTIC
POSTURE

The sacroiliac joints (see p. 110) are held together by strong ligaments. During pregnancy, hormonal secretions increase the laxity of these ligaments so that the mobility of the sacroiliac joints is greatly increased. This lasts up to five months after the birth. This extra mobility makes the pelvic joints less strong while the important role they play in weight transmission is increased. Therefore they are more vulnerable to injury and imbalance, and movement may result in the compression or inflammation of pelvic nerves. Lower back strain, disc problems or pressure as the baby's head engages may all contribute to sacroiliac pain and sciatica, and osteopathic advice is strongly recommended.

Careful attention to posture and keeping the feet parallel is vital (see Chapter 4). Avoid standing more on one leg than the other. While some women find one posture helpful, others may find it worsens the pain, so try them all and use the ones you find relieving, leaving out any postures which make the pain worse. The child's pose (No. 11) is usually helpful. It is important to avoid overextending any movement in the pelvic joints so keep well within your comfortable limit and focus on gentle release, avoiding strain.

Osteopathic treatment, along with yoga practice, is usually very effective. Also, make sure you are getting enough rest and are not overdoing it.

If you are caught by a spasm of pain in the sacroiliac joint or down the leg, it can be very difficult to move or to get up.

Try bending up one leg and gently holding the knee until the pain eases and then slowly roll over on to one side with your knees bent and rest for a few minutes before coming up slowly.

FIG. A8
EXERCISE
TO RELIEVE
SACRO-ILIAC
PAIN

RIB PAIN

The muscles of the abdomen attach to the lower ribs. As they stretch and are pulled tight over the enlarged belly in late pregnancy, pain may occur at the point of attachment to the ribs. Also, the baby may kick under the lower ribs in the last few weeks, causing discomfort.

The increasing weight of breast tissue at the front of the body also places some strain on the rib cage. Yoga practice, with the emphasis on lengthening the root of the spine downwards and releasing tension in the neck and shoulders, should help to free the rib cage. The ribs essentially protect your heart and lungs. Try to remember this regarding your daily posture and avoid slouching unnecessarily and thus constricting the rib cage. If you give yourself room to breathe and work on correcting general postural imbalance, rib pain should be eased. Osteopathic treatment is recommended.

PUBIC PAIN

In late pregnancy many women experience pain in the pubic area. This is not surprising since the pubic joint begins to separate (widening by as much as 1 cm) in readiness for the birth, just as most of the weight of the heavy uterus falls down on to it. Consequently this pain is often worse after walking or standing for a long time, or when you are tired.

Rest a lot and avoid all strenuous exercise, or standing any more than necessary. Avoid extreme spreading of the legs, making your yoga postures especially moderate and gentle, and avoiding any position which worsens the pain. Gentle practice of tailor sitting with cushions (No. 9) alternating with cow pose (No. 8) may be helpful. If pain is extreme a visit to an osteopath is recommended.

GROIN PAIN

There is an internal ligament which runs deep in your pelvis from the uterus to the vulva called the 'round ligament', which helps to position your uterus. As the weight of your baby increases, pressure on this ligament can lead to heavy sensations of pain resulting in spasms in the surrounding muscles. The result may be a colicky pain in the groin which gets worse when you exercise. If this is the case it is wise to stop doing any yoga postures or other exertion which make it feel worse, and visit an osteopath who will use gentle relaxation techniques to relieve the muscle spasms.

COCCYX PAIN

The joint between the sacrum and the coccyx is held together by ligaments. Pregnancy often causes dragging on these ligaments, resulting in muscle spasms which pull the coccyx inwards, and pain. As the coccyx normally tilts backwards to enlarge the pelvic outlet as the baby is being born, a 'hyperflexed' coccyx like this may result in injury during the birth. This can cause pain when sitting or defaecating postnatally and may give rise to problems in another pregnancy or birth. Osteopathic treatment is recommended before the birth as well as after.

ABDOMINAL PAIN

Women experience all sorts of harmless pains as the muscles of the uterus and abdomen stretch. They can be like a sudden stitch or a mild pain in the lower belly. Often, stitchlike pains or sudden muscle spasms can occur if you change position too quickly. Usually rest combined with breathing exercises, warm baths and massage are best until the pains pass. Severe or continuous abdominal pains can be serious, so always inform your doctor if you have pains of any sort, although they are unlikely to be significant.

PALPITATIONS

These are common in pregnancy even when you are at rest, due to the extra work your heart is doing, and they are usually not a problem. It is as well to check with your doctor, though, to be sure you are not anaemic. If there is no problem, yoga and exercise are helpful, as is attention to good nutrition.

PERINEAL MASSAGE

During the actual birth the soft tissues of your genital area expand and stretch amazingly as your baby's head emerges. The perineum is the fleshy bit between the lower part of your vagina and your anus. It has a wonderful capacity to release and stretch as you are giving birth to your baby.

Some midwives believe that massage of the perineal tissues using a pure vegetable oil in the last month of pregnancy is advantageous in increasing the stretchability of the tissues. It is a good idea to be familiar with this part of your body through massage, but not essential as the tissues are self-lubricating and soften naturally in readiness for the birth.

Half-squatting is a comfortable position to use for perineal massage (see Fig. 6.17 p. 182). You can see what you are doing if you place a mirror on the floor in front of you.

With your right leg up, put some oil on the fingers of your left hand. Then, using your left hand, place your thumb in the inner surface and your fingers on the outside of the lower part of the vagina. Then work your way down the right side of your perineum to the centre. Change legs and repeat on the other side with your right hand.

Starting with your left leg up, use the middle finger of both hands to stretch the perineum in a diagonal line from front to back. This can be done easily, if you tuck your left hand through from behind and with your right hand in front, pull the tissues gently in opposite directions until you feel a mild stretching sensation. Release and then repeat on the other side with your right leg up.

PILES – *see Varicosities*

PLACENTA PRAEVIA

If you have partial or complete placenta praevia you can do gentle yoga but should avoid full squatting (No. 12f). It is all right to squat on a pile of books or a low stool. Avoid all strenuous exercises and be moderate and stay well within your comfortable limit. Stop exercising if you have any spotting or bleeding until your doctor says you can continue.

POSTERIOR POSITION

The spine and head are the heaviest parts of your baby's body and are lying against your spine when your baby is in the posterior position. The all-fours kneeling position encourages them to rotate downwards towards gravity. Practise it as many times as you can throughout the day, while rotating your hips, in the last three weeks of pregnancy and also in labour to assist your baby to turn into the anterior position (see p. 182).

PRE-ECLAMPSIA

If you are diagnosed as having pre-eclampsia you must take the condition seriously. You will probably feel perfectly well, but if pre-eclampsia worsens into eclampsia this could be dangerous for you and your baby. You can avoid this possibility by following the advice given under High Blood Pressure. In addition, homoeopathic or herbal treatment and good nutrition can be invaluable. If you have mild pre-eclampsia it is quite safe to do gentle yoga, making sure you stay well within your comfortable limit. If bedrest is recommended, however see High Blood Pressure (p. 205) regarding exercise.

PROLAPSE – *see Vaginal prolapse*

RHESUS NEGATIVE

The Rhesus factor has no bearing on exercise in pregnancy and your midwife or doctor will advise you as to antenatal and postnatal care.

SCIATICA – *see Pain*

SEXUALITY

Sex in pregnancy will not harm either you or your baby, provided you are enjoying it. Choose comfortable positions which do not compress your belly. The kneeling forward with legs wide position may be comfortable (partner underneath) or lying on your side (partner behind) in late pregnancy. Orgasms nourish body and soul and prepare your uterus for birth.

In general, practising the yoga postures, especially those which focus on opening and releasing the pelvic area, helps to increase enjoyment of sex and improve orgasmic potential. However, bear in mind that some women go off genital sex during pregnancy. If this is the case, it is usually helpful to spend time enjoying other ways of enhancing sensual pleasure, such as massage. Avoid intercourse if your membranes have broken as the risk of infection is increased.

SKIN CHANGES

You will probably notice that your skin has a healthy glow in pregnancy, and your face and body may be more rounded and fuller. This is due to the increased fluid retained in the tissues just beneath the skin. Blood flow also increases due to the softening and widening of the tiny blood vessels in the skin. You are likely to feel warmer and to sweat more while you are pregnant. The warmth generated by the additional blood supply to the body surface ensures that you maintain a regular internal temperature. Sweating helps to eliminate waste products and also to regulate your temperature. The increased flow of blood in the blood vessels of the skin sometimes causes flushed cheeks or red spots to appear. These will disappear after pregnancy. Itching is also very common in pregnancy and may be an allergic reaction to washing powder or soap. In some women the skin of the breasts, belly or thighs may develop reddish streaks known as stretchmarks. They may appear on the breasts in early pregnancy and on the belly in late pregnancy as the skin stretches. These fade and become silvery after the birth. They are more likely to occur if you have delicate skin or if you are overweight. Yoga will help to enhance elasticity of the skin. Daily massage with a good stretchmark prevention oil from early pregnancy may help to improve elasticity of the skin and thus prevent stretchmarks. Sometimes, however, it is not possible to avoid them.

STITCHES AND SPASMS – *see Pain (abdominal)*

STRETCHMARKS – *see Skin changes*

SUPINE HYPOTENSION

This is a condition caused by the weight of the heavy uterus and baby compressing the large blood vessels when you lie on your back, resulting in a feeling of faintness. It is usually not a problem until late pregnancy, but some women do suffer from this throughout pregnancy. For this reason, yoga positions which involve lying on the back have been omitted from this book. However, if you enjoy doing them and do not feel faint or dizzy you can continue until the last six weeks of your pregnancy.

SWEATING – *see Skin changes*

TIREDNESS

A common problem in pregnancy, tiredness may be caused by the extra work your body is doing. Make sure that you are not adding to the tiredness by overdoing things. It is essential to accept that being pregnant does change your life and you need to slow down, to rest more and to pay proper attention to nourishing yourself. It is also important to check that you are not anaemic and, if you are, then increase the iron-rich foods in your daily diet, and take an iron supplement or iron-rich organic tonic.

Tiredness can also arise because of poor posture, stiffness or lack of exercise. Following the guidelines in Chapters 4 and 5 should make a difference to your energy level. Start very gently and gradually increase the amount of exercise you are doing so you can enjoy the benefits without putting yourself off! If you tend towards laziness, join a class or work with a friend or partner or use an audio tape.

Lack of sleep or emotional problems can also result in tiredness. If tiredness persists, acupuncture or shiatsu may help, and massage and plenty of rest are essential.

TWIN PREGNANCY

Carrying twins is a very special kind of pregnancy. I have enjoyed working with many mothers of twins and sharing with them the excitement of having two little people inside, as well as the special considerations and realities that having two babies at once entails.

A woman's body is designed to be able to cope with two or even more babies in pregnancy but, as the combined weight of both babies may be considerable, the demands on your body will be greater than with a singleton. Your uterus will enlarge faster and the greater size and weight may cause extra minor discomforts. While most women have completely normal pregnancies and births, the risks with twins can be greater than with only one baby, so good antenatal care is essential. Attention to posture is also vital (see Chapter 4). Practising yoga in a twin pregnancy is wonderfully helpful. Gentle practice of the most comfortable yoga postures will encourage your body to loosen and accommodate the pregnancy well. Take special care to stay well within your comfortable limit in the postures, and do lots of breathing and relaxation. Avoid any position which involves lying on your back and which makes you uncomfortable. Diet and nutrition need special care and extra resting is necessary.

In the last weeks of your pregnancy gentle yoga exercises such as 'tailor sitting', 'squatting' and 'sitting with legs wide apart' may be practised in a swimming pool if you find it difficult to move around.

The labour and birth positions in Chapter 6 can all be used for the birth of twins provided there are no complications and your attendants are agreeable. It is common for one twin to be breech and in this case gravity-effective positions are sometimes especially helpful in the second stage (see Breech Baby).

VAGINAL PROLAPSE

Yoga practice and pelvic floor exercises in pregnancy can help to prevent this uncomfortable problem which occurs when the supporting ligaments and muscles of the vaginal wall are too slack. Stress and 'extreme overdoing it' can contribute to excess slackness of the pelvic floor, which is a message of 'collapse' from your body.

If you are pregnant again after a previous prolapse, pelvic floor exercises (see p. 138) are vital to avoid a recurrence, as is a restful, stress-free lifestyle. It is also advisable to consult an obstetric physiotherapist to ensure that you are doing everything you can to avoid any weakness in the pelvic floor.

VARICOSITIES

These can occur in the legs, anal or vulval areas in pregnancy, due to hormonal softening of the muscular walls of the veins, combined with the extra weight of pregnancy. In general, yoga will not worsen varicosities at all and pain is the general warning that you should not be doing a particular posture. For self-help, you need to focus on improving circulation from the lower body up to the trunk by getting your weight off your legs as much as possible and putting your feet up whenever you can. When sitting on a sofa, for example, place a cushion on a chair in front of you and rest your feet on it so that they are slightly raised.

Aromatherapy massage is very helpful, avoiding pressure on the veins and working from the foot upwards.

VARICOSITIES IN THE ANAL OR VULVAL AREA

In pregnancy, lots of pelvic floor exercises in anti-gravity positions, such as the knee-chest or slowdown position (see p. 139), are the way to improve and cure these, by gradually improving muscle tone of the blood vessel walls and supports to the pelvic floor. Ideally you should do between fifty and 100 quickies (see p. 139) every morning before you get out of bed and every night before you fall asleep, and a few any other time you remember.

It is best to avoid full squatting (No. 12) and always use a stool instead. Also avoid all forward bends until the varicosities improve.

VOMITING – *see Nausea and vomiting*

VULVA – *see Varicosities*

WEIGHT

If you are overweight you are more likely to suffer minor discomforts, so pay careful attention to good nutrition without dieting. Your main problem will be fitness. If you are very unfit, start your exercising with gentle swimming as this is easy to do due to the buoyancy and weightlessness in water.

Begin your yoga with the postures which can easily be done in water and then start to do them on land as well, as your fitness improves. Then gradually introduce the other yoga postures to your exercise session without overdoing it. By learning to burn up calories in this health-giving way you can use your pregnancy to improve your overall health and change the patterns which led to being overweight in the first place.

If you are underweight, seek medical and nutritional help as your baby could be affected if you lose weight and your pregnancy must be carefully monitored.

WORKING

Pregnancy should be a time of health and it is possible for most women to continue working. However, you must remember that you will now be doing two jobs at once, and you do have a need to slow down and rest more when you are pregnant. Nourishing your baby should be your first priority. Your colleagues at work should understand this, so make sure there are facilities to lie down and rest at work and during the lunch hour.

Ensure that your posture is good if you are sitting at a desk and get up and walk around frequently. Build some yoga postures into your routine at work if you can, and pay extra attention to your nutrition and join a twice-weekly exercise class if you have no time at home. It will help you immensely to go swimming before or after work a few times a week.

If your pregnancy is more difficult than expected, or you are feeling exhausted, you may need to give up working earlier than you anticipated.

RECOMMENDED READING

ASHFORD, JANET, *Whole Birth Catalogue – A Sourcebook for Choices in Childbirth*, Crossing Press, 1983.

BALASKAS, J., *The Active Birth Partner's Handbook*, Sidgwick & Jackson, 1986.

BALASKAS, J., *New Active Birth*, Unwin Paperbacks, 1989.

BALASKAS, J., *Natural Pregnancy*, Sidgewick & Jackson, 1990.

BALASKAS, J., and GORDON, Y., *Water Birth*, Thorsons, 1992.

BALASKAS, J., and GORDON, Y., *The Encyclopaedia of Pregnancy and Birth*, Macdonald Orbis, 1987.

BALDWIN, RAHIMA, AND PALMARINI, TERRA, *Pregnant Feelings*, Celestial Arts, 1986.

DALE, BARBERA AND ROEBER, JOHANNA, *Exercise for Childbirth*, Century, 1982.

DAVIS, ELIZABETH, *Energetic Pregnancy*, Celestial Arts, 1988.

EASON, CASSANDRA, *A Mother's Instinct*, Aquarian, 1992.

HOARE, SOPHY, *Yoga and Pregnancy*, Unwin Paperbacks, 1985.

KITZINGER, SHEILA, *Pregnancy and Childbirth*, Michael Joseph, 1980.

KLEIN OLKIN, SYLVIA, *Positive Pregnancy Fitness*, Avery Publishing Group Inc., 1987.

LEBOYER, FREDERICK, *Inner Beauty, Inner Light*, Collins, 1979.

LEBOYER, FREDERICK, *The Art of Breathing*, Element, 1985.

NOBLE, ELIZABETH, *Essential Exercises for the Childbearing Year*, John Murray, 1980.

ODENT, MICHEL, *Birth Reborn*, Fontana, 1986.

ODENT, MICHEL, *Primal Health*, Century, 1986.

ODENT, MICHEL, *The Nature of Birth and Breastfeeding*, Bergin and Garvey, 1992.

PANUTHOS, CLAUDIA, *Transformation Through Birth*, Bergin-Harvey Press, 1983.

PETERSON, GAYLE, *Birthing Normally: A Personal Growth Approach to Childbirth*, Irvington Publishers, 1984.

PETERSON, GAYLE, AND MEHL, LEWIS, *Pregnancy As Healing*, Mindbody Press, 1984.

SCARAVELLI, VANDA, *Awakening the Spine*, The Aquarian Press, 1992.

STEWART, MARY, *Yoga*, Headway Lifeguides, Hodder & Stoughton, 1992.

STIRK, JOHN I., *Structural Fitness*, Elm Tree Books, 1988.

TISSERAND, MAGGIE, *Aromatherapy for Women*, Thorsons, 1985.

VINCENT-PRIYA, JACQUELINE, *Birth without Doctors*, Earthscan Publications, 1991.

VINCENT-PRIYA, *Jacqueline, Birth Traditions and Modern Pregnancy Care*, Element, 1992.

RESOURCES

AUDIO TAPE A 'Yoga for Pregnancy' practice tape by Janet Balaskas is available by mail order from the Active Birth Centre, 55 Dartmouth Park Road, London NW5 1SL.

VIDEO Water and Birth – the Video, is a 48-minute inspirational video made by Janet Balaskas and Amy Hardie, featuring the births of three women and interviews with their midwives. It is available by mail order from the Active Birth Centre.

TEACHERS For a list of certified active birth yoga teachers trained by Janet Balaskas and her colleagues, please write to the Active Birth Centre enclosing a sae.

MAILORDER CATALOGUE For aromatherapy products, books, tapes and videos – available from the Active Birth Centre.

WATER BIRTH POOLS Portable pools for hire, or installed pools to purchase – colour brochure available from the Active Birth Centre.

USEFUL ADDRESSES

ACTION AGAINST ALLERGY, 43 The Downs, London SW20 8HG.

ACTIVE BIRTH CENTRE, 55 Dartmouth Park Road, London NW5 1SL. Telephone: 020 7267 3006, Fax: 020 7267 5368.

AIDS AND PREGNANCY: Healthline. (Confidential telephone information service.)

AINSWORTH HOMEOPATHIC PHARMACY, 38 New Cavendish Street, London W1M 7LH. (Stockists and mail-order suppliers of homeopathic remedies.)

AROMATHERAPY OILS, 55 Dartmouth Park Road, London NW1 1SL. (Pure oils for pregnancy and labour supplied by mail-order.)

ASSOCIATION FOR THE IMPROVEMENT OF MATERNITY SERVICES (AIMS), 40 Kingswood Avenue, London NW6 6LS. Telephone: 081 960 5585.

ASSOCIATION OF RADICAL MIDWIVES (ARM), 62 Greetby Hill, Ormskirk, Lancashire L39 2DT.

BACH FLOWER REMEDIES LTD, Dr Edward Bach Centre, Mount Vernon, Sotwell, Wallingford. Oxon OX10 0PZ.

G BALDWIN & CO., 171-3 Walworth Road, London SE17 1RW. (Suppliers of dried herbs, herbal preparations and essential oils.)

BRITISH ASSOCIATION FOR COUNSELLING, 37A Sheep Street, Rugby CV21 3BX. (For a directory of counselling and psychotherapy organizations.)

BRITISH COUNCIL FOR COMPLEMENTARY AND ALTERNATIVE MEDICINE, Suite One, 19A Cavendish Square, London W1M 9AD.

THE COUNCIL OF ACUPUNCTURE, Suite One, 19A Cavendish Square, London W1M 9AD.

CRANIAL OSTEOPATHIC ASSOCIATION, 478 Baker Street, Enfield, Middlesex EN1 3QS.

GENERAL COUNCIL AND REGISTER OF OSTEOPATHS, 56 London Street, Reading, Berkshire RG1 4SQ.

HELIOS HOMEOPATHIC PHARMACY, 92 Camden Road, Tunbridge Wells, Kent TN1 2QP. (Homeopathic remedies supplied by mail-order.)

HOME BIRTH MOVEMENT, 10 Portrush Close, Woodley, Reading, Berkshire RG5 9PB.

INDEPENDENT MIDWIVES ASSOCIATION, Nightingale Cottage, Shamblehurst Lane, Botley, Nr. Southampton, Hampshire SO3 2BY.

INTERNATIONAL INSTITUTE OF REFLEXOLOGY, 28 Hollyfield Avenue, London N11 3BY.

LA LECHE LEAGUE, BCM 3424, London WC1N 3XX.(For breastfeeding counselling.)

THE MATERNITY ALLIANCE, 15 Britannia Street, London WC1. (For advice on using VDUs in pregnancy.)

NATIONAL CHILDBIRTH TRUST, Alexandra House, Oldham Terrace, Acton, London W3 6NH.

NATIONAL COUNCIL FOR ONE-PARENT FAMILIES, 255 Kentish Town Road, London NW5 2LX.

NATIONAL INSTITUTE OF MEDICAL HERBALISTS, PO Box 3, Winchester SO23 8AA. (Send SAE for list of registered practitioners.)

OSTEOPATHY PREGNANCY CLINIC, The British School of Osteopathy, Littlejohn House, 1-4 Suffolk Street, London SW1.

ROYAL COLLEGE OF MIDWIVES, 15 Mansfield Street, London W1.

SHIATSU SOCIETY, c/o Elaine Liechti, 19 Langside Park, Kilbarchan, Renfrewshire PA10 2EP.

THE SOCIETY OF HOLISTIC PRACTITIONERS, Old Hall, East Bergholt, Colchester CO7 6TG.

SOCIETY OF HOMEOPATHS, 2 Artisan Road, Northampton NN1 4HU.

THE TISSERAND AROMATHERAPY INSTITUTE, 10 Victoria Grove, Second Avenue, Hove, East Sussex BN3 2LJ. (For training and books.)

USEFUL ADDRESSES

USA

ACTIVE BIRTH AND PREGNANCY EXERCISE CONTACTS

INTERNATIONAL CHILDBIRTH EDUCATION ASSOCIATION (ICEA), PO Box 20048, Minneapolis, MN 55420.

SYLVIA KLEIN OLKIN, POSITIVE PREGNANCY AND PARENTING FITNESS, 51 Saltrock Road, Baltic, CT 06330.

BETSY MERCOGLIANO, 3 Wilbur Street, Albany, NY 12202.

OTHER USEFUL CONTACTS

AMERICAN COLLEGE OF NURSE-MIDWIVES (ACNM), 1522 K. St. NW. 110, Washington, DC 20005.

ASSOCIATION FOR CHILDBIRTH AT HOME, PO Box 1219, Cerritos, CA 90701.

BIRTH RESOURCES, 1749 Vine Street, Berkeley, CA 94703.

BIRTHWAYS, 3127 Telegraph Avenue, Oakland, CA 94609.

CAESAREAN PREVENTION MOVEMENT (CPM), PO Box 152, Syracuse, NY 13210.

CAESAREANS / SUPPORT, EDUCATION AND CONCERN (C/SEC), 22 Forest Road, Framingham, MA 01701.

INFORMED HOMEBIRTH, 3555 Pratt Street, Ann Arbor, MI 48103.

LA LECHE LEAGUE INTERNATIONAL (LLLI), 9616 Minneapolis Avenue, Franklin Park, IL 60131.

MIDWIFE ALLIANCE OF NORTH AMERICA, 30 South Main, Concord, NH 03301.

NATIONAL ASSOCIATION OF CHILDBEARING CENTRES (NACC), Rd 1, Box 1, Perkiomenville, PA 18074.

NATIONAL ASSOCIATION OF PARENTS AND PROFESSIONALS FOR SAFE ALTERNATIVES IN CHILDBIRTH (NAPSAC), PO Box 646, Marble Hill, MO 63764.

NATIONAL WOMEN'S HEALTH NETWORK, 1325 G Street NW, Washington, DC 20005.

AUSTRALIA

CERTIFIED ACTIVE BIRTH YOGA TEACHERS TRAINED BY JANET BALASKAS

JANE CAMPBELL-KAYE, 4 Eurella Street, Kenmore, Brisbane, Queensland 4069.

JO DADD, 33 Grand View Drive, Newport, NSW 2106.

PHILIPPA HOLLAND, 7 Old Beach Road, Brighton, Adelaide, South Australia.

ACTIVE BIRTH TEACHERS

JULIE PEARSE, Adelaide Active Birth Centre, 24 Dalton Avenue, Aldgate, Adelaide, South Australia 5154.

ANDREA ROBERTSON, Associates in Childbirth Education (ACE), PO Box 366, Camperdown 2050.

LEENA CLARKE, Centre of Awareness, 294 Smith Street, Collingwood 3066, Melbourne, Victoria.

GENERAL YOGA CONTACTS

AUSTRALIAN YOGA MASTERS ASSOCIATION, 183 Pitt Town Road, Kenthurst, NSW 2156.

INTERNATIONAL YOGA TEACHERS ASSOCIATION, PO Box 207, St. Ives, NSW 2075.

BKS IYENGAR ASSOCIATION OF AUSTRALIA, 109 Upper Avenue Road, Mosman, NSW 2088.

SIDHA YOGA FOUNDATION, 50 Garnet Street, Dulwich Hill, NSW 2203.

CANADA

ESTER MYERS YOGA STUDIO, 390 Dupont Street, Toronto, M5R 1V9. Telephone: (416) 994 0838.

INDEX